ΔNARCHiSTS
iN THE BOARDROOM

How social media and social movements can
help your organisation to be more like people.

BY LiAM BARRiNGTON-BUSH

MORE
LiKE
PEOPLE

morelikepeople.org

*Dear Matthew —
Thank you for your full
range of opinions — both that
that align + conflict with my
own. Really appreciate your
help in making this
happen!
Love!
LIAM*

What people are saying about 'Anarchists in the Boardroom'...

"Anarchists in the Boardroom is a disturbing book in so many ways. All of them good. It challenges us to rethink the dinosaur assumptions on which most of our organisations are built. It opens our minds to fresh and creative possibilities for treating ourselves and colleagues with trust and compassion. Above all, it places the qualities of being human at the heart of our endeavours, putting a better world within the reach of us all. A vade mecum for life!"

> - Roger Clark, former Secretary General of *Amnesty International Canada*

"We all crave meaning, agency and fulfilment at work. Too often we experience the very opposite; the idealism that drove us evaporates into disillusionment and boredom. If this is you, read this book! It's an inspiring and above all highly practical guide to how to change your workplace for the better. Thank you, Liam, for showing us the way."

> - Carne Ross, former senior UK diplomat to the UN, Author of *The Leaderless Revolution* and Occupy Wall Street activist

"I've lost count of the number of times I've been asked to speak on panels organized by NGO managers asking 'What can we learn from the success of Occupy/ UKUNCUT/Climate Camp/the latest grassroots movement hitting the headlines.' I tend to decline, politely responding that I don't think hierarchical organisations are able to do so. Since reading this book though, I will adopt a new approach and recommend Anarchists in the Boardroom instead. This book deserves to be passed around like contraband by charity workers committed to making their organisations part of - rather than simply observers of - transformational social change."

> - Tim Gee, Author of *You Can't Evict and Idea* and *Counterpower*

"Anarchists in the Boardroom is a powerful contribution to the growing chorus of voices calling for a new way of leading and managing our organizations. And Barrington-Bush goes beyond the boundaries of traditional management scholarship, drawing some critically important lessons from overlooked sources like the Occupy Movement and hip-hop music, and applying them in refreshingly practical ways to the real challenges we face in creating organizational cultures that work in the 21st century."

> - Maddie Grant and Jamie Notter, Co-Authors of *Humanize: How people-centric organizations succeed in a social world*

Dedicated to Paul – without whom I would not likely have had the confidence to run off to Mexico and write this book.

Thanks!

Liam

This book/ e-book was first published in the UK in September 2013 and was written by Liam Barrington-Bush.

The hard copies have been printed by unionised workers at ImprintDigital.com in the UK.

The costs for the book were crowd-funded by 161 people using StartSomeGood.com in March 2013.

For more about the book, check out morelikepeople.com or email me: liam@morelikepeople.org

Cover art by Steve Lafler – www.stevelafler.com

Edited by Dave Oswald Mitchell – www.daveomitchell.com

Lay-out and internal design by Serena Lee – www.serenalee.com

morelikepeople.com development by Majed Rostamian – www.artadesign.ca

Paperback ISBN number: 978-0-9926803-0-5

E-book ISBN number: 978-0-9926803-1-2

Table of Contents

Your more like people map

INDIVIDUAL CHANGE

1. Simple Starters
a. Tell someone that you appreciate something they did
b. Stop using jargon (and tell others you're doing so)
c. Get to know someone new in your organisation
d. Dress as you'd like to dress at work
e. Send fewer internal emails & talk to people in person
f. Have chats, not meetings (Ch.5)
g. Try more ideas than you expect will succeed (Ch.5)
h. Don't talk through the command chain
i. Bake cookies or make a meal for those you work with

2. Personal Development
a. Appreciate your role in contributing to tough relationships (Ch.2/7)
b. Practice 'conscious vulnerability' (Ch.2/7)
c. Speak up, but don't blame (Ch. 2/7)
d. Work when you are happiest and most productive
e. Address your own privilege and prejudice (Ch.4)

4. System 'Hacks'
a. Start a clandestine lunch group (Ch.5/7)
b. Launch your own 'more like people action week'
c. Proceed until apprehended! (Ch.6/7)

3. Social Media
a. Blog /Tweet about organisational learning (Ch.3/5)
b. Share your opinions and feelings online (Ch. 2)
c. Find likeminded colleagues online (Ch.4/6)
d. Use Twitter for learning and development
e. Ask for feedback and opinions (Ch.5)

6. Planning and Decision Making
a. Consensus/consensus-like decision making (Ch.6)
b. Involve everyone (Ch.3/5/8)
c. When you can't agree on one thing, try two (Ch.8)
d. Explore 'Developmental Evaluation' (Ch.9)
e. Avoid turning human stories into metrics (Ch.9)
f. Don't strategise! Pay attention and adapt! (Ch.1/2/8)

WORK CHANGE

5. Holding Meetings
a. Scrap the agenda (Ch. 1/2)
b. ...or write the agenda together, each time
c. Make everyone a chairperson
d. Hold meetings in parks, pubs, or someone's living room
e. Ask yourself if the meeting really needs to happen
f. 'Livestream' your meetings (Ch. 5)

7. People Management
a. Encourage failure (Ch.5)
b. 'De-specialise' your team (Ch.2/6/8)
c. Encourage personal social media (Ch.2/4/7)
d. Regularly ask staff what they want from the job (Ch.6)

8. Outside World
a. Make organisational learning 'open source' (Ch.5)
b. Support others in the movement (Ch.3/8)
c. Share funding, resources, media with others (Ch.3/6)
d. Let supporters find their own ways to support (Ch.6)
e. Question how you organise your events (Ch.4)

9. Working Parameters
a. Allow non-fixed working hours
b. Hold a 'Hack Day' (Ch.5)
c. Give staff a free day/week to follow their dreams (Ch.2/5/6)
d. Let staff choose how many hours they work (Ch.6)
e. Let staff take as much paid leave as they want (Ch.6)
f. Support staff to informally teach each other their jobs (Ch.6)
g. Start a Results Only Working Environment (Ch. 6)

10. Salaries
a. Establish a 'social justice waging' system (Ch.6)
b. Let staff set their own wages (Ch.6)
c. Pay enough, but not too much
d. Keep the salary gaps among all staff relatively low

11. Structures
a. Let go of 'Senior Management' (Ch.3/6)
b. Support ad hoc self-organising teams of 'Buddies, Bricks and Affinity Groups' (Ch. 3)
c. Support co-management among staff (Ch.1/2/6)
d. Scrap departments (Ch.6)

12. Hiring
a. Create project, not job descriptions (Ch. 6)
b. Emphasise perspective (Ch. 4)
c. Hire as a last resort (Ch. 6)

WORK CHANGE

STRUCTURE CHANGE

Introduction: A management book for people who don't read management books

I clearly remember the creeping feeling of despondence and disillusionment I felt while working at my second proper job for a national charity. My sense of what working for social change was all about was deeply shaken by the experience. Having spent my youth involved in a range of voluntary community projects and campaigns around Toronto, with only bits of paid experience before moving from Canada to the UK in 2006, I had no idea the culture shock my transition into the professional world would bring.

While there, I experienced a range of phenomena I had previously only associated with Dilbert comics and *The Office*, leaving home stressed in the morning, and only becoming more so as the day went on. In-fighting between teams, dog-eat-dog backstabbing amongst colleagues, vicious internal competition for organisational budgets, managers who couldn't seem to distinguish between a human being and the spreadsheet their name was found in.

Grievances were commonplace, stress and resentment were high, honesty and trust were low, and lots of things got counted, but few valuable things seemed to actually get done.

Those who unquestioningly followed orders quickly found themselves moving up the organisational ladder, while those who challenged the status quo were routinely ignored, disciplined, and often gradually manoeuvred out of their jobs.

When I put new ideas forward, they were rarely dismissed outright, but instead subjected to a bureaucratic churn in which my enthusiasm was slowly stripped away via countless re-drafts of a proposal that could have sufficed with a give-it-a-try nod. Eventually, I would give up, as the energy was sucked from the idea through unnecessary, time-consuming paperwork and sign-off processes.

What made this so much worse was discovering, over-and-over again, that others working in a range of social change organisations (particularly, but not exclusively in the big national organisations) were experiencing the same things where they worked. I gradually realised that I hadn't just found myself in a particularly dysfunctional workplace, but rather that the same patterns were playing themselves out in countless organisations focused on bringing about a better world.

The irony was not lost on me, but it spent a long time cloaked beneath layers of anger and resentment before I was able to see it as such.

I remember regularly reiterating the question, while out at the pub with fellow disillusioned colleagues, or after conferences with newfound allies from other dysfunctional NGOs, *How have we ended up creating organisations that are meant to create good in the world, but make so many of those involved in them so miserable in the process?*

What I gradually realised during this disillusioning experience was that the problems were much bigger than the particular individuals making our lives miserable. The assholes were a product of the organisational 'asshole-making machine,' of which I felt I came dangerously close to becoming a product myself, not long before walking out its doors for the last time.

I also realised that these organisations had become so calcified, so stuck in their ways, that *any change* – if only to get things moving again – was better than no change, even if it didn't answer all of the questions we wanted it to. Once we got things moving, we could continue to adapt, but as long as we remained stuck, we gave up the possibility of something better.

The experience left me asking a question that has come to frame my work over the three or so years since I finally left: how can we make our organisations more like people? In other words, how can those of us engaged in social change work, find structures that nurture the innovation, passion and sense of personal connection that first brought us into this work?

How we get there...

This is a book about social change, technology and how lessons from our most meaningful personal relationships can change how we relate to the world as a whole. I have done my best to write the book I wish someone had handed me while I was still at that last job – that would have armed me with the tools I needed to start making real change happen, regardless of how frustrated and powerless I felt at the time.

It is a book for staff and managers at non-governmental and voluntary organisations who may be frustrated by the kinds of experiences I describe above, but who still want to be an active part of changing those organisations for the better.

It is a book that moves between two spaces: the loose clusters of social justice activists working for a better world, and the non-profit, charitable and voluntary organisations whose mission statements espouse similar aspirations.

It's a push back against decades of the 'professionalisation' of the social change sector and its deeply patronising attitude towards grassroots activists and community groups.

It tells a story of the power of social media to start conversations, seed relationships and spark people-powered mass movements. It draws its inspiration from exciting new forms of collective action, asking how more traditional organisations can learn from these movements to mobilise passion, spark innovation, and encourage diversity.

It explores what it means to be human at work and why our organisations are so rarely equipped to support genuine human engagement. It asks questions about our organisations that, by extension, reveal further questions about ourselves (including the parts of us that exist beyond our nine-to-five personas), and the role we play in making our institutions what they are.

Finding your own way of reading the book

This is not a how-to guide for building a 'more like people' organisation. In my experience, cookie-cutter solutions are part of the problem. To offer a single prescription would be to undermine some of my core arguments. Instead I tell stories and highlight principles, leaving it in your hands to figure out what to do with them.

I've written each chapter to stand alone (while maintaining a start-to-finish narrative for those who prefer to read that way); I encourage you to jump around to the topics and ideas that interest you most. That said, I suggest reading Chapters 1 and 2 first for a more solid grounding in the problems and the principles.

On page i, you'll find your 'more like people' map, which lists a range of different kinds of change, ranging from personal habits to organisational structures, with suggestions for activities you could undertake in each of those domains. Most of the suggestions include a chapter reference with more information. At the back of the book you'll find a few more words about each suggestion in the 'more like people' legend, if you want the quick-and-easy explanation, without the longer narrative.

Whatever your organisation, whatever your role, I hope the book encourages and challenges you, professionally and personally, to see the ways your organisation might begin to change, and the actions you might take to change it – and yourself – wherever you sit in its ranks.

The journey ahead...

Chapter 1 makes the case for change. I argue that industrialism and professionalism have shaped our social change organisations for the worse, and social media and social movements are demonstrating a range of alternatives for better organising ourselves. This chapter explores the roots of many of the problems with our current organisational structures, while introducing the realms of knowledge in which the book will look for alternatives, many of which are underpinned by broadly anarchist ideas.

Chapter 2 outlines the 'more like people' approach, introducing the core principles of *humanity*, *autonomy*, and *complexity*. It introduces some of the changing understandings of science, management and philosophy and shows how these innovations offer a very different narrative by which to live and understand the world. It also highlights some of the benefits, personally and organisationally, of being ourselves in our work. Chapter 2 provides the basic compass from which the rest of the book can be navigated.

Closely linked to our ideas of professionalism and industrialism are our deeply ingrained assumptions and practices of organisational hierarchy. We assume that someone will have final say, that we always report to someone, and that someone should be earning more than someone else. But when it comes down to it, hierarchy doesn't sit well with the core values of most progressive people, even if we practice it throughout our working lives.

We no longer need to accept top-down structures as a necessary evil, undermining our lived visions of the world. There are too many other options available to us, being practiced by activists involved in local and global social movements the world-over, fuelled by the increasing ubiquity of social media. Chapter 3 tells some of the stories of those who are living and experimenting with self-organising structures. These stories challenge us to hear ideas from those we may never have expected to be learning from; a fundamental tenet of the world beyond our current hierarchical practices.

And while there are those from whom our organisations have often ignored valuable lessons, there are also those shut out by current methods. People with a certain level of opportunity and privilege often feel at home with the customs, attitudes and practices that are common in our organisations. However, these ways of working can be equally alienating to people who have travelled different paths in their desire to change the world. In Chapter 4 we will explore these questions of diversity and inclusion, and take a look at some of the ways we can re-centre our work to encourage more diverse organisations.

While opening our doors to a wider range of members, activists or supporters might be a challenge, we can't be afraid to try new things! Chapter 5 looks at the development of new ideas and practices, and explains some of the conditions that enable creative thinking. It also touches on the processes of open source software development, our understandings of failure, and the importance of non-directed, seemingly meaningless conversations, in the quest for new ideas and new ways of working.

Chapter 6 looks at the differences between people who are stressed and unhappy coming to work each day, and those involved in jobs and social movements where they feel motivated, passionate and in control of their own effort and direction. Perhaps unsurprisingly, those in the later group tend to do a lot more good in the world when they feel this way! Chapter 6 explores ownership, motivation, and the things that help us to find them.

Chapter 7 follows a similar thread, taking a broader view of our personal feelings about coming to work, and exploring how they relate to our organisational cultures. Through the lens of 'culture as a field,' it looks at the ways each of us plays a role – for better or worse – in creating the cultures of our organisations, while offering stories of improvement that have emerged from individual change, rather than top-down imposition.

While many would acknowledge that culture change cannot be orchestrated from the executive suite, fewer executives, keen to maintain control over organisational direction, would admit that their time spent developing strategic plans is equally ill-founded. Chapter 8 explains a bit more about complexity, networks, emergence and the futility of most of our strategic planning efforts. It also highlights the importance of organisational agility and responsiveness, and how we can waste less time and resources trying to predict the future, and more time responding to the present, as is the norm in so many social movements and online activities.

Another common but questionable top-down imposition is our obsession with numbers, convinced they offer us accountability. But accountability is much broader than the compliance measures funders and organisations tend to impose. Countless organisational compliance systems offer us the illusion of accountability, but not the practice of it. Trust-based relationships, on the other hand, can involve all members of a group holding each other to account. Trust is built through empathy, and empathy emerges from human relationships. Chapter 9 explains why, if we want real accountability, we need to trust one another, and make sure our systems reflect this trust.

But *real* trust is radical stuff. It doesn't come easily. In recent years, many organisations – from governments, to big businesses and NGOs – have begun to espouse the ideas of participatory democracy, only to clamp-down and re-assert control at the first signs of trouble. Let this be a warning: when you open things up, there *will* be trouble. But the benefits that are becoming clearer and clearer can outweigh that trouble tenfold if we give them a chance. In Chapter 10, we'll look at what to do when the temptation to get back in the driver's seat is at its strongest. Chapter 10 brings together a handful of key themes from the rest of the book, as it urges us all, half-facetiously, to swallow our pride and ask the hippies for help – to invite the anarchists into the boardroom and see what happens!

#morelikepeople

If you're already using Twitter, I suggest reading this book with the hashtag #morelikepeople close at hand, to share your reflections, thoughts and questions with other readers. (A hashtag is a sort of filing system for everyone in the world's Twitter updates, so we can find and contribute to the same online conversation as others who are reading the book.) As you read, you might be inspired by something, confused by something else, or think of an example that an idea here helps explain and want to share a link to it. You might read about someone I've mentioned in the book, and want to get in touch with them directly (via their '@ name' in brackets after I mention them for the first time). You might think something here is totally wrong and needs to be challenged. That's great – I would rather this book sparked positive conflict, than simply left all of its readers passively nodding away (or nodding off). (If you're not using Twitter, maybe this is a chance to experiment and dip your toes in the billions-strong world of social media that is so central to this book!)

Through the website (*morelikepeople.com*), we will be drawing together online responses, whether Tweets, blog entries, videos or articles. Just make sure to tag any content you create #morelikepeople. We have the tremendous privilege of being able to build a collective body of knowledge together online that can dwarf the pages of this book, if we want it to!

One of the amazing opportunities that social media makes possible is for authors and readers to convene an on-going conversation around a set of ideas. Instead of thinking of this book as a fixed and static piece of text, why not see it as a starting point – the beginning of a conversation among readers and practitioners. I hope you'll join me in discussing how we can make our organisations more like people, so that eventually, the many threads of that conversation can grow to dwarf the body of knowledge in the pages that follow.

The kinds of shifts the world requires of us are not easy ones, particularly for those of us who've been reasonably successful with the older approaches we may have become accustomed to. But the potential these changes could release is truly inspiring if we want to imagine a fairer, more just, and legitimately people-powered future.

Liam Barrington-Bush (@hackofalltrades)

The inhumanity of it all!

'Can organizations learn to sustain the energy and desire
that called them into being?' – Margaret Wheatley and
Myron Kellner-Rogers
'Let's treat each other as if we plan to work side by side in
struggle for many years to come.' – Naomi Klein, speaking at
Occupy Wall Street, 8 October 2011

1

The world is changing. But our twin organisational pillars of
industrialism and professionalism seem unwilling to change with
it. Even in so many social change organisations, where elitist,
undemocratic structures are directly at odds with their missions
and values, industrialism and professionalism remain strong.

Meanwhile, the growth of social media and new social
movements are highlighting the shortcomings of these systems
across all sectors of society, offering more effective organising
approaches which are also more aligned with the values social
change organisations have long espoused, but often struggled to
live up to.

Anarchist principles have long been at the core of countless social
movements, and have fuelled the growth of social media. As
we apply anarchism to our organisations, we begin to see what
'more like people' is all about, as both a practical and ethical
alternative to the systems of organising we've long taken for
granted.

'The most important thing in the world'

Many dismissed the ragtag encampment gathered in Lower Manhattan's Zuccotti Park in the autumn of 2011. 'They don't know what they want!' many a pundit of varied political stripes declared at the time. But writer and activist Naomi Klein (@NaomiAKlein) refused to join this chorus. Instead, when she spoke to the camp she described what they were doing there as 'the most important thing in the world.'

And she made a strong case for what might otherwise be dismissed as a bit of activist hyperbole: at that moment, Occupy Wall Street (@OccupyWallSt) really was the most important thing in the world. *Finally* were the core issues of an unjust world being confronted head-on, *finally* these issues were being addressed in a non-reactionary way, and *finally* the methods of change were becoming aligned with the kind of change we wanted to bring about in the world. And this was all happening just in the nick of time, as far as our used-and-abused planet was concerned.

The Occupy movement – like all movements before and after it – emerged from an unpredictable intersection of forces none could have masterminded in advance. A few months before thousands of people setup camp in Zuccotti Park, responding to a call from *Adbusters* (@adbusters) magazine to "occupy Wall Street" on September 17, thirty or so activists began meeting at Manhattan's 16 Beaver Street, just down the road from the workplaces of the world's most powerful financial elite. The group included activists from Spain, Greece, and Egypt, several of whom had recently taken part in their own movements for change, and wanted to bring that energy and experience to NYC. Many local activists, meanwhile, had recently come from 'Bloombergville' an encampment at City Hall to protest local budget cuts, not dissimilar to those faced by communities the world over since 2008.

Those initial meetings gave birth to the New York City General Assembly in August 2011. It borrowed a consensus decision-making model that had come to prominence in Spain's 15-M (15th of May) movement earlier that year, but which had roots tracing back to Latin American social movements and the indigenous traditions many of them had grown from. Linking the underpinning ethos of the model to its anarchist roots, former Yale professor and New York City activist David Graeber (@ davidgraeber) wrote, 'in the same way human beings treated like children will tend to act like children, the way to encourage human beings to act like mature and responsible adults is to treat them as if they already are.'[i]

When the group chose to heed Adbusters' call to 'Occupy Wall Street' on September 17th, what would happen beyond that afternoon was unknown. But when the General Assembly process kicked off that day, there was resounding support from the thousands present for the idea of striking a camp and staying the night.

What followed is now well known, but the nuts-and-bolts that allowed it to happen are less so.

Building on experiences of other social movements, and combined with the increasing interconnectedness of social media, Occupy shifted the global debate on a range of issues that had for decades remained the unspoken – but highly damaging – wallpaper of political discourse. They did so by modelling critical elements of the world they wanted to see, leaving massive space for individuals to find their own ways to get involved, allowing leadership to emerge from wherever it was best suited to emerge from, and raising a banner that others beyond New York City were able to take up and make their own.

They inspired nearly 1,000 cities to follow suit, each making the movement distinctly local. And they have spawned countless spin-off campaigns, addressing everything from predatory lending, home foreclosures, legal reform, and personal and student debt, to urban agriculture, military service, and many other pressing issues. In doing so, they paint a very different picture of how change happens than most non-profits and charities have operated from in recent decades, both in terms of its means, as well as its ends.

While there is no 'one-size-fits-all' approach to anything as complex as social change, there are important lessons that Occupy has helped surface, but which have been a part of activism for decades and centuries. Unfortunately, many of our social change organisations have chosen to walk a different path.

As we find ourselves at a juncture in which the old methods *simply aren't working*, it is time we start to look differently at those who are modelling something more effective, even if doing so might feel uncomfortable at first.

But where did our organisations go so wrong? And what can we do to avoid the threat that so-called change just brings more of the same?

'One Best Way'

Frederick Winslow Taylor was born in Philadelphia, Pennsylvania, in 1856, to a wealthy Quaker lawyer and an abolitionist mother with American roots tracing back to the Mayflower. He passed the Harvard entrance exams with honours in 1874, but surprised those around him when he declined placement at the prestigious university in favour of a machinist apprenticeship at a local factory run by family friends.

The apprenticeship led to a shop floor position at Midvale Steel Works, another company with which the Taylors were closely associated. In the years that followed, young Frederick flew through the Midvale ranks, due to some combination of skill, ambition, and nepotistic influence, eventually becoming its chief engineer.

Taking particular interest in the details of the manufacturing process, he began to note the countless minute inefficiencies that he felt characterised work on the shop floor at the mill. Thus began a long and mostly prosperous career aimed at weeding out such inefficiencies and increasing industrial productivity via a pioneering breed of micromanagement. Taylor's approach is perhaps best characterised by his fabled insistence on measuring individual shop floor workers' performance down to the hundredth-of-a-second with a stopwatch, to determine their actual and potential productivity, and the gap of 'wasted' time between the two.

Taylor is said to have been the world's first management consultant and the father of 'scientific management.' He was also a leading voice behind the Efficiency Movement, which believed that human organisations, like machines, could be optimised by discovering the 'one best way' each individual part of the system should be organised, and then standardising it.

'It is only through *enforced* standardization of methods, *enforced* adoption of the best implements and working conditions, and *enforced* cooperation,' wrote Taylor in his 1911 manifesto, *Principles of Scientific Management*, 'that ... faster work can be assured. And the duty of enforcing the adoption of standards and enforcing this cooperation rests with *management* alone.'[ii]

Taylor regularly described workers as 'stupid' and 'phlegmatic' (dull or apathetic), viewing them as animals harnessed in the pursuit of industrial production, like horses or oxen had been used in agriculture for millennia before.

Perhaps unsurprisingly, factories that imposed Taylor's methodologies often faced workplace revolts and strikes, though his writings tended to omit or minimize these occurrences. He also didn't give much space to the inefficiencies created by upsetting and abusing workers to the point of pushing them onto picket lines – a considerable cost to any company's production forecasts.

While not always popular, Taylor's ideas spread, influencing more and more of the industrial workforces in the US and Britain around the turn of the 20th Century.

But Taylorism was not unique to the forces of early industrial capitalism. Henry Ford, one of Taylor's intellectual progeny and famed inventor of assembly line production, was a hero to both Vladimir Lenin and Adolf Hitler, the latter of whom is said to have had a life-sized photo of Ford next to his desk in the Reich Chancellery. Joseph Stalin was once quoted as saying, 'The combination of the Russian revolutionary sweep with American efficiency is the essence of Leninism,' referring to the work of Taylor and Ford as the model adopted by so many Soviet factories after 1917.[iii]

Taylor's 'organisations as machines' metaphor persists over a hundred years after *Principles of Scientific Management* was first published.

Namely, this mechanistic worldview holds that:

1. The perfect system is possible.
2. The perfect system can be achieved by finding 'one best way' to run each of its parts.
3. That management alone is positioned to see and understand all the parts that need fixing.

In 1974, management guru Peter Drucker described Taylor as 'the Isaac Newton... of the science of work,'[iv] which seemed an appropriate description, given his rigid, mechanistic application of the linear, cause-and-effect relationships that characterised Newtonianism. But while Newton's theories have been both de-bunked and expanded upon in the time since his death, Taylor's core ideas have remained largely untouched by most of his successors.

Efficiency or resilience?

Taylor's thesis – like that of so many modern-day management consultants – rests on the notion that efficiency is the primary goal for any organisation to aspire to. In recent years though – and cutting across a whole range of disciplines – greater emphasis is being place in the importance of resilience.

'Resilience,' write ecologists Brian Walker and David Salt, 'is the capacity of a system to absorb disturbance and still maintain its basic function and structure.'[v]

The truth is, efficient organisations are often *less resilient* than their counterparts. Because their efforts are so heavily streamlined towards a specific goal, when context shifts and that goal is sidelined – whether through the market, government policy, or internal changes – they are least able to respond effectively. 'Being efficient,' Salt and Walker continue, 'leads to elimination of redundancies – keeping only those things that are directly and immediately beneficial.' Further, 'the more you optimize elements of a complex system of humans and nature for some specific goal, the more you diminish that system's resilience. A drive for an efficient optimal state outcome has the effect of making the total system more vulnerable to shocks and disturbances.'[vi]

This explains in significant part how large companies can go from leading their field to bankruptcy, almost overnight. When their processes have become so tailored (Taylored?) to a particular aim, an unforeseen change can more easily render them useless.

Even if it were possible to optimise the perfect system, finding the 'one best way' to do each and every thing that the organisation does, the world around it would ensure that it stopped being perfect within moments of its completion. 'Unforeseen circumstances' are a perpetual excuse for failure, yet, if we are honest, they are also the only things we can legitimately predict will occur in our various forecasts and strategies. The fact that we continue to make detailed plans *without* the expectation that things will change unexpectedly is really what's at fault here.

The assumptions of industrialism remain at the core of our work, whether we are building cars, or ending child poverty. It's clearly time for a new vehicle, but maybe we also need to re-learn how to drive it?

Professionalism: Industrialising our behaviour, one phrase or outfit at a time

Before robots existed, Taylor and other industrialists fetishised the possibility that they someday might. They dressed workers in matching overalls and work boots, enacting a disturbing role-play of a future in which free will had been subjugated to the infinite wisdom of expert planners, finally free to shape the world in their image, without humanity to get in the way.

And when these fantasy role-plays were applied to factory floors in the late 19th and early 20thcenturies, they achieved significant success. The combination of the repetitiveness of the tasks of an industrial assembly line, and the brute force which could still acceptably be used to punish insubordination, worked quite well together from a purely economic point of view. In other words, standardisation allowed people to build more identical things, faster, even if some of them died in the process, and countless more suffered a range of unpleasant illnesses, conditions, and unhappy lives as a result.

At an individual level, Taylor's expert planning was the foundation of a very specific standard for 'professional' behaviour that continues to proliferate in a growing range of jobs today. This behaviour pretends that the clothes you wear are a reflection of your skills and abilities, that your choice of language is a sign of your intelligence (or lack thereof), and that whatever you do outside of your nine-to-five routine miraculously vanishes when you sit down at your desk each day.

At the individual level, professionalism is the industrialisation of your behaviours and attitudes; it is what keeps you within the spectrum of 'manageability,' gradually sucking your sense of self and personal autonomy in the process. The thinking must have gone: 'If we make them all dress the same, speak the same, and deny their own feelings or preferences, they will all work with the same (equal) efficiency that the organisational plans we have created expect of them.'

While standardisation had previously been applied to the rote mechanical tasks of the shop floor, management needed to find ways to control people in a more diverse range of working environments. 'What could be transposed from the factory, to the office?' early organisational theorists asked themselves, as the West took its first steps into the world of supposed post-industrialism.

With a bit of creativity, matching overalls become identical grey suits, assembly lines became cubicles, and everything else pretty much continued as it had before. Punch clocks, time sheets, fixed hours, autocratic bosses, specialised roles, massive pay gaps between the top-and-bottom, exclusive hierarchical communication and upward accountability channels, rigid disciplinary methods, and centralised decision making remained.

Of course, we also got meetings: a clever way of managing conversations into the same control-freak pyramid that the rest of the organisation was based on. They were given a chair, a pre-set agenda, and a minute-taker, who shaped the official record of 'what had happened,' a powerful position indeed, while unsurprisingly subordinate to the whims of the boss.

Today you can still find much advice urging a dysfunctional breed of professionalism, like the following passage from 2012:

> 'You must learn to always be professional. Never lose your temper, never cry, never get impatient, never get upset, never show your weakness. If you are caving under pressure, run to the bathroom. ...by being emotional, you are making yourself a liability. No one wants to keep people who are flaky or break under pressure. The corporate world wants people of steel.'[vii]

While some of the language has loosened up in recent years, the professional spectrum remains a narrow one. Though less explicit, it subtly demands behaviours that whittle down our individual rough edges, encouraging conformity in countless aspects of our working lives. It also makes it much harder to involve people from diverse backgrounds in our work, regardless of their strengths and abilities. Professionalism made the walls of the office perpetually explicit, clarifying exactly who belonged and who was unwelcome in the new members-only club.

From 'the model professional' to 'I was just following orders'

In 2000 Jeff Schmidt published *Disciplined Minds: A critical look at salaried professionals and the soul-battering system that shapes their lives.* In it, he describes professionalism as a trait sought by employers looking for prospective staff who can quickly adopt the established protocols of their organisation, willingly subordinating their own values or beliefs in the process. In this sense, professionalism is not simply an abstract notion, or even a particular imposition, like a dress code, but rather description of the practical ways those in professional roles tend to act at their desks and in their offices.

Obedience, for example, is core to this notion of professionalism. Even if it doesn't make it to many of the lists of professional behaviours these days, it is still ubiquitous in innumerable workplaces where dissent is rarely encouraged or appreciated.

Marx (Groucho, that is) perfectly captured this notion when he quipped: 'Those are my principles. If you don't like them I have others.'

Schmidt describes these traits as results of the 'hidden curriculum' in public education, in which children are taught via the underlying structures and methods of their classrooms 'to follow instructions, adhere to a rigid schedule, respect authority, and tolerate boredom.' He goes on to describe the professional as 'one who can be trusted to extrapolate to new situations, the ideology inherent to the official school curriculum.'[viii]

Nowhere is this more obvious than the civil service, where regular changes in government and corresponding ideologies at the top of the organisation require total realignment on the part of those who are charged with turning these political statements into practical policies. When a government is replaced and its successor decides that countless ongoing policies were not in the national interest, a professional civil servant is the one who adopts the new mindset and continues work towards very different ends, with as little break in continuity as possible. Their own beliefs on whatever path they are told to walk become irrelevant. Work is not the place to share their views on the world. There is a job to be done. And they are professionals.

In September 2010 I spent a day work-shadowing an economist at the UK's Home Office shortly after a new government had come to power. While the previous administration had pushed the roll-out of a costly and vaguely Orwellian policy of mandatory ID cards, the new government immediately shelved the plans. For those at the Home Office whose roles had been to operationalise ID cards, their work was all of a sudden against the interests of their employer. Overnight many of their jobs did a one-eighty and they returned to work to undo much of their previous effort.

When I asked about this inconsistency it was met with the blanket response, 'all of our policies are strongly evidence-based.' The role of politics was not part of the discussion. The previous policy had been evidence-based, and the current policy was also evidence-based, even if they directly contradicted each other! Like the perpetual public announcements in Orwell's 1984 of 'We are at war with Eurasia, we have always been at war with Eurasia,' there seemed to be a collective inability to acknowledge the ethical transience of their work, necessarily moving at the whim of the government of the day, facts be damned.

But this phenomenon is not limited to the civil service. The same pattern is apparent in the loyalty of 'the company man,' one of the archetypes of professionalism, always going the extra mile for the firm. He will stick with the employer through thick and thin, placing his family, his values, and his opinions on the backburner until the send-off party, the gold watch, and the comfy pension give him the chance to regain his sense of self.

It is also found in so many military heroes, where the same unquestioning obedience is seen as a badge of honour.

Sadly, when leadership goes bat-shit crazy, as it often does, those who were considered heroes are left clinging to the 'I was only following orders' defence, while the former rebels and traitors enjoy a brief dose of accolades for *their* heroism, grounded in principled refusal rather than unthinking obedience.

Industrialism requires professionalism to standardise individual behaviour, keeping the gears of the organisational machine running as managers deem they should. Professionalism, in turn, requires the subjugation of our beliefs, and by extension, our humanity. When we can't be ourselves, bad things happen.

Meanwhile, in the 21st Century...

While the ethics of this damning pair of ideas have always been elitist, oppressive and undemocratic, at one point they provided a practical means of achieving certain rote large-scale tasks. Today the ethics remain problematic, but the practical value of these dated approaches is also being thrown into question by emergent events and actions organised around very different principles.

Big changes can be the result of small actions; a person with a laptop can launch a worldwide campaign; we don't need to put on a suit and tie to win the respect of those with whom we share a passion. Social change – among other things – doesn't require the structures and strategies we once thought it did.

When the New York City General Assembly decided to heed the call from *Adbusters* to descend on the city's financial district on September 17, 2011, they hadn't planned on spending the night.

...And when Tunisian vegetable seller Mohammed Bouazizi set himself on fire on December 17, 2010, in a final act of desperation over the poverty and violence he was faced with, authorities across the Middle East had no idea how far the repercussions would spread.

...And when senior officers of the London Metropolitan Police refused to meet with the peacefully gathered members of the Tottenham, North London, community on August 6, 2011, after the police had shot and killed local resident Mark Duggan, they probably thought they were avoiding confrontation when tensions were peaked.

In each of these contexts, for better or worse, none of us could have predicted what followed.

As you know, that New York City General Assembly action was the birth of the Occupy movement; Bouazizi's death, two-weeks after his self-immolation, is said to have kick-started the Arab Spring, and members of the peaceful crowd in North London, after many attempts to get an explanation for their neighbour's death, went on to spark the London Riots.

History is filled with stories like these – seemingly random, small-scale events, with massive and unimaginable implications. They are the social manifestations of what meteorologist Edward Lorenz termed 'the butterfly effect' back in 1969, describing the ability of seemingly insignificant and disparate parts of an interconnected environment to affect one another in wide-ranging and unexpected ways.

These are the kinds of events that countless social change organisations would desperately hope to help create or avoid, but the systems of organisation inherited from Frederick Winslow Taylor and his ideological kinsfolk couldn't be more poorly suited for the task.

While Taylorism relied on controlling, from above, every part and sub-part of a system to achieve the desired result, the emergent change characterised by the butterfly effect is the result of many individual parts of a system acting autonomously, creating emergent, rather than pre-determined results. It's the kind of change that happens when the people involved are free to be themselves, rather than to follow steps set out by others.

As mass communication moves from the hierarchical distribution channels of TV and newspapers, to the distributed networks of social media, infinite new spaces for this kind of emergence are opening up. Like the flapping of a butterfly's wings, a Tweet, a slogan, or a story can travel rapidly to places no one ever thought they could, shared and adapted repeatedly by those with whom they resonate.

So while few social change organisations would publically espouse the controlling values at the core of our organisational structures, we are also clearly invested in them. But their growing ineffectiveness in the face of more horizontal organising approaches – on the web and in the streets – is raising more fundamental questions about why we are using these systems in the first place. Is change finally on its way?

Why the social web is on a collision course with your organisational chart

On the surface, organisations across most sectors have embraced social media. They probably have a Facebook page, a Twitter profile, maybe even a blog, or a YouTube account. But fundamentally, they are still the machine-like organisations of yesterday, with a few motivational posters tacked-up by the water cooler to give the appearance of progressive management.

The issue lies in what we perceive social media to be. Do we see it as an extra budget line in a campaign strategy? A direct marketing channel? A 'keeping up with the Joneses' fad that must be tolerated until it goes the way of the pet rock or stonewash jeans?

Rarely is the potential of social media understood in organisations, because at its best it can unravel a range of deeper organisational assumptions that have long passed their best-before dates. This can be scary for people who have long relied on those assumptions. The implications of the power social media unlocks are far reaching, in ways we are still only beginning to understand.

At its core, social media is allowing people to find and do more and more things, directly, with more and more other people, in ways that would traditionally have required institutional intervention. And to institutions that have been largely created to play this in-between role (whether coordinating campaigns, or bringing donations to those who need them during disasters), this logic simply does not compute.

The good news is that our organisations don't have to face the level of redundancy of, say, the Mubarak regime in Egypt, before they can start to let go of the assumptions on the left side of the upcoming chart, and find practical ways of embracing those on the right.

The pages of this book are filled with examples of how this is being done: sometimes through radically different, non-organisational approaches, sometimes through brick-by-brick piecemeal shifts that cumulatively reshape an organisation's identity. The point is not to offer blueprints for change, but to highlight what makes these new approaches different from (and often, more successful than) much of what we've been doing, so we can think about what they might mean in our own particular contexts.

For all the challenges that the social web and its staggering pace-of-change have created, we have one major asset to keep us from stumbling, utterly clueless, into new situations and dynamics as we try to change the world: ourselves. Social media has become a deeply counterintuitive reminder of much of what it means to be human, as a range of social factors have, for decades, pushed us away from such fundamental understandings. For instance, who would've imagined that sitting in front of our monitors could help to reawaken some of our natural but dormant sociability? That websites, mobile phones and apps could help us relate to each other in a more personal way than we likely have in our work, or even other parts of our lives? That a website could provide an emergent breadcrumb trail that leads us into relationships with people who will change our lives, or us, theirs?

Here are a few ways in which traditional management structures are likely to be at odds with the underpinning principles of social media:

The Management/Social Media Conflict

Management Assumptions	Social Media Assumptions
Decisions should be made by someone more senior than the person taking the action	Decisions should be made by whomever is there to make them
Job titles and descriptions create a sense of order, which helps get things done	Job titles and descriptions prevent people from working to their strengths, passions and interests
Expertise and leadership are concentrated at the top of the organisational structure	Expertise and leadership are shared amongst everyone – inside and outside the organisation – and shift, depending on the situation
To get things done, we need to be able to control them at each stage	The most amazing outcomes are the result of the most people, working with the most autonomy, united by a broader shared sense of purpose
Resources should only be allocated to efforts that create a clear, causal return on investment	Seemingly meaningless conversations can be the glue of stronger working relationships, and need the freedom to happen
Internal communication should travel through the appropriate chain of command	Anyone can talk to anyone else, if it will help them get things done
External communication can be kept to office hours	External communication happens when people from outside your organisation engage with you
Clear hierarchy ensures information reaches the right people and parts of the organisation	Hierarchy distorts information and denies people the agency to share ideas on their own terms

Yet that is exactly what's been happening.

As Jamie Notter (@jamienotter) and Maddie Grant (@maddiegrant) put it in *Humanize: How people-centric organizations succeed in a social world:*

> One of the most important reasons social media has been so successful and grown so quickly is that it has tapped into what it means to be human... Social media has given all of us the power to do what we as humans always wanted to do. Social media allows us to be more of who we are.[ix]

So let's reconnect with our instincts and ask ourselves:

> *What kind of organisation would I most enjoy being a part of?*
>
> *What could my working relationships learn from how my best personal relationships work?*
>
> *How would I do this job if my colleagues were my friends, and our office was a park or cafe?*

A brief history of organising for good causes outside of institutions

While social media represents a key shift in how people do things in groups, it is unique primarily in its scale, rather than its principles. The concepts that fill the right-hand column of the table above are assumptions that have been seeded, nourished and grown in social movements all across the globe for centuries.

While we often hold a certain reverence for the movements that have brought about countless significant gains we now take for granted – from women's suffrage, to the end of Apartheid in South Africa – we rarely see those involved in social movements today as people who could teach us how to get things done. But it was movements, not simply organisations or individual leaders that:

- Secured women's rights to vote all over the world
- Helped end the Vietnam War
- Brought Apartheid to an end

- Won civil rights for African Americans
- Won healthcare, welfare and workers' rights for millions of citizens
- Overthrew innumerable oppressive colonial dictatorships

These are victories that no organisation could have achieved on its own. So as we move headlong into a world that is increasingly enabling the emergence of new movements, what can our organisations do to be effective and constructive agents of the change we want to see?

One thing we can do is start listening to those we have traditionally ignored, and open our doors to those who might have different ideas about how change happens. They often don't look, act, or sound like the management gurus we've been told we should look to for guidance, but they may still have critical insights to offer our organisations.

Enter: *Anarchism!*

While perhaps not as widely demonised as the ideas of socialism in 1950s America, anarchism has pretty negative connotations these days. Images of black hoodies and bandanas from one international protest or another, brick or bottle in hand, smashing a corporate storefront, understandably make some uneasy with the phrase. While in keeping with the spirit of anarchism I don't believe it is my place to denounce others, the Black Bloc tactic is not where the focus of this book lies.

In spite of the stigma that surrounds anarchism, variations on its ideas have been the ideological underpinnings of many social movements around the world, and are also useful in understanding the rise of the social web. Much of this stigma arises from our collective conflation of *order* and *control*. In a nutshell, anarchism places the highest faith in human potential, arguing that we do not need outside structures to create order. Anarchists believe that social order is the result of individual autonomy and self-organisation, rather than the imposition of control by some over many, whether through violent dictatorship or liberal democracy. As we've seen, belief in the centrality of control has criss-crossed much of the political spectrum, placing

Our abusive relationship with our organisations

When you met, things were good.

An initial boost of confidence; someone thought you were worth taking a chance on! Some consistency in your life, some firm patterns to keep you moving forward, a sense of the possibility of the things you'd do together, the financial security they offered.

But it didn't take long for all that to change. Almost before it started, the honeymoon was over.

You remember the first time you suggested something new, something you hoped to do. They didn't take you seriously, told you to 'be realistic.' Then eventually they just ignored you... so you let it go.

The next time you had an idea, their patience was shorter; they made fun of you for even thinking of such things. The next time, you just kept it to yourself, not wanting to face the judgment again, not wanting to feel so bad about yourself.

You told yourself they'd change, if you just stuck it out. You could change them, if you really tried.

At some point, you realised you weren't achieving your potential in the relationship. You offered to do more, you tried to take on different roles, but they weren't interested. They told you to 'know your place' and to 'mind your business.' You gradually forgot that you could do these things; that you had more you could offer. You felt like it was them, not you, that defined who you were. You stopped feeling like you could grow, or even like you had the potential to grow.

After a while, the consistency and the patterns became a burden – same ol', same ol'. Financial security started to feel like financial dependency, the sense of possibility was narrowed to what they told you was ok for you to do.

To be continued

anarchism at fundamental odds with the ideas of capitalism, communism, fascism, and of course, the vast majority of management theory.

'I am not myself free or human,' wrote Russian anarchist Mikhail Bakunin, 'until or unless I recognize the freedom and humanity of all my fellowmen.'[x] It is probably safe to say that Frederick Winslow Taylor wasn't a fan.

Anarchism discourages the individual leadership and cult of personality that has been so central to so many political and organisational systems, instead seeing leadership as a collective trait, encompassed by the many individuals who make up a society. Systems of leadership that make some people submissive to others, inevitably impede individual autonomy, stifling collective potential.

Anarchist ideas are not as isolated as you might think. World-renowned linguist Noam Chomsky describes himself as an anarcho-syndicalist, while Carne Ross (@carneross), former UN diplomat to Tony Blair, who resigned over the Iraq War, and has since gone on to author a book called, *The Leaderless Revolution*, calls himself a 'gentle anarchist.' Ross describes anarchism as 'a new and more durable order... built from the ground up, by people acting on their beliefs and engaging with each other.'[xi] While still not popular, there are several established and respectable names across a range of fields and disciplines that have associated themselves with these beliefs.

Perhaps more accessible to some are the ways that our engagement with social media is demonstrating anarchist principles, as countless individual autonomous efforts can coalesce into something bigger, often creating political and social power where before there had only been isolated voices. Even the forward-thinking companies and organisations you'll hear about here are beginning to talk about the principles of autonomy and self-organisation at the core of anarchist philosophy.

So if you're wondering what 'more like people' is all about, think of it as 'anarchism for your organisation.' But how do you introduce anarchism to a Taylorist machine?

Our abusive relationship with our organisations (continued)

Your friends kept telling you that you had to get out. But you couldn't imagine what it would be like to wake up without having them to go to.

Each day it wore on you a little more, but each day you found it a little harder to imagine anything different. There was always an excuse to keep going back, if only for the security, the stability of it.

Occasionally you'd still try to change them, try to make them what you had always hoped they would be, but eventually, after things had gotten especially bad, you decided you'd had enough.

So you left them. And look where you've ended up:

You're free to be yourself – not just as you are, but as you hope to be. You're free to grow – encouraged, even, to pursue new aspects of yourself.

This new relationship pushes you, in the best possible ways, to try new things, experiment, even if that means you make mistakes sometimes. They don't hold it against you.

Maybe you don't have the same financial security this time around, but it doesn't bother you – you are happy, you are pushing yourself and you are doing good things. Money somehow doesn't mean as much when these other pieces are in place.

You don't stay because you feel you have to, but because you want to.

Your days, your outlook, your world, all look different now. It's not that you're without conflict, but that you can both handle it constructively, learning and emerging stronger in yourselves through the process.

Occasionally, you look back and you think: 'How did I stay in that awful job for so long!'

How organisational change happens

So much traditional management theory has focussed, perhaps unsurprisingly, on the role of managers – usually senior ones – in bringing about organisational change. This model is based on the same assumption that is at the core of our organisations themselves; namely, that power lies at the top of the organisational chart and emanates downward from there. But this is only ever partly true.

Like the belief that all power in a country rests in its government, the idea that power rests with the leader is a deeply disempowering notion for everyone else within the system, whether it is a society or an organisation. Our problem has been that we so often forget the changes that have occurred *in spite* of traditional power bases, rather than because of them.

Different kinds of power exist in different parts of a system, thus change can come from many places and take many forms. Sometimes change happens through formal channels, but many other times it will creep around the edges, starting informally, gradually establishing legitimacy on its own terms. Often it will be the result of 'hacking' the existing system, re-purposing the old structures in ways they were never intended. But whether formal or informal, it will never emerge or be driven solely from above.

The pages that follow look at organisational change as the result of four different approaches:

1. **Top-Down:** Management literature suggests that power rests at the top of the pyramid, and like trickle-down economics, organisational change will cascade its way from the head to the toes of any institution. This kind of change can be useful for progressive directors wanting to get old structures out of the way (ideally with clear staff mandate to do so). However, it tends to have more limits than benefits in most 'more like people' scenarios, but still has its place, in combination with the other approaches below.

2. **Bottom-Up:** Much Marxist thought has championed the bottom-up power of the masses, demonstrating the change

that can come from large groups of people coming together to challenge the traditional powers of the state and big business, often securing changes that benefit a wider layer of those affected. Collective power in the most oppressive of working environments is often captured through unionism, though unions have too often come to model the worst bureaucratic structures themselves. Organisationally, this approach runs the risk of reinforcing us-and-them workplace dynamics that, even if traditionally true, get in the way of all involved finding common ground and working together towards shared goals.

3. **Collaborative:** While there can be value in both of the above understandings of power and change, there is also a more collaborative approach, which, at its best, can utilise some of the traditional power of the formal hierarchy, as well as the groundswell of collective power. This has been seen when leftist governments and social movements in Latin America have been able to bring about greater change, through complimentary approaches to different social problems. Within an organisation, it can be about representative democratic change, but requires a certain amount of existing shared vision, trust and power across the organisation to be most useful.

4. **Emergent:** This is the change that happens regardless of top-down or bottom-up efforts. It is the change described by the concept of the butterfly effect, when a shift in one part of a system leads to an unexpected shift in another part of that system. A chat at the water cooler leads to a policy being scrapped. A Tweet leads to a closer relationship between different teams. A batch of homemade cookies leads to someone treating the person they manage more nicely because they're in a better mood. This kind of change is hard to track and impossible to coordinate, but happens every day and offers each of us the chance to influence the broader organisation through our individual choices and behaviours. At times it can amble along without much broader impact, while at other times it can take off at lightning speed as a new idea goes viral and shifts a broader system in the process. It is the heart of 'more like people' change, though it doesn't discount the roles the other approaches can play in any complex system.

Emergent change is the only approach that can have a place in the full range of organisational contexts, and thus is the primary approach of the book. However, it is far from the only way and different chapters and stories will look to understand change through each of the four approaches above.

While Top-Down still plays a role, this book aims to smash its often-perceived monopoly on organisational change and paint a picture of changes that can come from anywhere within a system. 'more like people' is management for anyone who manages or is managed in an organisation that is trying to improve the world. We all play a part in making our organisations what they are, and can thus play a part in making them what they could be.

So what does an organisation that is 'more like people' look like?

Since I started describing my work as 'helping organisations to be more like people,' I've often been confronted with the retort, 'What *kind* of people?' This is often conveyed in a slightly snarky tone of voice, which I've felt carries an assumption of the worst amongst humans– that people will be mean, selfish and inconsiderate, if given half a chance. Without unpicking the philosophy of this assumption right away (I will in Chapter 3), I generally respond with a dose of anarchistic optimism: 'The good ones; the ones we aspire to be.'

It goes without saying that not all human qualities are things we want to consciously emulate in our institutions. We all have the capacity to be rude, impersonal, cruel, petty, but we also have the potential to be the full spectrum of more positive attributes. And these are the adjectives that are rarely used to describe our organisations: trusting, flexible, understanding, and creative.

For years, management literature has been 'helping organisations to be more like machines' – more rigid, more hierarchical, more predictable and inflexible. The assumption is this will bestow the same virtues that assembly lines did for automobile production on everything else we do: that we will get more for less.

But we don't. It's a nice idea, but I'm sorry to say, Mr. Taylor, it doesn't work in most of the real world. Even its applicability to building machines has been thrown into question by people we'll hear from later, who build machines, but do so through processes that don't resemble them.

An organisation that is 'more like people' is constantly changing, learning, adapting, questioning. Its processes and systems are not the assembly lines of industrialism, but the swarms and clusters of people who come together on their own accord whenever they discover a shared passion and decide they need to make something happen. For instance, an organisation may start by working to improve children's diets in a poorer neighbourhood, but end up working with new parents on confidence issues, or pushing for government policy to support new childcare options. It may hire someone to do graphic design work, but realise that, because of *who* they are, they are better equipped teaching kids about positive life choices. It may avoid writing a five-year strategy in favour of a more ad hoc approach, constantly checking its collective pulse, asking questions of, and listening to, those inside and outside its walls to ensure it is on the right track, radically adjusting when it is not.

An organisation that is 'more like people' is one that people enjoy or appreciate coming to work at, being in contact with, or being supported by. It emphasises strong relationships. It encourages staff to try new things and work to their passions. It assumes that knowledge, expertise, new ideas and solutions can come from everywhere, not simply those who have words like *director, head* or *leader* in their job titles.

The vision acknowledges that even in our more aspirational moments, people are still messy, relationships need conflict, innovation needs failure, and change needs chaos. Most of our organisations go to great lengths to produce systems that deny, discourage or cover-up these unsightly realities, rather than embracing them for the natural part of life that they are. In their efforts to be 'more like machines,' (or 'more like paper,' as my friend Paul [@PaulBarasi] has often described them) they blind us to certain realities. Like an ostrich with its head in the sand, our professional systems of planning, organising and reporting go to great lengths to give us the illusion of control in a deeply complex – and ultimately uncontrollable – world.

Just like people, no two organisations that are 'more like people' will be the same. Their aims, their contexts, their sizes, their locations, will all have meant they will have grown and adapted very differently, even if their core values are similar. Like the tastes of two wines, grown from the same grape seeds but planted in different soils and exposed to different weather, no two 'more like people' organisations can emerge identical to one another. But the seeds, the world over, can be rooted in three simple 'more like people' principles:

- **Humanity**: Being ourselves, while growing and learning to build stronger relationships.
- **Autonomy:** Having the freedom to find our own best ways of doing things.
- **Complexity:** Understanding that life is as emergent, non-linear, and interdependent as we are.

Beyond these three principles (which we will explore in detail in Chapter 2), a range of qualities, including trust, purpose, empathy, collaboration, diversity, flexibility, and risk will be regularly revisited throughout the book, as cornerstones of the 'more like people' approach.

There is nothing perfect about a 'more like people' organisation – far from it! Things will always go wrong along the way. But as we begin to move in the right direction, we'll hopefully be able to notice them, respond to them, and try a range of new choices more easily than we traditionally have. I hope that by connecting with the humanity, the autonomy, and the complexity that are the hallmarks of groups of people doing amazing things, we'll continuously find it easier to improve along the way.

Reminding ourselves what it's all about

Social change organisations have a natural disposition towards the 'more like people' approach. Our purposes are those that people *voluntarily* choose to be involved with. Our visions describe the kinds of world that most of us would like to live in, and we offer support and voice to those who have often struggled to get or have either. Yet as we've seen, many have drifted away from what these ideals should mean at an operational level, borrowing our blueprints from institutions set-up with no aim other than to maximise cash profits. (A goal that has broadly served to *undermine* the visions many of our organisations were set-up to achieve!)

While predisposed to these values, social change organisations have nothing like a monopoly on being 'more like people.' In fact, several forward-thinking corporations around the world are doing a better job of modelling more people-centric approaches than their non-profit counterparts by trusting their staff, getting out of the way of new ideas and encouraging more autonomous models of working among the people they employ.

More commonly, however, the best examples of 'more like people' organisations are not coming from organisations at all, but from informal community and activist groups that have come together to challenge injustices, address collective needs, share solutions and model alternative and sustainable ways of getting things done together in the process.

From worker-occupied factories in Argentina and non-violent environmental direct action groups in the UK, to spontaneous democratic uprisings across the Middle East and massive online global protest movements, the chapters ahead brush away our preconceptions and start a new conversation about how we do things worth doing. We'll look at how these unlikely management gurus are practically living 'more like people' approaches, and what that might mean for social change organisations at different points on their journey towards more human ways of organising.

And while there is a clear ethical imperative for organisations that promote social change to be 'more like people,' there is also a very practical one: we can be better than we have been. As the Occupy movement and so many more local counterparts have demonstrated, when committed individuals are left to their own devices, with a shared sense of purpose, they are capable of amazing things.

As we fly headlong into a world we have yet to fully comprehend, rather than looking to the so-called experts to guide us safely into a radically different way of doing things, let's not forget that we can be our own best compasses in the journey. If we can stay grounded in the things we feel, the ways we respond, the dynamics we want to share with those we work with, we are likely to be better equipped for the new, emergent world than the many organisations who hire 'change managers' to transition them into something strangely resembling what they've always been.

[i] David Graeber, 'Enacting the impossible: Making decisions by consensus,' in *This Changes Everything: Occupy Wall Street and the 99% Movement*, Berrett-Koehler, 2011, p. 23.

[ii] Frederick Winslow Taylor, *Principles of Scientific Management, cited by Montgomery, The Fall of the House of Labour*, Cambridge U P, 1989: p. 229 (italics with Taylor).

[iii] Thomas Hughes, 'American Genesis,' University of Chicago Press, 2004, p. 251.

[iv] Peter Drucker, *Management: Tasks, Responsibilities, Practices*. Harper & Row, 1974, p. 181.

[v] Brian Walker & David Salt, *Resilience Thinking*, Island Press, 2006, p. 7.

[vi] Ibid, p. 9.

[vii] 'How to be a professional at work,' *eHow.com* (since removed).

[viii] Jeff Schmidt, *Disciplined Minds*, 2000, audiobook, chapter 2, 07:43.

[ix] Jamie Notter & Maddie Grant, *Humanize*, Que Publishing, 2011, p. 91-92

[x] Mikhail Bakunin, 'Man, Society, and Freedom,' 1871.

[xi] Carne Ross, *The Leaderless Revolution*, Blue River Press, 2011, pp. 60.

Transition Diagram

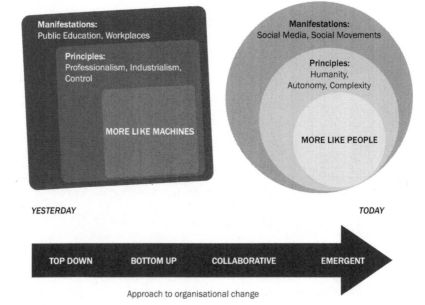

Manifestations:
Public Education, Workplaces

Principles:
Professionalism, Industrialism, Control

MORE LIKE MACHINES

Manifestations:
Social Media, Social Movements

Principles:
Humanity, Autonomy, Complexity

MORE LIKE PEOPLE

YESTERDAY   *TODAY*

TOP DOWN   BOTTOM UP   COLLABORATIVE   EMERGENT

Approach to organisational change

The 'more like people' principles: humanity, autonomy, complexity

2

'I believe really strongly in bringing your personality to work. I think you get the best out of people if they know something about the people that they're working with.' – Peter Wanless, Big Lottery Fund

'Every situation is different; things are always changing. It's a complex world.' – Brian Walker and David Salt

We know the case for change. We know our traditional organisational alternatives are no longer either desirable or tenable. But what can we do differently? What is the alternative?

There is, of course, no single alternative. Contrary to the assertions of men like Frederick Winslow Taylor, there is no 'one best way' forward. The world is a complex place, and complexity is key to understanding the changes that are happening all around us. When we can relax the rules around how our organisations should operate, and how we should operate within them, we are far more able to live up to both the demands of the 21st century and the ethics that brought us into this kind of work. We need the autonomous space – inside and outside our organisations – to pursue our desire to better the world in whatever ways we feel inspired to. This kind of change has no blueprint, but is guided by certain principles.

Social media and social movements, at their best, can align the deeply inter-related 'more like people' principles of humanity, autonomy and complexity, showing us new ways of organising ourselves beyond the remnants of Industrialism we still find ourselves practising. Chapter 2 outlines each of these principles in greater detail, providing a lens from which to understand the specific problems and solutions outlined throughout the rest of this book.

Complexity: Moving from cogs to consciousness

'Put your hand on a hot stove for a minute and it seems like an hour. Sit with a pretty girl for an hour and it seems like a minute. That's relativity.'[i] Thus was Albert Einstein's down-to-earth explanation of the theory for which he became most famous.

As was the case with Sir Isaac Newton's classical mechanics centuries before, lessons from Einstein's take on natural science started to find homes in far-flung fields and disciplines, gradually transforming the way we saw the world. While the theory of relativity demonstrated a newfound subjectivity in our understandings of time and space (acknowledging the influence of the observer in any form of scientific measurement), it also offered a scientific basis for the philosophical notion of relativism, incorporating the centrality of subjectivity into a wider range of life questions.

In contrast to the black-and-white worldview of absolute objectivism and rationality popularised during the European Enlightenment, relativism emphasises the observer in interpreting and participating in what they see, based on their previous experiences and understandings of the world. Relativism may well be captured most succinctly by the popular phrase 'perception is reality,' three words to make Frederick Winslow Taylor turn in his grave, undermining the absolute authority of an expert's all-seeing eye.

Since the days of Einstein, a range of other disciplines have also picked up on aspects of relativity and relativism. In stark contrast to Newtonian objectivism, Chilean biologists Humberto Maturana and Fransisco Varela discovered that human visual perception is 80 percent -based on what we personally already know and believe, while only 20percent is the result of the outside world we are observing. Previous science had presumed that our eyes objectively converted visual information from the world around us, into something our brains could understand, yet Maturana and Varela demonstrated that most of what we 'see' is actually the result of our brains putting together a picture from information they already have, with a relatively small new input from the world beyond.[ii] Thus, at some level, subjective perception applies even to the seemingly fixed notion of eyesight, going some way to explaining the frustration that occurs when two people, experiencing the same phenomenon, come to wildly different conclusions about it.

Applied to organisational life, relativism chucks Frederick Winslow Taylor's scientific management out the window of a tall building. From handling management-staff relations, to writing standard policy documents, the objectivism that frames so many organisational practices is thrown into question by the idea that the real human beings involved in such processes probably don't all see them in exactly the same way.

Chapter 2:
The 'more
like people'
principles:
humanity,
autonomy,
complexity

The science legitimised by Einstein and others laid some of the early bedrock for our relatively recent understanding of complex systems. Several key concepts, however, make complexity different from most Newtonian science. Among these is its emphasis not on material things or people, but the *relationships* between those things and people. This means understanding whole systems, and not simply the arbitrary parts (teams, subjects, disciplines) we so often divide them into. So, when applied to organisations, rather than simply producing an organisational chart visualising a hierarchy of managers and workers, complexity tells us that it is the ever-subjective line connecting the two roles that is most determinant in understanding the work that will occur.

What the organisational chart also misses – much like the linear management approaches it is based on – is that organisations have infinite relationships, inside and outside their walls, which collectively play a strong role in shaping what the organisation *actually does* and how it *actually does it*. The chart cannot tell you, for instance, that Zoe in Finance is a close friend of James, the Head of Human Resources, creating a mutually beneficial connection (between Finance and HR) that supersedes the official organisational processes when either of them – or their respective teams – need to get things done. Or that a one-night stand gone ugly between Sophie in Campaigns and Alex in Policy has had ripple effects, with both teams involved taking sides on the matter. In a complex system, relationships are central, meaning cogs (or people) cannot simply be replaced, as their job titles might suggest they could, and be expected to create the same results.

Complexity is...

- The importance of the whole, rather than simply its component parts
- An emphasis on relationships between parts and people, rather than just the parts or people themselves
- Life's ability to self-organise at every scale
- Emergent, rather than predetermined outcomes

Additionally, complexity – based on countless studies of living systems at every scale – tells us that life constantly self-organises, whether we like it or not. Our uniquely human systems of top-down management fly in the face of countless other living systems, from bacteria to whole ecosystems, not to mention the things people achieve when they don't have organisations to tell them what to do.[iii]

Deeply connected to the notion of self-organising systems, is that of *emergence*, the idea that results grow and develop organically, through random on-going interactions, rather than as the result of pre-determined top-down plans. While the Taylorist machine metaphor has offered us the illusion of control, emergence offers us something far greater: endless possibility beyond what any of our leaders could have predicted in advance.

The online and offline social movements that appear throughout this book are practical examples of this emergent phenomenon. They are the unimagined results of a dovetailing of countless small, self-driven actions, drawn together by a shared sense of purpose, and an ever-growing ability to connect that purpose with others in so many diverse corners of the world. While our societal belief in the wide-ranging applications of Newton's physics initially makes it very difficult for many of us to view this kind of activity as a serious alternative to current organising structures, its effects are all around us, if we choose to see them.

At its most basic level, with the above characteristics in mind, complexity theory defines questions and problems in one of three ways:

- Simple
- Complicated
- Complex

Brenda Zimmerman, in her 2006 book with Frances Westley and Michael Quinn Patton, *Getting to Maybe: How the world is changed*, has provided an archetypal understanding of the differences among these designations, exemplifying the distinctions as follows:

- Making a cake is simple
- Launching a rocket is complicated
- Raising a baby is complex[iv]

A cake – if the recipe is good and the correct ingredients available – can be made by almost anyone, regardless of skill or talent. It is primarily a good recipe that makes a good cake.

A rocket is also launched using a relatively fixed formula, but it is unlikely that you or I could walk into NASA's Cape Canaveral and make it happen. While the recipe is key, so are skills and experience related to rocket-launching– without these, the formula won't get us very far.

A baby, on the other hand, is an entirely different story. Once she or he is born there is no reliable how-to guide. Nor is previous experience necessarily an indicator of being able to raise a healthy, well-adjusted adult. In fact, the step-by-step guide and past experiences may well *work against you*, if you rely on them too heavily, as many parents have lamented after their second child has entered the world.

This is where the relationship stuff comes in. A baby doesn't exist in a vacuum. It is impacted by, and has impacts on, the world around it – a hallmark of any complex system. A baby born during a recession to two suddenly out-of-work parents will be impacted by such early experiences. A baby with health problems that cause them to cry all night, keeping their parents awake, will impact on those parents in a range of ways. They may in turn have less patience, or less energy for other things in their lives, which will likely influencing the child as well.

When the baby gets to school age, their teachers, their neighbourhood and their classmates will all influence their development. As the child becomes more independent, little by little, the range of relationships around them all begin to have an effect, just as the child does on those same relationships and the others involved in them.

What do babies have to do with my work?

The world of social change has a lot more in common with the baby than it does with the cake or the rocket ship, yet looking at how we organise ourselves would suggest otherwise.

The international development world has often described issues of complexity as 'wicked problems,' those 'without form, structure, or solution.' The Overseas Development Institute (ODI/@ODI_development) identifies three components to so-called wicked problems:

1. What is needed to address them is not found in any particular organisation or agency, but in a combination of several different institutions,

2. They are hard to predict and often spring-up, seemingly out of nowhere,

3. Many stakeholders aim to address the same questions in radically different ways, often working against each other in the process.[v]

While a step in the right direction, this kind of analysis and its corresponding recommendations are still one among several examples of more traditional organisations trying to fit a complex reality into a 'complicated' framework. Complexity science tells us that when two or more independent variables come together, we can't say for sure what the outcome will be. When an infinite number of independent variables are constantly bumping into one another, there's no point even trying to predict the results. Doing so will likely only blind us to what's actually going on.

Now, if we think of something that our social change organisations might do – trying to end homelessness, for example – what kind of problem or question do you think this would qualify as: simple, complicated, or complex?

We know that people become homeless for a wide variety of reasons (grief, mental illness, poverty, housing policy, substance use, domestic violence, trauma, etc.). We also know that it is rarely just one of these reasons, but often the combination of two or more of them interacting with each other that finally push people onto the streets. We know that the longer someone lives in the streets, due to the additional problems that arise from the experience (health deterioration, abuse, trauma, etc.), the longer it is likely to be before they are able to be happily housed again. We also know that different people respond to different kinds of support differently, due to a range of factors we can only begin to imagine about their lives before we came into contact with them.

Chapter 2:
The 'more
like people'
principles:
humanity,
autonomy,
complexity

If your aim were to get just one homeless individual off the street, you would be dealing with complexity. When you work in an organisation that aims to change the living arrangements of literally thousands of rough sleepers, it certainly doesn't get any simpler. Good workers and volunteers involved in ending homelessness know this at a visceral level, adapting what they do to fit each particular person's situation, at whatever stage they are at in a difficult process.

Yet our organisations' approaches seem perpetually stuck somewhere between dealing with 'simple' and 'complicated' problems. We write a business plan to describe each of the steps we will take before we've taken them. We measure our work against the completion of these predetermined steps. But like the how-to guide and expert advice for child rearing, the more we tell ourselves that following these steps is the way to achieve our aims, the less likely we are to notice that the road has curved under us and our linear trajectory has driven us off into the bush somewhere.

'Disasters can occur when complex problems are managed or measured as if they are merely complicated or even simple,' write Zimmerman, Westley and Quinn Patton, in *Getting to Maybe*. Describing the reliance on pharmaceutical solutions in so many mental health services, they continue,' The fact that many patients are too ill to adhere to their prescribed drug regimens is ignored as it demands of our specialists a level of interaction and adjustment most are not equipped to deliver.'[vi] Rather than developing more personalised provision, based on particular needs, too often the response is to impose new ways of forcing people to take their medicines, which then invariably leads patients to finding more creative ways of avoiding them, sparking a costly downward competitive spiral, rather than a solution.

In such examples we find the ripple effects of Frederick Winslow Taylor's 'one best way' still playing themselves out, hopelessly patching band-aid on top of band-aid, so thoroughly committed we are to our initial approach being right that we keep reinforcing its faulty logic, unwilling to try something different, when something different is often exactly what is needed. Without change, systems eventually fall apart.

The way most people handle the complexity of raising a baby is instructive: *be flexible, adapt, accept that things will go wrong along the way, and allow for new interactions to occur. Don't expect you can transfer your knowledge of life to a child without them having to learn things for themselves that you already knew. Pay attention to what goes wrong and what goes right, but don't assume the same pattern will repeat next time. Notice things in the moment, and don't let yourself get too distracted by your long-term objectives along the way.*

This is the essence of successful work in a complex world. It is not about linear thinking or following rules, but about adaptive flexibility in the moment, and accepting the need to shift when the world tells you something isn't working. 'more like people' means learning to accept that we will see the same things differently and should not impose our particular theory of change on the world around us unquestioningly, just because it made sense to the few of us who were a part of the strategy meeting that developed it however many months or years ago.

The first time I ran a workshop on the theme of complexity, after months of reading and preparation, I spent almost a full afternoon lecturing those who came along on the importance of flexibility and adapting to new information. Unfortunately, I did this while ignoring the fact that my audience had come to do something a bit more participatory, had told me so at the start and at the break, and had mostly dozed off or left before I completed my in-depth sermon on the complex world around us.

After that event I realised how thoroughly my means and ends had become unaligned, and was able to take the lessons of my own hypocrisy into future workshops. I did this by making sure I had a co-facilitator to work with who would happily cut me off if I went too far into lecture mode. Gradually, I got to a point where I could let groups direct themselves, offer their own insights, and shape their own session, with only sporadic input from myself when I felt that new information would enrich their process. Unsurprisingly, as I became more flexible, the feedback improved, as participants were able to shape their sessions along the way.

We can practice working with complexity both individually and organisationally. A first step might be in appreciating that someone else's perspective is still a perspective, and that, just like our own, an infinite number of experiences will have shaped it. Personally, I have found this helps avoid non-constructive conflict in working relationships. By remembering the complexities that have produced someone else's differing views, I can breakdown the black-and-white understanding that easily leads to vilifying a colleague who seems to be undermining or criticising me at every stage. If you can find the space to discuss your differences at a less operational level (for example, the deeper question of why someone supports doing 'x'), it might provide the chance to get a better understanding of where each of you are coming from, easing some of the tensions between you.

In what parts of your life do you accept complexity as a given?

When do you find it hardest to let go of your plan?

What helps you pay attention to what is happening around you in the moment?

Humanity: What we can learn from ourselves?

While approaching the world as a complex system can help us adjust the ways we work from an intellectual point of view, it doesn't necessarily shift us at that more visceral level where individual change is more likely to occur. For this kind of change, we might have to dig a little deeper.

Humanity is...

- Trust of and empathy with others
- Awareness of what we bring to any relationship
- Learning from the rest of our lives
- Being ourselves!

The stifling and dehumanising processes of professionalism have embedded themselves so deeply in so many of us that re-learning to *be ourselves* may be the hardest aspect of change this book encourages.

As complexity explains why the relationships between parts of a system, or people in an organisation, are more important than the roles themselves, we need to think about what we are contributing (or taking away) from the many relationships of which we're a part.

Luckily, there are plenty of experiences from other parts of our lives that we can learn from – especially our personal relationships, whether with our families, our friends, our children, or our partners. The straightjacket of professionalism we talked about in Chapter 1 has made it much harder to bring learning from our personal lives into our organisational ones, but this is precisely what is needed.

> *What could a pick-up football or basketball game teach you about facilitating group dynamics?*

> *What could an argument with your teenage daughter teach you about working differently with people of another generation?*

> *What could a passion for improv theatre or jazz teach you about adapting your work plans on the fly?*

The more personal the source of the learning, the harder it can be to think of it outside of that relationship. A series of trial-and-error efforts to learn from the things that make your personal relationships the best they can be, is really the most effective way to kick-start this kind of change.

What I hope to offer are a few principles, mostly gleaned from the less-manipulative end of the relationship and pop-psychology back catalogue, and from my own life and those of people around me, which I find just as relevant to a range of organisational issues as they are to relationship issues.

The biggest difference between our personal relationships and our working ones is the level of trust present in each. The more trust we share, the easier it becomes to work together, whether in strengthening family bonds, or winning a campaign. Conversely, the less trust we share, the harder these things become.

While it never fails to raise eyebrows when I first suggest it in workshops or seminars, I strongly suggest experimenting with what I've called *conscious vulnerability.* Essentially, this is giving someone else the chance to hurt or take advantage of you, on the assumption that they won't. It might mean admitting that you made a bad choice on a particular project, or acknowledging that you don't have as much experience as one of your staff does in a specific area. It might mean something a little more personal: telling your team, or members of it, that you're struggling with conflict at home, and that you'll do your best to keep it from affecting your work, but that it is occupying a lot of your thoughts at the moment.

As economist Tim Harford (@TimHarford) has written, 'many people respond to trust by becoming more trustworthy.'[vii] If we can develop more trusting working relationships, we can open countless other doors in our organisations.

The uglier flipside of this is, of course, that many people respond to even subtle hints of mistrust ('Can you send me the draft of that email before you send it out?' or 'Here is a list of bullet points to make sure you get across in this meeting') by becoming *less* trustworthy.

Conscious vulnerability is not a failsafe methodology and can open you up to being taken advantage of. But the alternative is superficial relationships where difficult dynamics remain buried just below the surface, making good work the exception, rather than the rule.

If I work closely with someone, there are both practical and human arguments for why I would want to know a bit about big things that are affecting them. Practically, it means I can step in, if they need to rush out of the office on short notice, or work out alternative arrangements with them if they need time off. More fundamentally, I want them to know that they don't have to pretend they're fine at work if they're not. Empathising with someone's situation, rather than simply ignoring it, or telling them to 'check it at the door,' is another strong way to foster more trusting relationships. Just as ignoring unhappiness in someone you are close to is unlikely to do good things for your relationship, the same dynamics apply at work.

Beyond trust, I have often found that self-awareness (or lack thereof) can be a major determinant in being able to build strong relationships. We all have blind spots around our own attitudes, behaviours, and actions. But unlike a machine, which lacks the consciousness to see the consequences of its actions and adjust accordingly, people can develop the psychological and emotional tools to better understand what we are bringing to the table, and thus to begin to address our less constructive habits.

Greater self-awareness helps to breakdown blame culture, which is equally a problem in both organisational and personal relationships. Blame culture tends to result from our own blind spots: we can easily see where someone else has done something wrong, but it's much harder for most of us to see our own shortcomings and contributions to a shitty situation. Organisational hierarchy doesn't help, and, if anything, further conditions us to avoid responsibility, because of its one-way, upward accountability channels, and the potential disciplinary implications if we are seen to be in the wrong.

Marriage counsellors deal with the blame associated with intimate relationships every day. If you were to hear two people from a troubled marriage recount what they felt was wrong with their dynamic, odds are good that you'd find reasons to empathise with and criticise parts of what both were saying. When Partner A says, 'I want more space to myself and Partner B won't let me have it!' we might think, 'Fair enough – everyone needs a certain amount of space to pursue their own interests.'

Then, moments later when we hear Partner B exclaim with equal sincerity, 'I just want us to have some quality time together,' you might say, 'Of course! Both people need to make an effort to be together if the relationship is going to work!'

In any relationship, both people are always making choices that make the dynamic better or worse. In our intimate relationships, we can often justify the work involved to improve things because the payoffs of better intimate relationships are so great. However, when it comes to the place we spend most of our waking hours, from Monday to Friday, we are rarely willing to put in the same efforts to improve things. As part of our professional notion of separating work and life (as if the former was not simply part of the latter!), we relegate ourselves to having less-than-ideal working lives, as though forty or more hours of our average week is not worth the personal effort to improve things.

How often have you looked at a lousy working relationship and thought: 'What could I do differently here?' rather than reverting to the more common knee-jerk response: 'how can I make *them* do something differently?'

Dr. Harriet Lerner (@HarrietLerner), in her 1990 bestseller on relationship patterns, *The Dance of Anger*, wrote, 'It is tempting to view human transactions in simple cause-and-effect terms,' harkening back to the Newtonian ideals that have infiltrated so much of our lives. 'If we are angry,' Lerner observes, 'someone else *caused* it. Or, if we are the target of someone else's anger... we may conclude that the other person has no *right* to feel angry.'[viii]

Clarifying the blame question, she adds, 'We are responsible for our own behavior,' along with the critical disclaimers, 'but we are *not* responsible for other people's reactions; nor are they responsible for ours.'[ix] Successfully distinguishing our own emotional responses from other peoples' actions is basically the Super Jedi Ninja standard of emotional intelligence, but is still one we can all be working towards.

Closely related to letting go of blame is one of the golden rules of basic relationships psychology, passed along to innumerable sobbing friends in miserable situations over the years: *You can't force someone to change, if they don't want to change themselves.* While these words are often a precursor to encouraging someone to leave a relationship, sometimes a more constructive alternative is still available: if the other person isn't willing to change in the way you want them to, you can work to improve yourself, taking the steps to shift how you respond and what you give to a dynamic that isn't making you happy. Like in a miserable marriage, there are times when leaving a job is absolutely the best thing you can do, but in either situation, understanding your own role in the conflict is important, and might help to keep you from reliving the same experience in a new job or new relationship, further down the road.

This is not about compromise, as it is so often portrayed in relationship literature. It is more about the pragmatism of finding the part of a destructive dynamic that you have the power to affect, rather than wasting your efforts on the points you have no control over, where no amount of blame will create the outcome you want. Being aware of the ways we subconsciously make a dynamic worse through our behaviours – with aggression, passive aggression, silence, or self-blame, to name a few – can help us to break the patterns that make our working dynamics untenable.

More colloquially, if a colleague tells me to piss-off, and I respond by telling them to piss-off, I haven't done anything to open up a more constructive relationship, even if it felt like what they deserved at the time. I've only accentuated the negative, validating their rationale for the initial comment (and their likely follow-up) with my response. To pass along a question my mom once asked me during a difficult time early in my marriage, in which I thought I had my wife's side of our problems completely figured out: *Do you want to be right, or do you want to be together?*

While we may not be quite as committed to a manager or colleague, there is some value in getting past the winning-the-debate-with-the-correct-argument approach we easily fall into. There's a certain logic in wanting to prove we're right during conflict, yet it only tends to make both sides of a dynamic feel less engaged in their relationship, in part because both are likely equally committed to their own versions of what is right.

If there were one best way and we were entirely rational machines, 'winning' might make the other person see what was wrong with their approach. However, too often, winning an argument just leaves the other person feeling more resentful as the loser in the relationship, rather than building a better dynamic together by understanding each of our own contributions to the problem, and thus, the solution.

Rather than trying to win, why not think about how we could improve ourselves?

To take it to a more practical level, let's say you're a manager. Your administrative assistant is uncooperative with your instructions, regularly late, and argumentative when you challenge them on it. You first kept your frustrations with these behaviours to yourself, but then started into a series of efforts to change them – to make them more cooperative, more punctual, more abiding. But matters worsened. You moved into more formal disciplinary action. Some of the most measurable problems – lateness, for example – went away, but the ones it was harder to keep track of simply got worse.

Now, let's say you're the administrative assistant. You've done this job for years, and a new manager is telling you to do things their way, even though you're sure you've got the best systems in place, and that this is just about them not wanting to change their own working habits. You've also been struggling with childcare lately, but haven't wanted to make an issue of it because you don't want your personal life to be seen as interfering with your career. No one seemed to mind that you were a bit late sometimes, but then, all of a sudden, you were receiving grief for slight infractions. These griefs seemed to escalate very quickly, and soon, you were facing a formal disciplinary process. Worried for your job, you pony-up and hire someone to take your son to school for you in the morning, to avoid any further lateness. You're out-of-pocket and more frustrated than ever with your manager, but you're on time now.

Both parties want the other to change. Both parties have legitimate reasons for wanting the other to change. But neither is going to get what they want from their current approaches.

While there is no guarantee that any of these would have radically altered this situation, there are several points where either person could have shifted their own behaviour to avoid *worsening* the conflict:

- The manager might have begun by asking what they could do to help the situation, rather than staying quiet about the lateness issue. *Silence is not a constructive responsive to conflict.*

- The administrative assistant might have asked to compare different ways of working, rather than sticking to their guns about the superiority of their previous methods. *Opening dialogue, rather than only stating opposition, strengthens relationships.*

- The manager might have thought about an experience where they felt they knew how to handle a situation better than their boss, and given the administrative assistant the chance to prove themselves, even if it meant adjusting their own working habits. *When we put ourselves in the shoes of those we are in conflict with, we might start to empathise with where they are coming from, rather than simply opposing them.*

- The administrative assistant might have been more open about their needs in the situation, and the external factors affecting their ability to do their job. *Honesty opens up the opportunity for an honest response, which can be discussed more openly than if both sides are holding their cards close.*

There are, of course, an infinite number of possible variables here that we haven't explored, but this example highlights the ways in which we might subconsciously be making a situation worse without realising it, and what we can do to change the dynamic.

> *What has helped build or re-build trust in your personal relationships?*

> *What helps you to actively reflect on the contributions you are, or could be, making to a relationship?*

> *What helps you to relax when you're not at the office?*

Autonomy: Trusting ourselves and others to be brilliant

One of the fundamental tenets of both self-organising complex systems and being yourself is autonomy. Our human desire to find our own distinct paths is not the waste a Taylorist would argue it to be, but instead the place from which our greatest potential emerges.

Organisations have traditionally sought to suppress or steer individual autonomy, through the imposition of professionalism, job descriptions, command-and-control management, top-level strategies, and the many subtle hints that tell us what is and isn't acceptable behaviour. This is because autonomy is antithetical to control, and control is at the core of industrial organising.

But is it possible that individual freedom is in fact *complementary* to organisational success? That letting a large group of people in an organisation act independently, as they see fit, can actually foster a stronger whole?

That's what Google believes. It underpins their 'twenty percent' policy, in which staff have the freedom to choose how they spend a day out of every working week, to focus on whatever inspires them.

Similar policies are at play in more and more web and software companies, because they realise that their staff are talented, and, if left to their own devices, will create great stuff without being told to.

The organising successes of horizontalism (a form of leaderless organisation in which decisions are made, and actions taken, collectively), in so many recent social movements – from the Zapatistas in Mexico, to workers' factory occupations in Argentina, landless peasant organising in Brazil, to the global Occupy movement – are giving a new dimension to the importance of individual autonomy in the world of social change. Autonomy operationalises equal opportunities far more effectively than most organisational policies of the same name do, simply by offering wide-open space for anyone who cares about the same issues to do what they want about them.

Implicit or explicit in each of these alternatives is the notion that 'If we free people to follow their passions, they will be brilliant,' rather than assuming, 'If we don't impose rigid structures, our staff will do the wrong things.' As we saw in Chapter 1, this faith is at the core of anarchist thought, and more and more brave and forward-thinking groups and organisations are demonstrating its value. No longer simply the naive mantra of a smoked-out hippie, autonomy is increasingly proving its worth as a bedrock principle of organisational and social change.

Margaret Wheatley and Myron Kellner-Rogers, two pioneers in applying the lessons of naturally occurring complex systems to the field of organisational development, put it this way:

Stability is found in freedom — not in conformity and compliance. We may have thought that our organisation's survival was guaranteed by finding the right form and insisting that everyone fit into it. But sameness is not stability. It is individual freedom that creates stable systems. It is differentness that enables us to thrive.[x]

To put it simply: people have the potential for brilliance, if we don't let our systems get in the way.

> *What practices help you let go of the need to control things, in any parts of your life?*
>
> *When have you been pleasantly surprised by yourself or others, acting independently to achieve something meaningful?*
>
> *What scares you about letting go?*

Why social movements and social media are like people

These 'more like people' principles are in direct contrast to the 'more like machines' principles outlined in Chapter 1:

- In mindset, *complexity* challenges the orthodoxy of *industrialism*
- In values, *humanity* is a juxtaposition to *professionalism*
- In relationships, *autonomy* is the opposite of *control*

Social media and social movements exemplify these three 'more like people' principles. Each of the chapters that follow will contrast the mindset, values, and relationships of our old organisations, with those of newer, more social ways of organising, as well as putting forward ideas and questions about moving from the former to the latter.

We've recently reached a point where some of our more traditional organisations have begun to engage with social media and social movements, but without the deeper shift in orientation this chapter talks about. A Facebook page is setup and left in the hands of an intern without the authority to post to it without sign-off; a conference is titled 'Occupy[blank]' but fills its schedule with keynote speeches by white men in suits. The window-dressing of change is there, but the old building remains intact.

A couple of years ago I started telling a story about this clash, and it always seemed to get the point across, so rather than theorise, I'll let this imagined exchange paint the picture of the conflict our organisations are so regularly stumbling into.

Meeting agendas at the pub

Imagine for a minute it's early Saturday evening and you're meeting a few friends at a local pub. It's not a special occasion, just a chance to catch up, relax, share a few drinks.

As the last of your friends arrive, you clear your throat loudly and thank everyone for coming. You remove some paperwork from the briefcase you've stealthily concealed under the table and hand everyone a copy of the evening's agenda.

'Alright, we've got twenty minutes to hear about Paul's family troubles, ten for a quick update on the last football game, another twenty to vent about public sector cuts, and I believe James wanted a few minutes at the end to tell us all that he's going to be a father. Was that it? Any other business before we get things started?'

Eyebrows are rising. James is visibly annoyed. A few awkward laughs and glances from side to side, hoping to make eye contact with someone who knows what you're doing. You continue.

'If everyone is settled with their drinks, I'd just like to lay out a few ground rules before we get into things. Most importantly, respect the speaker; everyone will have a fair chance to speak. I'll be keeping time to make sure nothing runs over, and if all goes according to plan, we should be out of here before eight.'

At this point you're ruffling feathers. Someone quizzically asks you what you're doing, but you keep going, unimpeded by a question asked out of turn. Eventually, separate conversations pickup around the table amongst those lost by whatever you're attempting to pull here. Paul is at the jukebox, hoping some music will break the tension. At some stage you realise you're talking to yourself. Everyone else is engaged elsewhere. Your meeting has become a meeting of one.

It's awkward even to think about, isn't it?

Ridiculous as it is to imagine applying our stuffy professional habits to such an explicitly social setting, that's what most organisations do on the Internet. Professionalism, applied to social media, is like minute-taking at the pub – a bit cringe-worthy, to say the least – and a thorough misreading of the right tool for the job. (The social movement equivalent would probably be to show-up at a sit-in in a corporate store with health and safety waivers and evaluation forms for those taking part.) The difference is that since most of the people who follow our organisations online aren't really our friends, they might find it harder to call us out when indeed they should. Instead, many choose to unfollow or simply ignore us until we figure out what we're doing there.

Too often, our organisations – both through official accounts and staff's personal profiles – are reluctant to engage others through social media with anything less than a policy team-approved press statement, should something remotely opinionated ever come back to haunt them. Even with the increasingly ubiquitous 'these views are not the views of my employer' tacked on, countless charity staff are still unlikely to express anything that could be seen as controversial. I've suggested that when we go out on the weekends, we should wear a badge that reads, 'these clothes are not the clothes of my employer,' to avoid any ambiguity about who dressed us for the evening. We can then assume that those without a badge are still maintaining their company dress code, since they haven't said otherwise.

Chapter 2: The 'more like people' principles: humanity, autonomy, complexity

Further, many organizations are averse, in their online activities, to the social qualities that nourish active networks, such as:

- Humour
- Humility
- Asking questions
- Sharing valuable stuff from other organisations
- Engaging in banter
- Learning from the audience

I recently heard a story about a national charity that became deeply divided over the use of emoticons in organisational Tweets, with senior managers arguing vociferously that such frivolity was *not* the professional image the organisation wanted to convey. Ironically, it was the kind of sociable practice that had helped their lower-ranking staff build up a significant social media presence in the first place, without senior managers even noticing.

My friend and colleague Paul Barasi often jokes about the countless non-profits whose Twitter biographies include words like *engagement, participation, involvement,* or *user-led,* yet who only follow other organisational, party political, or celebrity accounts, and who refuse to engage in online conversations with those who approach them. Like other places where our professionalism comes up against our stated values, actions speak louder than words, and tend to be what people remember about us.

Bass player and social media consultant Steve Lawson (@ solobasssteve) explained to me once 'the importance of talking bollocks,' a phrase I have included in countless workshops since. He initially brought it up in response to the all-too-regular accusation of social media being 'all about telling people what you had for breakfast.' 'Sure,' Steve might say, 'it's a conversation, it doesn't have to always be about something serious. Breakfast Tweets are the stuff we build relationships around.'

When I first heard him say this, it resonated immediately. It's not as though the conversations we have at lunch, around the water cooler, or in the stairwell at the office generally start with some profound work-related exclamation or insight – they usually start with the weather, a meal, or maybe the plans we've made for the weekend. From there, they could stay superficial, or lead us to sorting out a shared problem, trying out a new idea, or getting some feedback on something we've been working on lately.

Imposing professionalism on social media makes sure that we miss opportunities, and look a bit lost to those more comfortable with online spaces. But if we approach social media the same way we might approach our many other office conversations, we might come to see it a bit differently. Simple, human interactions are the stuff that builds the relationships that help us work better with people, inside and outside our walls. Without them, we're both missing an opportunity and sending a deeply anti-social message to the people who would like to engage with us.

And as on social media, so in our workplaces, where we are too often guilty of the same practices, putting forward a face that isn't really who we are. This fosters superficial working relationships, but also creates a massive power imbalance in countless services, where beneficiaries or clients are expected to open up about the most personal details of their lives, while we, in our professional roles, are justified in sharing nothing about ourselves in return. Such attitudes, online or off, reinforce elitist hierarchy at the most individual levels of our work.

Alternatively we might open up a new range of opportunities if we can:

- Appreciate the complexity of our world, in which answers might come from unexpected places we wouldn't normally engage with,
- Remember our own humanity, and the good stuff that happens when we don't have to pretend we're people that we're not, and
- Embrace autonomy, for ourselves and others, because we can't predict what insights might arise or where they might lead us.

Chapter 2:
The 'more
like people'
principles:
humanity,
autonomy,
complexity

Can more natural social media use help us to make the case for spreading the values of more natural communications across and beyond our organisations?

Have you had any experiences in social media engagement that demonstrate the effectiveness of less-formal communication?

We've got as many choices as we can imagine!

While the solutions that have dominated our traditional organisational outlook and practice has have been about as narrow as Taylor's 'one best way' logic, we have nothing so restrictive shaping our possibilities moving forward. We no longer need to rely on a hegemonic unity to survive together, instead embracing a plurality of answers, finding strength in our diversity, not our singularity.

Embedded in each of the three 'more like people' principles is the importance of diversity. The world is a diverse place, so successful organising within it should be, too. This means it's up to us! We don't need to come up with a new 'one best way,' we just need to find lots of different good ways, that work for the many different things our particular organisations need to do, whether campaign emails or payroll, internal communications or media engagement.

Social media is offering some inroads to new approaches that can apply more generally, as it is still relatively new and more people are willing to admit they don't get it yet, often leaving space for experimentation. I have used it as a Trojan Horse with several organisations who had budget lines and skills audits for social media training, but really needed to be talking about professionalism and management. It is fair to say that if an organisation is serious about using social media effectively, they have to also be serious about letting go of many of their established professional standards – the two can only coexist for so long before one will proclaim victory. Luckily, when people have had a taste of the freedom offered by these new ways of organising, they are unlikely to go back to the old ways without a significant fight.

Unlike the bureaucratic routes of the past though, 'more like people' changes should not feel like a long drive in neutral, plodding away but getting nowhere. If we try to simply use our old systems to bring about new systems (submit proposal, seek approval, etc), odds are good they will intentionally or inadvertently be suffocated before they can see the light of day. As many of the organisational stories throughout this book highlight, critical change often happens without permission, and emerges wherever a need exists. If we don't rely on our old processes, we won't be restricted by their limitations.

If this chapter has done anything, I hope it has highlighted the sense of possibility that exists for positive change in even the most entrenched of bureaucracies. Now let's get into some of the specifics, shall we?

Chapter 2:
The 'more
like people'
principles:
humanity,
autonomy,
complexity

i Susan Kruglinski, '20 Things You Didn't Know About… Relativity,' *Discover Magazine*, 25 February 2008. http://discovermagazine.com/2008/mar/20-things-you-didnt-know-about-relativity

ii Klaus Krippendorff, 'Afterword,' *Cybernetics & Human Knowing*, Vol.9, No.2, 2002, p. 95–96.

iii Margaret Wheatley has written extensively about the relationships between quantum science, living systems, and human systems of organisation. For those who are looking to explore the philosophical and scientific sides of complexity in more depth, *Leadership and the new science* is her most complete work on these relationships.

iv Frances Westley, et al. *Getting to Maybe*, Vintage Canada, 2006, p. 9.

v Adapted from Harry Jones, 'Taking responsibility for complexity,' ODI Briefing Paper 68, August 2011.

vi Westley, et al., 2006, p. 10-11.

vii Tim Harford, *Adapt*, Little Brown, 2011, p. 228.

viii Harriet Lerner, *The Dance of Anger*, Harper Element, 1990, p. 123.

ix Ibid, p. 124.

x Margaret Wheatley & Myron Kellner-Rogers, *A Simpler Way*, Berrett-Koehler, 1996, p. 41.

The myth of hierarchical necessity and what we can do for ourselves

3

'If people are machines, seeking to control us makes sense. But if we live with the same forces intrinsic to all other life, then seeking to impose control through rigid structures is suicide.' – Margaret Wheatley, Leadership and the New Science

'My role is that of a catalyst. I try to create an environment in which others make decisions. Success means not making them myself.' – Ricardo Semler, Semco

Underpinning the twin problems of an industrial mindset and the stifling imposition of professionalism is the deeply ingrained notion of hierarchy. For centuries, we have been telling ourselves that in order to do big things, we need to impose systems of control to make them possible. But a range of examples based in the recent growth of both social media and social movements have begun to make the alternatives increasingly clear. When we apply the 'more like people' principles introduced in Chapter 2 (humanity, autonomy and complexity), we can achieve things that our hierarchies would never have imagined possible.

Hierarchy, self-organisation and the differing politics of human nature

In Chapter 1 I mentioned the most common initial response to describing my work as 'helping organisations to be more like people': the smirks, the raised eyebrows, the condescending assumptions of naiveté that have tended to accompany the 'what *kind* of people?' reply that so often follows my introduction. Let's unpack this for a moment.

I work (and live) from the assumption that people *are good* and *want to do good*, if given the chance. This can absolutely be corrupted, and we have all experienced and demonstrated moments where this becomes painfully obvious. But when it comes down to it, we are good, and want to improve, as it is in all of our personal and collective interests to be so and to do so.

Working from this belief determines the ways I choose to work with others. If I assume the best of them, I am more likely to trust their intentions. If I trust their intentions, I am more likely to accept their actions. If I accept their actions, I probably won't tell them what to do. And if I don't tell them what to do, they will be freer to achieve things I never would have imagined possible. Trust liberates human potential.

Now let's try starting from the opposite perspective, and assume that people are greedy, selfish, petty and individualistic.

If I view others with this negative understanding, I am less likely to trust their intentions. And if I don't trust their intentions, I am less likely to accept their actions. And if I don't accept their actions, I may well try to tell them what to do, so they don't go and fu*k it up, through some combination of ignorance and malicious intent. And if I tell them what to do, they'll probably get quickly annoyed with my lack of trust in their initial intention or judgment.

Enter *the organisation!* A machine built with these latter assumptions at its core, assuming the worst of those who fill its cubicles, and – surprise, surprise – often getting it in return.

As Margaret Wheatley puts it:

> If we believe that there is no order to human activity except that imposed by the leader, that there is no self-regulation except that dictated by policies, if we believe that responsible leaders must have their hands into everything, controlling every decision, person, and moment, then we cannot hope for anything except what we already have— a treadmill of frantic efforts that end up destroying our individual and collective vitality.[i]

*Chapter 3:
The myth of
hierarchical
necessity and
what we can
do for
ourselves*

In 1960 MIT professor Douglas McGregor published a book called *The human side of enterprise.* In it he described the view I hold of human nature as Theory Y, and the view that dictates the vast majority of our organisational structures and policies as Theory X. McGregor argued that Theory X organisations were fundamentally misunderstanding people by creating organisations that assumed the worst of them. Not only did the application of Theory X limit our potential, it made us worse than we would naturally be if left to our own devices.

But a half-century on, Theory X is still the dominant operating system in most of our organisations. So let me put it bluntly. Your employer thinks you are stupid, thinks you are untrustworthy, thinks you will get it wrong if given half a chance to do so.

'But,' you may protest, 'they hired me – they *must* have faith in what I can do!'

Hiring you – or someone else – was a necessary evil in producing whatever it is they produce. Some great individual was unable to do all of the great things they wanted to do with the time they had on this planet, so they resorted to paying someone else to do some of them on their behalf. If they believed in you, at an institutional level, you would not have a line manager, but would be part of providing and receiving collective support, direction and accountability for and from those you work with. If they trusted you, you would not have fixed hours to fill each week at your desk, but could work wherever you felt best equipped to do the job, and would know enough about the institution as a whole to reasonably set your own salary and holiday time in

The SNAFU principle and why hierarchical communication is a broken telephone

In the Army, acronyms and foul language can be found in surplus. Some of both find their way out of the closed ranks of the military and into common usage. The term 'snafu' is not uncommon to describe any number of , screw-ups and mistakes, however, most of us don't think about what the letters initially stood for.

> **S**ituation:
> **N**ormal.
> **A**ll
> **F**uc*ed
> **U**p!

It was coined to describe the near-inevitable communication breakdowns associated with the military hierarchy. Imagine a fire fight in which a squadron is in way out of their depths. They know they can't hold their position much longer without reinforcements, and radio back to their commander that without help, they're going to lose their position (colloquially translated as 'it's all fuc*ed up out here!').

Their commander receives their message, but not wanting to take the blame for people in his command failing at their mission (even if it was impossible), he waters it down a bit: 'Our boys are in a bit of trouble on the front; some reinforcements'll get 'em back on track.'

The Division Head gets this message, and in the same vein as his subordinate, twists the message to avoid the inevitable blame that would go along with a failure taking place under his watchful eye: 'It's a bit rough out there, but the boys'll pull through.'

By the time the message has reiterated itself through a half-dozen rungs of the command chain, the person who could actually do something about it has been told that everything is going according to plan: 'Situation: Normal'.

So a SNAFU is not simply a mess or a mistake, but the inevitable real-world results of how power and individual blame culture distort information and communication across hierarchy.

accordance with the work you were doing. If they cared about you, they would trust and believe in you.

These organisational machines were not designed to care, trust, or to believe. People, however, are. And because we are, we can do things that machines can't. This is what 'more like people' is all about.

It may seem like a no-brainer, but until recently – and still almost universally in many fields – we assumed organising big things was beyond human capability, requiring the imposition of these untrusting, uncaring structures to make them possible. But if we get past the fallacy of Theory X, do we necessarily need those structures, or the managers that exist to prop them up?

The day the bosses packed up and left

What do you think happened when foreign investment fled from Argentina after the country's IMF-poster-child economy collapsed in 2001, shutting down many of the country's factories overnight?

For one, the Argentines ousted five presidents in the first months of 2002 to voice their displeasure. But rather than simply protest, a movement of suddenly unemployed workers emerged to reclaim abandoned workplaces and run them as democratic workers' collectives.

Recovered businesses, as they were innocuously termed, spread across Argentina as workers returned to their old factories, clipping the chains on the gates that stood between them and their jobs. Their slogan, 'Occupy, Resist, Produce,' highlighted the radical nature of the movement, which threw private property rights into question, as more and more workers began to assert that their right to work trumped the employer's right to own an empty factory.

Occupied factories took on different forms. Some remained relatively traditional, with clear job titles and hierarchical salary structures, while many others began to change the nature of their workplaces in a range of deeper ways. Assembly decision-making processes, equal salaries across the workforce, and collective administration of the business, in sales, pay role, budgeting, and production forecasts, were but a few of the shifts that began to take hold in many of the factories.

Recovered businesses would support other recovered businesses, giving each other the first contracts they needed to get machines operational again, supplying the different parts that other factories needed to make whatever it was they made. Even in the face of a severe economic downturn, several of the two hundred-plus occupied workplaces began to turn profits surpassing those achieved by the previous owners, often doubling everyone's pre-occupation wages in the process. As one worker highlighted in Naomi Klein (@NaomiAKlein) and Avi Lewis' (@avilewis) 2004 documentary, *The Take*, 'What we've learned is that in a business, participatory democracy is more efficient.'[ii] For example, when the recently jobless Unión y Fuerza piping factory workers voted to occupy their old workplace, their union's lawyer told electrician Roberto Salcedo there was no way they could get the bankrupt factory up-and-running again. 'If the owner, with his entire team of professionals and all his experience, ended up bankrupt, how could fifty workers with no experience manage to make it work?'[iii] But the men – not a university degree among them – formed an assembly where all decisions were made, registered as a workers' cooperative, turned down loans from eager banks and investment from former clients, and did just what they were told they couldn't.

In a diving Argentine economy, these workers carried out a market evaluation, determined potential income and expenditure (minus the costs of all the long-gone managers), and decided together to opt for an equal waging system for all. Unión y Fuerza soon became the biggest domestic pipe supplier in Argentina.

'You have to break through many fears, like the idea you can't take over a company like this one,' says Salcedo. 'Actually, you learn how. And then you have the satisfaction that you are doing it for yourself.'[iv] If our social change organisations are committed to practicing the democratic values we speak about, it is hard to imagine why senior management teams still exist at all. The notion that staff in any organisation are unable to come together to make responsible decisions is an elitist remnant of Frederick Winslow Taylor's time that needs to be thrown away if we hope to align our means and ends for social change.

But if the notion of scrapping Senior Management still seems excessive, why don't we think for a minute about some other important events in our shared histories that have transpired without a single manager orchestrating peoples' actions. While countless Argentine companies went bankrupt in Argentina, but became financially sound without managers, if we had tried to achieve the changes brought by social movements through our organisational management structures, we can almost guarantee we would – at best – have gotten in the way. All of which should lead us to ask whether, even with the best of intentions, management itself might be the problem?

Micro-managing the Arab Spring

Imagine the first strategy meeting amongst an imaginary coalition of NGOs involved in strategising for the delivery of the 'Arab Spring 2011' programme. Probably in about April 2002:

'Our vision is: A series of mostly peaceful revolts across the Middle East and North Africa in the spring of 2011, overthrowing longstanding dictatorships and kicking off a process of bottom-up democratisation throughout the region.'

'Great. What are our targets gonna be? Have we identified strategic partners in each of the countries? What will we accept as a democratic victory? Do we have a system of risk management? How will we measure the impact?'

If they had somehow managed what we now know was achieved by less strategic or coordinated means, think for a minute how the follow-up meetings might have gone:

'Do we have a figure on total persons liberated yet?'

'What if that figure goes up after the funding period is over? Think we could fudge it a bit to boost the numbers?'

'We're probably gonna want to avoid mentioning Syria in the final report... Bahrain too.'

**Five reasons – in no particular order –
why hierarchy sucks**

1. It assumes the worst of people, and thus is likely to foster it

From the basic premise of having to start at the bottom and work your way up, hierarchy doesn't give us the credit to be able to do the amazing things that people constantly demonstrate the ability to do.

Hierarchy denies us the autonomy to use our judgment and figure things out in our own ways.

Formalising accountability – especially when it only flows in one direction – breaks down trust, because it assumes we won't be honest about our strengths and weaknesses. In doing so, we are pushed to play up our strengths and gloss over our weaknesses, reducing opportunities for learning and improvement, both individually and organisationally.

'We'll have to talk about Libya, but is there a way we can avoid giving NATO too much credit on that one? If we make it look like they were the critical success factor, they'll get all the funding in the next round.'

'Can we reshape the vision statement to reflect Tunisia and Egypt more strongly? If we were aiming to liberate the whole region and only two dictators were ousted, it'll be easy to say the programme was a failure. What if we said it was something about 'supporting peaceful revolts in Tunisia and Egypt'? Then we can credit the other stuff as unexpected fringe benefits of our interventions. And maybe we can build the next funding app around some of the other countries that have been primed for future peaceful revolutions?'

There were of course many organisations that played roles within the various uprisings across North Africa and the Middle East in early 2011, but there was no organisation that could effectively or meaningfully take credit for what took place in any single country, let alone the entire region.

Organisations as we've known them (clearly structured, hierarchical institutions) have, throughout history, played important roles in countless social movements (looser, larger, emergent and wholly autonomous masses of people), yet have repeatedly failed to understand the differences between the two forms.

The organising principles that underpin organisations and movements are almost diametrically opposed to one another, even if from the outside (and generally through the condensed lens of history) their aims and beliefs appear perfectly aligned.

An organisation in a movement is too often like the friend of a friend at a high school house party who hasn't grasped the etiquette of the group they've stumbled into. They do inappropriate things, hit on people they should know not to hit on, say things they shouldn't say... and ultimately end up too drunk for their own good, being looked after by some sympathetic stranger who wants to keep them from getting beat up.

Five reasons – in no particular order – why hierarchy sucks

2. Its power dynamics foster dishonesty and poor information sharing/ coordination/ learning

By centralising power and control, you distribute the desire for power and control. When power and control are more evenly shared, there is less reason for most people to want more of it.

Everyone needs to make themselves look better than someone else, if they want to progress their career, improve their income, etc. The hierarchy pits individual interest against the collective interest, which can't be a good thing for any organisation that hopes to have some kind of future.

Maybe that's pushing the metaphor a bit, but anyone who has participated in a movement without their organisational hat on knows the tension that emerges when an institution tries to impose hierarchy on something for which there are simultaneously no leaders *and* an ever-changing plethora of leaders coming and going, based on the specifics of the situation.

This tension might be sparked by unannounced organisational recruitment drives at broader movement events or actions. It might be in the domination of organising meetings by particular agendas and aims. It could be the prevalence of a particular organisational face in media coverage or publicity, taking disproportionate credit for something that had in fact been a much broader effort. In the case of reclaimed Argentine factories, it was often leftist political parties hanging their own banners all over occupied factories that rubbed many workers the wrong way.

Chapter 3: The myth of hierarchical necessity and what we can do for ourselves

Of course, the people who work for organisations can bring just as much value, energy and experience to a movement as any of the rest of us. However, too often this requires their aims as individual activists to trump their aims as employees of an institution.

The desires to build brand recognition, to secure funding, to promote awareness of a particular agenda or individual name are practically speaking at odds with actually working towards a better world. They distract from the tasks at hand. We began by explaining them to ourselves as necessary evils in the world of organising, until they gradually assumed a considerable bulk of our work. The tail is wagging the dog.

We have put the cart before the horse when the structures created to *help* achieve change become the institution's primary reasons for being. Over time, almost without fail, those 'helpful' structures end up practically at odds with the change they were meant to support – often at the point of engagement between the organisation itself, and the bigger movement it is a part of.

Our organisations need to be more sensitive to their environments, and accept that we are guests in broader movements for change, rather than the stars of the show, as

Five reasons – in no particular order – why hierarchy sucks

3. It expects its leaders to be superheroes

It elevates individuals to positions in which the unattainable is expected of them. Because their job title is 'x', they are expected to do 'y'... A promotion to 'w' means they are expected to do 'y+1'... which makes sense... until it doesn't.

Many argue that the people in leadership positions of massive multinational institutions can in no meaningful way know enough about their organisation to justify the difference between their salaries and the salaries of those below them. The rises follow a linear progression, but have no grounding in practical reality.

At a certain stage 'y+1' becomes the straw that broke the camel's back, surpassing human ability, or the number of hours in a day, and becoming inherently unachievable. But we pretend this isn't the case, and all the 'failed' leaders have failed due to their own shortcomings, not something inherent to our expectations of them.

so much organisational campaigning, publicity and fundraising efforts have pushed us to try to be over the years.

Becoming aware of the ways our organisational hats might be at odds with the aims of a movement is a critical step towards making a positive difference in this emergent world. If we want to be meaningful and constructive contributors, we need to understand the principles that help movements to thrive, even if they seem immediately at odds with the principles that have driven our organisations for so long.

Chapter 3:
The myth of
hierarchical
necessity and
what we can
do for
ourselves

As you read this, there are countless emergent social movements that could benefit from the people, experience and resources that our organisations have within their walls. Finding ways to work constructively – rather than antagonistically – with these looser networks will be a defining distinction of established organisations that remain important in the movements of the not-so-distant future.

But doing so means learning to take on some of the qualities of these looser networks.

Trafigura and the physics of censorship

It's August 2006. Trafigura – a company that lines its shareholders' pockets by moving oil and related substances from Point A to Point B – has cut a deal to dump a multi-tonne load of highly toxic hydrogen sulphide near the port city of Abidjan, in West Africa's Ivory Coast. Consequently, more than 30,000 people in the region fall ill, and come together to launch the largest group lawsuit in British legal history against the company.

By the time October 2009 rolls around, Trafigura has secured the services of Carter-Ruck, libel solicitors who specialise in suing the media. In this case, though, they didn't *sue* the media, but instead managed to get a judge to tell the *Guardian* newspaper that they would be breaking the law if they mentioned any of the pertinent details of their client's Parliamentary investigation (from the company's name and the MPs involved, to the questions being asked of them).

On the evening of Monday, October 12, *Guardian* editor Alan Rusbridger (@arusbridger) left the office after hearing word of the injunction, but before leaving, tweeted:

> 'Now Guardian prevented from reporting parliament for unreportable reasons. Did John Wilkes live in vain?'[v]

Rusbridger, editorialising what followed two days later, went on to say:

> By the time I got home, after stopping off for a meal with friends, the Twittersphere had gone into meltdown. Twitterers had sleuthed down [the MP's Parliamentary Question], published the relevant links and were now seriously on the case. By midday on Tuesday 'Trafigura' was one of the most searched terms in Europe, helped along by re-tweets by Stephen Fry and his 830,000-odd followers.
>
> Many tweeters were just registering support or outrage. Others were beavering away to see if they could find suppressed information on the far reaches of the web. One or two legal experts uncovered the Parliamentary Papers Act 1840, wondering if that would help? Common #hashtags were quickly developed, making the material easily discoverable.
>
> By lunchtime – an hour before we were due in court [to challenge the super-injunction] – Trafigura threw in the towel.[vi]

Just like that, a campaign emerged, achieved critical mass, and won, in well under a day, and with no leader but the idea that people have a right to know what happens in Parliament. Not only had the Tweeting masses undermined the gag order itself, they had demonstrated that the most aggressive and highly paid libel lawyers in the business still had nothing on the potential of a well-timed dose of people power.

The lesson? If you plug the big hole in the dam, an infinite number of smaller weak spots will burst under the added pressure. It's the physics of censorship in a deeply interconnected world. The *Guardian* – one of the most reputable newspapers in the world – all of a sudden became a relatively minor player in breaking a news story it had been following for several months. Twitter (and by that I mean many thousands of independently minded Twitter users) was the key distributor of the news that morning.

This is just one of countless examples in recent years of institutions being bypassed by ever-more-connected swarms of individuals, joined up only by common cause. And it was not just the institutions of the British courts, or Carter-Ruck, that were bypassed, but also the non-profit organisations we have traditionally turned to, to hold these systems to account.

Where were the civil liberties NGOs? The organisations concerned with freedom of the press? Probably at home for the evening. The story transpired largely outside of office hours, meaning that it was up to people – I'm sure some of whom worked for or volunteered with some of those same NGOs during the day – to carry this campaign without institutional buy-in, long before a policy could be drafted or approved, any formal statement made, or a letter-writing action launched.

So what could those organisations have done differently? It's clearly much harder to plan for a campaign when you:

- Don't know when it might happen
- Don't know exactly what it's going to be about, and
- Don't know what contribution you might be making to it.

That said, there are still at least a few specific shifts that organisations could make, but which would mean reframing our relationships with the wide-ranging, spontaneous movements of people who are concerned about our issues in a particular moment.

- Make sure you've already got the relevant information available online – reports, stories, interviews – so you can start to link to it and share it around, as soon as the topic appears to be taking off. If lots of people are linking to your information it builds a collective sense of trust that your messages carry some authority in the given area. Trust will make your next steps that much easier.

Five reasons – in no particular order – why hierarchy sucks

4. It wastes time, pretending we live in a linear and controllable world that only exists in a Taylorist fantasy

Strategic planning suggests that if you get the correct executives in an expensive enough room for an extended period of time, you will be able to predict the future.

Important people (according to the hierarchy) spend a great deal of time together in organisations, writing documents that declare, in spite of everything outside their walls: A will lead to B will lead to C.

Additionally, they write further documents to detail how others will ensure that A will lead to B will lead to C.

And then something unexpected happens – as it invariably does – and all their hard work is at best swept aside, or at worst, followed to a T, in spite of a radically changed reality.

- Ensure someone – or ideally several people in the organisation – are on call for such situations when they do arise, getting the Twitter updates direct to their phones, receiving Google Alerts at home, or being available for other staff or volunteers to contact, should something big come up when you're not at the office.

- Quickly figure out who the others are who seem to have some authority on the issues. As much as this cuts against the old organisational logic of building yourself up as the sole authority on your subject, sharing good, relevant content via Twitter, a blog, your website, or a Facebook page, wherever it may come from, is key to being taken more seriously online. Reciprocity is an important tenet of social media culture and will inevitably benefit both your work and your cause if you can demonstrate that your involvement is bigger than just your organisational aims.

Chapter 3:
The myth of
hierarchical
necessity and
what we can
do for
ourselves

- Lastly (and most importantly), be prepared to offer tangible support to those in the campaign who are most active and vocal. Maybe this means providing a meeting space for activists looking to move their online actions into the real world? Or making an introduction to a relevant politician whom you've already built a strong relationship with? Your contributions in such a situation could be endless, but your returns could be greater than those of many of our most successful traditional campaigns. *So don't be afraid to ask how you can help.*

Buddies, Bricks, and Affinity Groups

Further advice on enabling self-organising systems might be gleaned from a group of British activists who announced plans to shut down the Ratcliffe-on-Soar coal power plant in 2009.[vii] Having seen years of organisational lobbying for stronger environmental protections and better regulation of high-polluting industries make little progress, these activists were committed to put their bodies on the line to keep one of the worst climate criminals, the coal industry, from being able to continue with business as usual.

Explained in Emily James' (@emily_james) 2011 documentary, *Just Do It!* (@JustDoItFilm), public organising meetings for the action were based on the simple premise of trying to shut down one of the largest polluters in the country, to draw attention to the need for sustainable energy. With this starting point the draw for those who hoped to be a part of the action, the planning time could then be spent working at much smaller scales of organisation.

If you were one of the activists involved, your first step would be to find a 'Buddy' – a person who you would work most closely with, sharing the various tasks associated with the action along the way. If you were a good runner, you might pair up with someone stronger than you; if you were prepared to be arrested, you would pair up with someone else who was also willing to face arrest; if you wanted to cut through a metal fence, you might want to pair up with someone who was happy to carry any food or supplies you were hoping to bring with you. Whatever you did, you would do your best to stick with your Buddy.

Once you have a Buddy, you would find another pair of Buddies to form a 'Brick' – four people with whom you and your Buddy would be slightly less connected, but would try to stay close with.

Finally, a handful of Bricks would form an 'Affinity Group' – a dozen or two individuals who would approach the same section of the fence together, but with still less connection to one another than the members of any Brick.

The key within this system lies in the autonomy of everyone involved to do what they feel needs doing, in the moment. In the course of an action, Buddies will separate from Bricks, Bricks will separate from Affinity Groups, but the shared overall focus means that everyone can take the steps they see as necessary to achieve the goal.

You and your Buddy are responsible to one another and to your shared sense of overarching purpose. The rest is up to you.

> *What if you replaced 'shut down the power plant' with your latest project outcome?*
>
> *Could project groups be based on similar principles?*

The shadow side of self-organisation:
The London Riots

Just as hierarchical organisations can be created with broadly positive or negative aims, so too can self-organised networks emerge for better or worse causes. In fact, some of the most effective examples of self-organisation in recent years have manifested as reactionary violence.

Margaret Wheatley writes: 'effective self-organisation is supported by two critical elements: a clear sense of identity, and freedom.'[viii] And just as the Occupy movement and the Arab Spring have captured a sense of shared identity amongst millions of disparate individuals and allowed them the space to turn this sense of identity into action, this phenomenon is by no means inherently positive. When the extrajudicial killing of Mark Duggan by London Metropolitan Police sparked violence in Duggan's home of Tottenham, Northeast London, in August 2011, few expected such a local incident would spill beyond the neighbourhood immediately affected.

Chapter 3:
The myth of
hierarchical
necessity and
what we can
do for
ourselves

Two days later, I was cautiously wandering around the Pembury Estate in Hackney, several miles from where Duggan had been shot, as cars, dumpsters and scooters burned on the streets around me. Hackney was but one of dozens of neighbourhoods around the UK that had caught the spark and erupted into violence since the Tottenham incident. The scene was a mix of nervous energies; some angry, some visibly excited by a sense of control that was clearly not a regular part of most of the active participants' day-to-day lives. Countless half-litre tubs of Ben & Jerry's – stolen from a local business by those who probably never imagined spending five pounds sterling on ice cream – appeared alongside the rubble and the chaos, painting a deeply conflicted picture of children being children, in an environment that rarely allowed them to do so.

Hoodies up, bandanas masking identities, the group of mostly teenagers demonstrated that they could control this patch of East London, no matter what the police did to try and reassert their usual authority. Meanwhile, parallel scenes were playing out in predominantly poorer neighbourhoods across London and throughout England.

Five reasons – in no particular order – why hierarchy sucks

5. It denies the centrality of context, assuming that the best decisions can be made from outside the situations where they will be applied

If we think the best decisions can be made by the people furthest away from their application, we've got another think coming...

Given what we know about how information moves through hierarchical systems (see the first two points), we can't really believe such systems provide the stuff of good decision making, can we?

Good decisions must be grounded in the realities they will apply to. This is also why scaling up of good local ideas almost never works; context is everything, and replacing particular situations and relationships with others and expecting the results to be the same, only makes sense if you are far enough from the ground for the critical details to have become invisible.

Though after three days the riots did die down, they also demonstrated that the same phenomena that could be harnessed by broadly middle-class Twitter users to slice through a super-injunction on Parliamentary reporting, also had other uses. Namely, it could be used by those who have repeatedly received the short end of the stick in a wealthy but unequal country like England, to lash out –erratically and without clear direction– at a world that had treated them unfairly.

Chapter 3:
The myth of
hierarchical
necessity and
what we can
do for
ourselves

In other words, people are self-organising whether we like it or not, and the technology that is helping it happen is becoming more ubiquitous by the day. If we are not adopting methods that can work with self-organised groups and individuals, we will be left as impotent as the London Met – and many youth organisations – during those long days and nights in August 2011.

But the organising methods themselves, it bears emphasising, are not the problem. Indeed, they're probably our best hope for addressing the social unrest that fuelled the riots, if we take them seriously. And they were on display in London in a more positive form not so many months before. Let's look now at a hands-on example of non-hierarchical mobilisation that managed to shift the public debate around an issue NGOs had been trying to tackle for decades: tax avoidance.

How UKUncut put tax justice on the radar

In May 2010, the UK Conservative Party – having not won the electoral seats needed to form a government on their own– were forced to cut a deal with the third-place Liberal Democrats to form a coalition government in which both the 'liberal' and the 'democratic' elements of the junior partner were entirely subsumed by a dominant Tory ideology. In the months that followed, Britain experienced a dose of austerity that made the country's Thatcher years look like a half-hearted warm-up exercise in neo-conservative slash-and-burn economics.

Shortly after the 'emergency budget' was announced by Chancellor of the Exchequer, George Osborne, in June 2010, the Treasury decided to forgive Vodafone, one of the world's largest mobile phone providers, the vast majority of a backlogged tax bill totalling roughly six billion pounds.

As it turned out, Vodafone was one of many household-name multinationals that had gone to great lengths – often with tacit or explicit Treasury approval – to hide their earnings in offshore subsidiaries and make sure their profits would do nothing to tackle the deficit for which the public was being mercilessly held to account.

From a government whose most popular slogans since angling their way into office were 'There is no alternative' (to unprecedented public spending cuts), and 'We're all in this together,' the estimated £69.9 billion lost each year in the UK to corporate tax avoidance schemes – many with the blessing of the Tax Man himself – came with an extra dose of bitter irony.[ix] Stand-up comedian and southeast Londoner, Chris Coltrane (@Chris_Coltrane), was just one more frustrated citizen when he happened across a Tweet that read, 'If you want to take direct action against the cuts, email this address.'

'I think I liked how cryptic and mysterious it was,'[x] Chris mused, looking back on his random entry point to a movement that helped shift the public debate and practical realities of corporate tax avoidance across Great Britain in 2010.

On October 27, Chris was one of about seventy people who walked into Vodafone's UK flagship store on Oxford Street and decided to sit down together at the shop's entrance, until it had no choice but to close up for the afternoon.

'Tax avoidance actually proves that the government is lying about there being no alternative to austerity measures. If Vodafone hadn't dodged six billion pounds in taxes, then almost every single cut to welfare for a year could have been reversed,' said Chris, as to why he'd decided to take action. But it didn't stop with a single occupation. And Chris – like many others – became much more active in what followed.

The next day activists in Leeds staged their own Vodafone occupation. That following Saturday saw fifteen other cities around the country organise their own actions. No longer targeting Vodafone alone, activists went after a shortlist of well-researched multinationals who had been engaged in similarly nefarious financial practices, including TopShop, Barclays and several other big name retail outlets and banks.

Word travelled quickly via the #UKuncut Twitter hashtag, and the group who had orchestrated the first action opened up the process. Chris described the organising process that followed as a 'collaboration with activists all around the country':

> The *UK Uncut* account [@UKuncut] on Twitter would suggest a date for a nationwide day of action, and then ask the question: who should we target, and why? From there, people would tweet their thoughts, and a decision was made collectively. It was very democratic, because everyone was able to read all the tweets on the hashtag, so there was this real transparency and openness which I think was extremely refreshing.... Seeing an elegant decision-making process really helped to inspire people and also made them more empowered, because decisions weren't being made from on high that had to be obeyed. They were being made by activists all around the country. Even when the target was announced, people were free to target them how they liked. Dress up in costume, give out home-made flyers, do some theatre in store, play music, dance, sing, scream, whatever people wanted to do, as long as it was peaceful and fun and disruptive.

Chapter 3: The myth of hierarchical necessity and what we can do for ourselves

UKUncut became a Saturday afternoon fixture for countless outraged Brits that autumn, spawning weekly actions spread across over seventy British cities by the end of 2010 and inspiring US, Canadian and other national movements in early 2011.

Front-page coverage – even from some of the country's most conservative newspapers – helped amplify the pressure that was being created on the streets and the social web, pushing tax avoidance into the realm of national policy debates (a place it had rarely been in the decades beforehand).

On December 6, 2010, 27 Members of UK Parliament signed an Early Day Motion to propose 'that this House congratulates UK Uncut for the role it has played in drawing attention by peaceful demonstrations to tax evasion and avoidance and to the need for firm action to secure tax justice.'[xi] By March 2011, the American sister movement had seen Uncut actions in over a hundred cities, including a three-day protest at the state capitol building in Phoenix, Arizona, and a US Facebook page with over 13,000 fans.

The movement also made some less-expected friends, as tax lawyers leveraged the grassroots success of the activists, to launch a legal case against Her Majesty's Revenue and Customs (HMRC), for writing-off a (minimum) ten million pound tax bill to financial giant, Goldman Sachs, not long after the Permanent Secretary for Tax was extensively wined and dined by the company.

While the energy eventually died down, as it will in any movement, Chris highlighted a spin-off benefit that none of the movement's originators could have predicted:

> We have been told by friendly sources in government that companies actually went to HMRC and told them that they wanted to make sure their tax affairs were in order, because they didn't want to become the target of a campaign. It's all anecdotal, we weren't told names, but that fear must have cleaned up a few previously dirty tax deals, and we can only imagine how many millions of pounds came into the treasury that would previously have found its way to Jersey via Luxembourg.

Let's summarise for a moment. In the course of a few months, what began as a handful of activists frustrated about the overly cosy relationship between a Conservative Government and big businesses looking to minimise their 'tax burden,' managed to:

- Kick-off the mobilisation of thousands of people and hundreds of actions, shutting down the stores of some of the worst tax avoiders in the country, time after time, in place after place

- Achieve press coverage from the full spectrum of UK media channels, including those that have traditionally ignored protests and more progressive causes, sparking a massive public debate about both tax avoidance and the faulty logic of government austerity measures

- Inspire a parallel movement in the US, which came to outgrow its British counterpart

- Launch a legal case against the UK Government, challenging the cronyism of its relationship with investment bank Goldman Sachs

- Encourage other multinational companies to settle their tax bills to avoid the kind of embarrassment and cost of being targeted by UKUncut.

For organisations that have been working hard on issues of tax justice and getting the rich to pay their fair share, this reads like the wish list they'd been sitting on for decades.

When I asked Chris what he thought had helped UKUncut to achieve what it did, he spoke of the democratic manifestations of the movement at its every stage of being: 'It can't be stressed enough how nice it is to empower people, and to give them a genuine feeling of having a voice that matters, of being able to make decisions and act on them. It's like a gateway drug onto bigger and more radical activism!'

Self-organisation isn't perfect

As lovely a picture as Chris paints of the processes that helped UKUncut to flourish, I feel it's important to throw in a few disclaimers:

1. UKUncut, like many movements, started from a small core of committed activists who got the ball rolling with the first action. Brave organisations willing to stick their necks out might be able to take on this kind of role, but doing so requires both the confidence to do something bold (and quasi-legal), and the ability to let things take whatever shape those outside your walls want them to, as they become something bigger than their instigators. Maybe a small group of autonomous staff working at arm's length from the organisational structure to try riskier ideas could help to set this kind of thing in motion?

2. In groups without formal leadership, informal leaders almost invariably emerge. This has been described as 'the tyranny of structurelessness,'[xii] as no formal accountability channels exist for these kinds of leaders. Self-organisation requires a fairly high level of maturity and honesty amongst those involved to keep strong personalities from dominating by default.

3. Movements come and go, unlike organisations. There is an argument for the consistency that traditional organisations can offer, persisting through the ups and downs of social change, maintaining pressure when there is less public energy to do so.

However, movements offer something different – permanent networks. As groups emerge around a cause, the relationships are not lost when that movement dissipates. Chapter 8 will explain more about the resilience of activist networks that were spawned during the anti-globalisation movement (and before) which have gone on to help create several social movements since, though seemingly disappearing for periods in between. While not necessarily a replacement for organisational consistency, these networks offer an alternative approach to maintaining presence and avoiding having to start from scratch each time an issue bubbles to the surface.

Where do we go now?

But let's not lose Chris's story, because it's one our organisations too often lack: *People discovering a shared sense of belief or identity, finding their own ways of taking it forward, and getting inspired to do the next thing.* We do this in so many parts of our lives already – amongst friends, families, our own various communities. It is remarkable that these ideas don't find their way into management literature more often.

It's instructive to think how differently a hierarchical organization would have approached the scenarios described above. If we think about the 'more like people' principles described in Chapter 2, we can begin to see how the *Trafigura* phenomenon, for instance, could not have been organised hierarchically – it was an emergent example of the complex world we live in that left the traditional systems that surrounded it sitting on their hands. The right factors, spiralling together at a particular moment in time, can create results not only *bigger* than any of the individual parts, but also new and distinct from their components – birthing a movement where there had previously been only scattered voices.

Chris Coltrane's story of UKUncut's unprecedented series of direct actions conveyed a sense of fun and excitement that countless traditional organisations would likely have quashed at the first risk assessment. People were free to come together in whatever ways they could imagine, and through so many people freely expressing their own creative energies, a movement grew. Similarly, each of the stories above could not have taken place without countless individuals feeling free to respond to a common sentiment in whatever ways they saw fit, rather than being instructed from above as to how they should do so. The autonomy present in each of the examples described was unquestionably at the forefront of their combined successes or impacts.

In studying the successes of social movements, we can ask ourselves,

Chapter 3:
The myth of
hierarchical
necessity and
what we can
do for
ourselves

> *How could we work to make ourselves a part of the movement, rather than trying to convince ourselves we need to be at its head?*

> *And, How can we become more comfortable just letting things happen, rather than trying to shape the world in exactly the ways we think is best for it?*

Hierarchy rarely collapses in one fell swoop, but more often through the gradual chipping away of established practices, assumptions, habits and beliefs over time. One manager or staff person starts to do something a bit differently, maybe it catches on; someone else sparks a change elsewhere, it encourages others to question something they had always done in a particular way, and gradually these shifts grow together, like the ripples of so many rain drops on an open pond.

Just like the kinds of systems we need going forward, the changes to our existing organisations cannot be orchestrated from above, but must emerge as more and more people start to unpick their old world assumptions about how we get things done. In brief, hierarchy cannot create self-organisation.

There is no silver bullet, but there is a silver lining: we can all play a meaningful part in the transformation we want to see. All of us, in varying ways, help to maintain the old top-down ways of working, wherever we sit in the pyramid, and thus we can make many small shifts in how we choose to engage with the structures around us.

'more like people' organisation

Humanity: People give generously when they aren't being told to do things they care about, often not needing to be paid or coordinated, if their passion and purpose are clear.

Autonomy: The possibilities of self-organisation are limited by any attempts to interfere with individual action. The diversity that autonomy enables gives space for success to emerge from unexpected places.

Complexity: Self-organisation is not the result of plans, but of complex contexts and relationships. Responsiveness and awareness, rather than strategy and expertise, are central.

The thing with systems built to work like machines is that they are full of cracks, oversights and loopholes, and thus always leave room for motivated people to discover and create alternatives within – or between – their particular silos or cubicles.

I invite you to take a moment to reflect on the stories you've read, in relation to your own work and your own organisational experience (and if you feel like it, share those reflections online using the Twitter hashtag #morelikepeople):

- How does the Trafigura revolt relate to that email newsletter you'll be sending out next week?
- What do reclaimed Argentine factories tell you about job titles, specialisation?
- What can the London riots tell you about organising a public event amongst your supporters?
- How would UKUncut activists coordinate that meeting you've been stressing about?

If one thing is clear at the end of this chapter, I hope it is that the pages of this book – or any other book, for that matter – will not provide answers to these kinds of questions, yet it is precisely in response to such questions that change begins to occur.

[i] Margaret Wheatley, *Leadership and the New Science*, Berrett-Koehler, 1992, p. 25.

[ii] Naomi Klein & Avi Lewis, *The Take*, Hello Cool World, 2004.

[iii] Lavaca Collective, *Sin Patrón*, Haymarket Books, 2007, p. 188.

[iv] Ibid. p. 193.

[v] Alan Rusbridger, 'The Trafigura fiasco tears up the textbook,' *Guardian*, 14 October 2009. http://www.guardian.co.uk/commentisfree/libertycentral/2009/oct/14/trafigura-fiasco-tears-up-textbook

[vi] Ibid.

[vii] Emily James, 'Just Do It!,' 2011, 43:05.

[viii] Wheatley, 1992, pp. 87.

[ix] Mark Jenner, 'Tax avoidance costs UK economy £69.9 billion a year,' *The New Statesman*, 25 November 2011. http://www.newstatesman.com/blogs/the-staggers/2011/11/tax-avoidance-justice-network

[x] Interview with the author, 8 June 2012.

[xi] http://www.parliament.uk/business/publications/business-papers/commons/early-day-motions/edm-detail1/?session=2010-12&edmnumber=1146

[xii] Original essay by Jo Freeman, 1970. Wikipedia description here: http://en.wikipedia.org/wiki/The_Tyranny_of_Structurelessness

'Not for us': The privileged bias of 'more like machines' organisations

'Being white means never having to think about it.'
– James Baldwin (attributed)

4

Professionalism is a personal and organisational straightjacket. But beyond its false ways of being, its emphasis on uncritical obedience, and its reliance on trust-killing bureaucracy, it is also a system of privilege and exclusion. Professionalism keeps old power structures intact. It keeps those who haven't learned its subtly refined practices out of the decision-making circles that often affect them. And it keeps organisations far more homogenous than they might otherwise be, with both ethical and pragmatic costs.

Luckily, there are things each of us can do, and it starts with delving into the challenging territory of exploring our own privilege. These steps rely on the 'self-awareness' element of the 'more like people' humanity principle, as well as embracing individual and group complexities, and making sure we are working in ways that provide space for individual autonomy, even if doing so can feel deeply uncomfortable at first. While organisations will never be perfect, we should do everything we can to open our doors and 're-centre' our work to help it connect with the vast majority of people who currently feel alienated by the ways we chose to organise.

Stepping outside of our comfort zones

There are things that will always stand out to me when I visit the East London neighbourhood where I lived with my wife when I started writing this book. The middle-aged gentleman who mutters loudly but incoherently to himself, just beyond our front doors; the horses running laps around the paddock across the river; the deep bass of the latest grime (a gritty UK variation on American hip-hop) singles wafting from a nearby apartment.

But there are also elements that almost don't register. They're as inconspicuous to me as I'd imagine they are ubiquitous to those who make them a regular part of their lives. The Turkish social club, the Ghanaian barber shop, the working man's cafe, still seemingly untouched by the 21st century. These are the places that as a) Canadian, b) relatively young, c) white, and d) middle-class, I'll subconsciously dismiss as places so distant and irrelevant to my life, as to hardly acknowledge their presence.

But then I take a minute and think about it: what if I walked into that club or barber shop? I imagine considerable awkwardness. *Lanky white dude with a North American accent walks into a bar....* The joke could write itself in any number of ways.

Luckily – at least for the sake of my short-term comfort – I can have a meal, meet my friends and get my haircut in several more comfortable settings. Basically, I can do these things with people who are more like me. On the one hand, this is deeply closed-minded, but on another, very much human. We like to be around people with whom we have things in common: interests, language, opinions, or cultures. Commonality often makes time together easier for all. It's at least part of why we hang out with ex-pat communities abroad, live in particular neighbourhoods, or go to the same local pub, year after year. It's also why so many peoples' Twitter feeds can give them the impression that the world is full of people who see things much like they do.

Culture is invisible, as long as you're a part of it. As soon as you're not, you know full well it's there. The slang, mannerisms, dress codes, power dynamics, gender roles and other assumed knowledge of any group can leave us feeling like a sore thumb when they are not our own. When you don't have a lot of these awkward out-of-your-element moments, it means you have the privilege to live your life within your particular comfort zone. It is a privilege relatively few people in the world have, with most regularly having to venture into difficult domains to do a range of basic things that others take for granted.

'Culturelessness'

There is a white western liberal tendency to bemoan 'culturelessness.' 'If only I had some of what all those other ethnic groups have...' – you might find that sentiment written in the subtext of so many indie music lyrics and alternative webzine commentaries.

What this tendency ignores is that white middle-class Anglo culture is far from cultureless – those of us who have it just seldom see our own culture because it is 'normal' to us. To: "It is the relative obsession with time-keeping, a dominant sense of pragmatism, an emphasis on individualism, privacy, and 'busyness as an indicator of personal achievement.' It is the championing of intellectual accomplishment (over, say, physical or spiritual gain), scientific rationalism, emotional distance...and the list of defining cultural characteristics could go on.

When positions of power are dominated by white, wealthy men, the things that define a white, wealthy, male culture generally go unspoken. They are the wallpaper in discussions of culture – the background that underpins conversations, activities and beliefs; rarely subjects of scrutiny in their own right – at least if you're a white, relatively wealthy man.

As activist and author James Baldwin is rumoured to have said, 'Being white means never having to think about it.'

Defining 'white privilege'

This invisible field of comfort and ease for some, discomfort and challenge for others, is sometimes called 'white privilege' – but its principles can be applied to a range of dominant social groups (e.g. - male/hetero/English-speaking privilege). Tim Wise (@ timjacobwise), one of the leading (white) voices working to make visible the subtle ways in which whiteness still provides countless advantages for those who have it, describes white privilege as 'psychological money in the bank, the proceeds of which we cash in every day while others are in a state of perpetual overdraft.'[i]

What does this 'psychological money in the bank' look like in practice? It is not being followed by security when you walk into a department store. It is running for the presidency of the United States and not having your birth certificate questioned as a forgery. It is believing – without reservation – that the police will be on your side when you need them. It is the benefit of the doubt.

White/male/wealthy cultures not only exist, they still dominate. But they dominate in ways that are often invisible to those who benefit. Culture is like the air we breathe, it's the habits and daily choices we take as normal: going to a pub after work, living in a nuclear family, the sports we play and watch.

What do personal habits and hobbies have to do with building more diverse organisations, you ask? They highlight some of the things people can easily take for granted about themselves and the world. And taking things for granted is not something that is limited to our personal lives.

'Learning to be white'

I remember working with a colleague, Maurice McLeod (@ mowords), at a charity some years ago. He was one of only a few black people in a relatively large organisation. We shared a few stories about our disillusionment with parts of the sector we worked in; namely, the distance between its rhetoric and its realities on a spectrum of issues, including diversity. Many organisations in the social change sector were keen to espouse the importance of diversity, but unlikely to practice it in more than a tick-box way.

Maurice grew up in Southeast London public housing, but unlike most of his childhood friends, had gone on to university. He had started his own business and done regular pro-bono work for community groups before moving into the voluntary sector himself.

While white and reasonably privileged, I had spent my formative years in the hip-hop community in Toronto, giving me some exposure to a tiny proportion of the realities faced by people born with considerably less than I'd had growing up. Street violence, police harassment, hunger, drugs... none of these phenomena were more than a few steps away in the community I considered my home for several formative years. The insights I gleaned there hit me hard. I carried them with me into my more formal working life, keeping those perspectives in the front of my mind when working on projects and campaigns over the years, while still clearly benefiting from the array of privileges I was born with.

While Maurice's and my experiences were vastly different, we found some connection when our paths crossed. We shared a sense of frustration with organisations that claimed to support particular people and communities, but did so from ivory towers, out of touch with the day-to-day issues so many people faced.

I vividly remember a discussion we had early on while working together. I had mentioned feeling out of place in certain office discussions because I didn't have a university degree. While this had largely been the result of my own choices, it created certain gaps in the assumed experience of most of those working in NGO offices, making me part of a very small minority of staff there who had educated ourselves through other means. My lack of post-secondary education left me in a bit of a lurch when discussions of university came up at the office ('What did you study?'). I didn't have the reference points, or have much to contribute, and there was little recognition amongst most colleagues that these conversations could make people feel uncomfortable.

This resonated with Maurice, who was very conscious of the differences that his time at university had instilled in him.

'I went to university and learned how to be white,' he stated, matter-of-factly.

He elaborated that coming from a poor community in a predominantly black part of London, he had to learn how to speak differently in order to be working in the job he was in at this point. As 'proper' English wasn't spoken where he grew up,

Chapter 4:
'Not for us':
The privileged
bias of 'more
like machines'
organisations

he saw these cultural adaptations as critical learning in his post-secondary education, the keys to a world of relative advantage compared to the one he'd grown up in.

When he goes home, sees childhood friends, spends time in his old neighbourhood, he might slip back into a way of speaking that most of his colleagues wouldn't recognise as that of the man they work with. Maurice is conscious that since he went to university, he has, in some ways, distanced himself from his own community in order to be accepted in the dominant culture of the workplace. This is too often the unspoken subtext of organisational inclusion efforts: the hiring of people of colour who have learned to act like white people, in order to be accepted within their ranks.

While equal opportunities and affirmative action measures in many countries ensure that there are certain criteria on which you cannot deny someone a job, they have also allowed us to realign subconscious prejudices. It is no longer a person's ethnicity, per se, that keeps them from getting hired, but maybe that their way of speaking or writing 'isn't sufficiently advanced' for the role. Too often, the result – who gets hired– is the same as it's always been.

A range of cultural cues, from language to image and dress, form an unspoken narrative aimed at a range of non-dominant communities. It reads, 'if you want to succeed, you have to be like us.' While adapting to differences can be both individually and collectively challenging, it is necessary if we are to re-shape our organisations to both *reflect* and *benefit from* the diversity of the world outside our walls.

From inclusion to re-centring

The US anti-violence collective *INCITE! Women of Color Against Violence* has described this kind of work, not as *inclusion*, but *re-centring* what we do to help it connect with a wider range of peoples' lived realities. Re-centring is about putting the onus of change on the organisation, rather than on those whom it aims to connect with. *INCITE!* Co-founder Andrea Smith writes:

Inclusivity has... come to mean that we start with an organizing model developed with white, middle-class people in mind, and then simply add a multicultural component to it... Instead of saying, how can we include women of color, women with disabilities, etc., we must ask what our analysis and organizing practice would look like if we centered them in it.[ii]

Chapter 4:
'Not for us':
The privileged
bias of 'more
like machines'
organisations

Smith describes the process through which the group developed their analysis of violence faced by women of colour as having initially focused on domestic and police violence, and aimed to involve the medical profession in their support work. However, she says, 'when we re-centered the discussion around women with disabilities, we saw that the medical system was as punitive as the criminal justice system, and we needed to work on developing alternative strategies.'[iii]

These kinds of insights are often lost in organisations more homogenous than *INCITE!* For example, youth organisations that work closely with the police without critique or sensitivity, often shut their own doors to young people who have experienced regular abuse and humiliation at the hands of local officers. Another common example is when organisations require programme participants who struggle with English, or whom have not received the same level of education that staff likely have, to fill in even basic paperwork.

When I was coordinating a student exchange, I made the mistake of requiring applicants to house a visiting young person on their return trip. Whereas the middle-class university students were often living away from home, and happy to have someone crash on their sofa, the working-class college students tended to be studying locally, still living with their parents, and thus lacking the same flexibility to accommodate someone. Unfortunately, I only heard that this was an obstacle through the grapevine, after the fact, so was unable to do anything about it beyond tell the story and involve more perspectives in future planning processes.

The fundamental point here is that the inclusion agenda is not enough and often serves to assimilate, rather than involve others as equals. Re-centring requires us to look at the nuts and bolts of our work and to make an effort to learn from how other groups and cultures do the same things, from organising events to holding meetings; doing recruitment to delivering services. And to do this, we'll need to be actively seeking out and hearing what others, who already do things differently, have to suggest. As hard as this can be to accept for many forward-thinking staff and volunteers working towards social change, all of us need to be more aware of the subconscious barriers we might be erecting that keep others from being a part of what we do.

> *Who do you involve, at what stage, when you're planning a new project?*

> *When have you felt excluded, or felt that you've had to change or hide something about yourself to feel a part of a group?*

Whom we hire and whom we support

While professional language and culture can be major barriers to those applying to and being hired by our organisations, as Andrea Smith made clear, these same traits can also have implications for those who feel comfortable joining our organisations or receiving our support. If our organisations really want to work with a wider range of people, we need to make a stronger effort to connect with their life experiences and adapt our work accordingly.

'Professionalism,' as a culture, not only requires a certain kind of education, but also certain ways of working. It promotes working systems seeded and nurtured in formal education, such as written presentation of ideas, fixed hierarchy, linear cause-and-effect project planning, and strict timetabling. Outside of the realms of formal education and office environments, these systems (and the assumptions they breed) are far from universally understood. In fact, rather than being considered positive attributes, these same traits can be seen as negative, threatening, or deeply suspect to those who are not used to them.

When I first met Richard Gordon, a father of five approaching forty and living in the same neighbourhood where he had grown up, in Brent, Northwest London, he had recently received a grant to deliver multimedia training to young people deemed 'at risk' of becoming involved in local gangs. Richard had been there himself and had the scars to prove it. The story of his early years was the story he was trying to help those young people avoid repeating.

The grant let Richard pay himself a modest salary. This accomplishment set him apart from anyone else in the immediate community, where a combination of welfare benefits and illegal activities provided the vast majority of local income. Richard was proud to be his own boss, in an area where the others who could claim that success had done so through quasi-legal means. He would hang the certificates from each training course he was able to attend on his new office wall, pointing them out to the youth in the programme and reminding them that such achievements were within their reach. In the context of the Church End housing estate, this was groundbreaking stuff.

Chapter 4:
'Not for us':
The privileged
bias of 'more
like machines'
organisations

While Richard and I were working on a grant application together in 2009, he explained to me the problems with something as seemingly innocuous as a registration form for the youth involved in his work:

> Our funders expected us to give registration forms to all the youth who come through our doors. Now, what would happen if we asked youth to do these forms themselves? Most of them have been kicked out of school – basically, at 14, 15, told, for whatever reasons, that they were failures at education. Since then, they haven't had to fill out any forms, done any kinds of paperwork, because it's no longer part of the world they live in. If we give them one of these forms, what kind of associations do you think that has for them? Do you think they're going to feel comfortable here still? Do you think they are going to want to come back to a place that reminds them of being told they were failures? So we explained the situation to our funders and now only ask the youth to put their signatures down, and gradually get them to accompany us in filling in other details, as they feel more comfortable with the programme.[iv]

While this may seem worlds away to some, I have heard similar stories from people working directly with refugees, ex-offenders, mental health services users, and a range of communities that don't speak English as a first language. In most organisations, circulating a registration form for a funder wouldn't so much as raise an eyebrow. But if the people you support are anything like those Richard works with, those forms might be the difference between them accessing what you have to offer, or not. Richard's background helped him to instinctively re-centre his work, in the face of funder pressures to do otherwise, and the questions and challenges he raised are not unique to his particular London neighbourhood.

Why individuals seem less homogenous than the groups they are part of

In the world of good causes, most of us would be devastated by the suggestion that we were racist, sexist, or guilty of any other form of discriminatory 'ism.' But the challenging reality is that by being myself – a middle-class white male – in many workplaces, I run a strong risk of contributing to excluding others.

When I first blogged on some of these ideas, I was challenged on my assertion that 'professional' office culture is broadly Oxfordian – white, wealthy, and male. A former colleague commented on the piece, suggesting I was in danger of stereotyping a group based on where they had been educated, which didn't recognise the diversity that exists, even within the privilege of somewhere like Oxford University.

While certain kinds of diversity will always exist, even in the most elite circles, when we form groups we come together around what it is we have in common, around sameness. We're unlikely to share the parts of ourselves that aren't part of the shared office culture if we assume colleagues won't be able to relate to them. If I worked in an environmental NGO, but still had a thing for high-polluting cars, I probably wouldn't discuss this much at work, even if it wasn't a conscious secret.

This creates a stronger perception of homogeneity amongst the group; people from outside only see what they have in common, giving the impression groups are more homogenous than they in many ways are. This is a big part of why the Ghanaian barbershop near my London apartment seems so distant to me. It's not that the men who hang out there are by any means a homogenous group – I would assume they have different jobs, interests, families – but from the outside, I see what they share with each other and what I don't share with them: nationality, ethnicity, possibly language.

In another setting, I'm sure I could easily come up with a list of things we did have in common, our neighbourhood being the most obvious starting point. But when they are in a group that is a lot harder to do – our differences dominate my perception.

Chapter 4:
'Not for us':
The privileged
bias of 'more
like machines'
organisations

What separates my personal discomfort with that barbershop, and the challenges of many qualified would-be staff from other backgrounds who might want to work for a charity, is that all I have to get over if I want to walk into that barber shop is my own discomfort. There is no hiring process in which I will be judged for my acceptability, as many of the men at the barbershop would likely have to face before being hired by one of the organisations I work with on a day-to-day basis.

In an office, like any community, we forget that the very things that can make us feel okay there, can be the differences that push away or exclude others. This is what I mean when I say that by 'being myself' in many offices, I might be reinforcing others' sense that this office is not for them.

At one level, this throws a contradiction into the 'more like people' approach; what if 'being ourselves' puts others off? But let me clarify: being *a small part* of who I am, as most of us are at work, can easily put others off. It's an important question though, and one that brings up another part of the 'humanity' principle – our ability to be self-aware. What can we do to embrace more of who we are at our work? By co-developing a sense that we are all more than what we have in common, we may open up new inroads for others who might otherwise have dismissed our workplaces as not for them.

This might mean dressing how we do on the weekends, organising a different caterer for an event, booking a venue in a different neighbourhood, or dropping some of the jargon and acronyms from our workplace vocabularies. These steps will not change the organisation overnight, but they might make others more comfortable breaking their own established patterns, thus helping to break down potential barriers in your work.

'Culturally white'

Veena Vasista (@seeandconnect), a friend, colleague and someone with a lot of important insights into ethnicity, privilege, and culture, wrote a report for the Runnymede Trust (@RunnymedeTrust) in 2010 on ethnic minority leadership in the UK private sector. The least surprising finding of the report was that the higher you went in a business, the fewer non-white faces could be found on the organisational pyramid. This is an important indication that many of our institutions are still a long way off achieving employment equality, years after so many pieces of legislation were passed in order to address this. (Though, as Veena has said, it wouldn't take several months of research to see this was the case!)

What was more interesting – and worrisome – about her report was that nearly all of her respondents (men and women of non-Caucasian identification working in senior roles in the private sector) described themselves as 'culturally white.' Veena writes:

> Some Black and minority ethnic individuals may feel as if they have to choose between bringing their true character to the office and meeting the cultural norms of the organisations. While the workplace may look diverse, e.g. more women, more visible Black and minority ethnic professionals, this 'diversity' is superficial. Getting to the top might require conformity in style, perspective, ways of working, cultural interests.[v]

So while some gains have clearly been made for these respondents to have the jobs they have at all (when previously, more explicit racism would have kept them out), the process of acceptance came at a cost, with the implicit requirement to assimilate with the dominant workplace culture in order to get in the front door.

Deconstructing the Digital Divide

While walking into the Ghanaian barber shop or Turkish social club would require some leap of faith on my part, social technology is making it infinitely easier to get beyond the comfort zones of interacting primarily with 'people like us.' While Twitter has the potential of re-creating the same closed circles we often create in the real world, it also makes it much easier to move beyond those circles, if we choose to.

Chapter 4:
'Not for us':
The privileged
bias of 'more
like machines'
organisations

Imagine the ten staff members at a fictional NGO are all white, wealthy and male. We know now that the office culture is very likely to reflect their shared reality, and their shared privilege. However, one of them is really into sustainable food, another is in a salsa band, another is a member of an environmental direct action group, and yet another has spent a lot of time in Nigeria. If each of them were on Twitter, they might each be confident enough to share thoughts and links related not only to their jobs, but also to their respective personal interests, even if those interests would make them obvious minorities in the workplace.

So let's assume those ten colleagues follow each other's updates. They see information related to their work, but are also getting each other's updates on a range of interests and activities that they would never normally chat about. And not only are they getting these updates from each other, they are seeing the updates of people who their colleagues follow and have re-tweeted, introducing new perspectives into their timeline. With each re-Tweet, a potential new world opens up.

There has been much discussion amongst social change organisations about the 'digital divide,' a notion that those online are the elite of the world, talking amongst themselves in greater detail than ever before. While there will always be an element of truth in this assertion, as new technology has an uptake lag amongst those with less opportunities and means, this lag is disappearing faster than most of us could have imagined.

In the United States, for instance, African Americans and Hispanics have consistently polled at more than twice as likely than white Americans to use Twitter.[vi] And in many developing countries, the use of low-cost mobile phones to access the

Internet is significantly narrowing the digital divide associated with global poverty, influencing national elections and crowd-sourcing important local information in countless development efforts. Juba, the new capital of South Sudan, is being described by some as 'the world's first digital capital city,'[vii] and some expect that within five years, half of all Africans will have their own smartphones.[viii]

In brief, we are moving faster than we could ever have imagined towards a global online conversation that includes many voices that have traditionally fallen below the radar of our old methods of communication. This isn't to suggest that the digital divide doesn't exist, simply that it is increasingly a social divide. It is less a question of technology than it is part of the same question of why most of our organisations, our groups of friends, and our communities remain disconnected from those who are different from them.

The critics who've devoted so many words to the 'elitism' of Twitter, Facebook, and a few other social platforms in recent years have done so largely based on their own online social circles. Because the networks they've crafted for themselves have likely emerged in their own image, the countless parallel networks forming elsewhere on the same platform have repeatedly passed them by.

But as with me walking into that Turkish social club, only a mental shift is needed to start to open up new social circles online. And it's a simpler shift than it's ever been: *follow people who are different from you.*

For those less familiar with Twitter, you can start by clicking on an unexpected and out-of-place re-Tweet in your feed and following the person who initially posted it. You can check the 'trending topics' to see a totally random scattering of users (though be prepared to be potentially offended if you choose this route). You can search a term that interests you and find people looking at it from countless different perspectives. And follow them.

More specifically, you can search the area where you work and connect with others who are talking about it. The #Hackney hashtag introduced me to a range of people in East London I'd never crossed paths with before, representing a fair share of the borough's diversity at any given time.

To be clear, a Twitter community is not the same thing as a real community, but it can be an inroad to conversations and perspectives from outside our social comfort zone. Think of it as a complement to a range of other non-online efforts to re-centre our work.

'When they see that what we are doing works, they shut us down'

Not long after I moved to London in 2006, I organised an event amongst community leaders who used hip-hop music and culture in youth programming around the city. There had been a widespread feeling amongst several I had met that their contributions to addressing local issues such as gang violence and crime were not being taken seriously by local authorities and bigger youth organisations. But the problem was bigger than I had realised. The level of mistrust of authority, in the broadest sense, cut to the heart of most of our organisations.

The meeting involved almost twenty local organisers, from across the London boroughs: Hackney, Brent, Newham, Southwark, Lewisham and more. These recognised community leaders were rappers, filmmakers, DJs, poets, fashion designers and music producers. There was a seventeen year-old concert promoter and a sixty-something pastor in the room. In hip-hop terms, this was a meeting of the Ol' Skool and the New Skool, East and West, North and South (of the River Thames, at least). This was a very diverse group, were it not for being all male and for me being the only non-Afro-Caribbean person in the room.

As the conversation moved towards ways of making their case, demonstrating their impact and leveraging greater support for their work, one of the participants cut in:

> 'When they see this stuff is working, they shut it down. They don't want us to succeed. They'll throw us a bone here and there, but they still want to know that our positions aren't

*Chapter 4:
'Not for us':
The privileged
bias of 'more
like machines'
organisations*

going to change; that we'll stay poor, keep killing each other and rely on them to keep us afloat. The only thing we can do is start to make our own money.'

At that point the rest of the group started to nod enthusiastically and another member cut in:

'We need our own businesses; grocery stores and everything. We make the money, we hire our own community and we put the profits back into supporting all of our work. We know that they'll just pull the plug if we start to really make a difference.'

Again, this got an enthusiastic response from the room, no one opposing the statements being made.

Finding myself in the rare position of thinking more conservatively than the rest of the group, I suggested that maybe the key wasn't in public money, but foundation funding, which didn't necessarily have the same puppet masters as the public sector and wanted to really make a difference in poorer communities.

The response was lukewarm, at best, with the first speaker countering that it didn't really matter what sector the money was coming from. Big charities, he said, were as bad as government and just as uninterested in supporting real, progressive, bottom-up change in their communities. And once again, the room agreed; charities were not only seen as ineffective, but were seen to be working *against* the interests of the communities they claimed to support, bar a few well-intentioned individuals.

Now let's think about this for a moment. I won't claim this group would be representative of *most* communities in London, but think about the implications of nearly twenty community leaders, of a range of ages and from an array of London neighbourhoods, agreeing that not only government, but the charitable sector as well, were instrumental in *maintaining* the problems they saw in their communities.

I don't want you to feel the need to defend your work as you read this, just to think about what this might mean for it. These were all people who had given their blood, sweat and tears to helping address devastating social ills – youth violence, unemployment, poverty – yet they wanted little to do with most of the institutions that claimed to be there to help them do it. This suggests there's something seriously wrong with the current approach. As hard as it may be to acknowledge, our organisations aren't viewed as universally positively as we might think, a reality which goes some way to explaining why people from some groups apply for non-profit and charity jobs disproportionately more than others.

Change our hiring criteria, not the people we hire!

My first formal charity sector job was with the Scarman Trust, an organisation that provides small grants to individuals across London to setup their own community projects. I had just moved to the UK from Canada, unable to get any work in the field there despite several years of experience setting up community projects, organising activist events, and running a small-scale hip-hop promotion company.

After being shortlisted, I walked into my job interview with a backwards baseball cap on.

What can I say, in retrospect, except that I thought it was a good look. I didn't realise people interviewing me for a job that had nothing to do with my sense of style would be bothered by something so superficial. I've learned since that many are. They hired me, though my boss – half-jokingly – never let me live down the baseball cap incident, reminding me that countless other managers, in most other organisations, would have written me off the second I sat down in front of the interview panel.

Fortunately the Scarman Trust was different – more so than I could have known at that stage in my working life. The staff – particularly at the London Office – were not reflective of the staff of most charities I've worked for or with since. Namely, we had travelled many different paths to be there together. We were from Canada, Georgia, Mauritius, Germany, Rwanda, Bangladesh... but, more importantly, what many of us had in common was that we had been in the positions of those we supported at some stage: setting up something new, taking initiative, learning practical community and youth work by doing it. We could share that perspective with the people we worked with, which was often the crucial difference in being able to build strong relationships with them. This kind of perspective doesn't come from formal qualifications.

Dorothy Newton, Regional Director for the London Region, had made a conscious effort when she came to the role years earlier, to *help the organisation adapt to people*, rather than expecting people to adapt to the organisation. This is where so often our organisations' diversity efforts fall short. By expecting those who come to us to adapt to us, we will continue to model workplaces after those who have been there before, rather than growing and changing to reflect the differences in the world around us. Dorothy and others at Scarman practiced the 're-centering' described by Andrea Smith of INCITE!, long before Smith's article on the subject had been written.

This alternative approach was reflected in the grant process, where a simple three-page application form was almost always followed up by an in-person interview for those who struggled expressing their ideas in writing. It was also reflected in staffing, hiring those of us who had not been given work opportunities elsewhere, but had relevant, if unconventional, experience. Volunteer recruitment reflected this approach as well, letting volunteers get involved in various ways, rather than pre-prescribing particular roles for them to fill.

Fundamentally as well, the Scarman Trust, and the Community Champions award programme it managed, were doing viral marketing before it had a name. There was an initial outreach period in 1999, based on hiring a core of staff with strong grassroots connections in different local communities across London. But after that, most of the outreach was done by former grant recipients and the groups many of them had gone on to create. This was formalised into a 'partners' programme in which former recipients and local organisations that had supported them could encourage people in their own networks to apply for grants. These trusted local partners supported new applicants through the application process and sat on the awards panels each round, along with partners from various other communities, making the case for those they had brought forward.

In roughly a decade, the grants reached nearly 2,000 individuals in London, most of whom had never received grant money before, and who represented many of the communities most detached from wider institutional funding or public services. Without formal targeting, the programme reached into most of London's more deprived neighbourhoods. This was an achievement for the ways the organisation worked, allowing those who could make best use of the money to find it, through well-nurtured word-of-mouth, rather than from a strategic choice to get the money into the city's poorest areas.

E-Democracy.org (eventually) connects with the Minneapolis Somali community

But it doesn't always happen like that. Dorothy's connections and a career spent actively working to connect with and tirelessly support the city's least-heard voices had laid the foundations for this programme many years before it was officially launched. While the methods were sound, they were made much easier because *a lot* of background work had helped make it what it was.

Steve Clift (@democracy), founder of E-Democracy.org (@edemo) and someone who hadn't spent his career as Dorothy Newton had, can attest to the work involved in crossing social boundaries. E-Democracy.org is a network of over fifty online local community forums in the US, UK and New Zealand, for neighbourhood-based community conversation and civic engagement. These are online spaces for neighbours to talk to neighbours about things that matter to them, from lost dogs, to small-p politics, and everything in between.

Though its first Minneapolis online community launched in 1994, before most people knew there was an internet, until 2010, E-Democracy was a deeply middle-class project. Early fora served as platforms for those with varying degrees of privilege to connect with one another and organise around local issues, online. And while the local achievements in the project's early years were indeed impressive, new tools or opportunities also reinforced inequalities by strengthening the power of those who already had it.

Too many organisations tacitly accept this, but Steve's deeply held belief that everyone should be able to be active in their community helped push him to do something about it.

In 2010, E-Democracy.org started a project to launch a forum in Cedar-Riverside, Minneapolis' largest immigrant community, just east of the city's downtown. Of the neighbourhood's eight thousand-plus residents, roughly half lived below the national poverty line, and nearly two thirds were not white, representing a significant contrast from the existing E-Democracy communities.

Steve's first step? Going to the mosques, the coffee shops, the community centres, and chatting with anyone who had any interest in community or social technologies about the kinds of projects E-Democracy ran. From these forays, Steve began to find out what local people wanted from the Internet, vis-à-vis local communication and engagement.

He spent the better part of six months this way, building trust and getting past peoples' apprehensions before meeting a young Somali guy and a well-connected Kenyan woman, to manage an online community for the neighbourhood.

Initially, Steve and his new team experienced a lot of hesitation, both towards outside input (lots of organisations had come to 'help them' before, but hadn't inspired much confidence doing so) and towards online community (community was not viewed as something that happened online).

Poverty and discrimination, as anyone who's worked with them knows, make trust much harder to come by. But this small, emerging team kept going where people were, knocking on doors, making their faces known and encouraging people to sign-up on the spot, needing only an email address to do so. Numbers on the forum gradually grew, through relationships with the local public housing association, and a range of Somali businesses and cultural organisations.

When I asked Steve what had helped to break through the initial scepticism, he was clear: 'We stuck around,' he said, highlighting the hit-and-run nature of so many other organisational outreach efforts.

When a forum manager was witness to a shooting at a local convenience store, all that groundwork began to prove its worth. Initially, people shared their shock and grief online, and began discussing funeral arrangements. But quickly this led to plans for a candlelight vigil in which the forum helped to bring a broad cross-section of over 300 community members together on short-notice to pay tribute to those who'd been killed. This was the first link between online community participation and face-to-face action, which in Steve's experience with dozens of local online communities, is when real change starts to occur.

Chapter 4:
'Not for us':
The privileged
bias of 'more
like machines'
organisations

Following the vigil, a young Somali man posted to the forum about the lack of police protection in the area, arguing that it was necessary for community members to arm themselves if they wanted to be safe in their own neighbourhood. This brought many passive forum participants out of the woodwork to comment, sparking countless in-person debates in the local youth centre and other community hubs, bringing to the surface a widely accepted sentiment that had remained mostly silent and thus unchallenged to that point.

The forum, Steve told me over Skype, voiced 'an honest feeling... among young Somalis that they needed to protect themselves and couldn't trust the police.' Further, 'it gave it a platform to be heard by those who could then say, "there are alternatives to that."'[ix]

The sentiment voiced by the young person on the forum was the kind of attitude, like those expressed in the meeting I held with hip-hop community organisers in London, that remains hidden from many of the professionals meant to be working with a community. Sharing those kinds of thoughts publically calls for a level of trust that doesn't always come easily in communities that have experienced violence and discrimination.

The debates that followed those shootings would likely have remained isolated without that online forum. And the forum would likely have remained empty, if not for the trust-building work Steve and his team had carried out, going where people already were and responding to their needs, rather than expecting the opposite.

While far from effortless, E-Democracy's work dispels the commonly held belief that only privileged communities will use a local online discussion forum. What the project in Cedar-Riverside highlights is perhaps that only privileged communities *initially assume a local online forum will benefit them*, because they start from the assumption that most systems will. For others, a local online forum may have to work a little harder to prove its worth, amongst a plethora of systems that have failed to live up to their promise.

In a similar vein, People & Planet (@peopleandplanet), the UK's biggest student activism network (and one of the most 'more like people' organisations I've known), has begun to challenge a similar stereotype about non-white, non-middle class disengagement with environmentalism. Having organised in UK universities since the late '60s with the broadly white, middle-class base you'd expect from a student environmental organisation, they decided that their issues were too important to be left in the hands of relatively privileged activists. Instead of simply making statements about inclusivity to their existing membership, they began to actively seek-out workshop opportunities in Britain's Further Education Colleges – the largely trade-based educational facilities where more mixed student bodies were generally found.

While doing so required certain shifts in terms of how content was pitched, how ideas were framed, and what kind of actions would be popular, the most important thing was that they were there at all, setting them apart from so many other NGOs and student organisations. Through broader organisational events, the College audiences have become better connected with more of the traditional university activist base, and vice versa. This process has helped create spaces for learning across difference for all parties.

Like Steve Clift's efforts in Minneapolis, People & Planet highlighted the difference between 'inclusion' and 're-centring,' placing the burden of change on organisations and staff, rather than the people they were hoping to involve in their work. While it can be difficult, awkward and time-consuming stuff, the onus to re-centre an organisation's work is both ethical and practical, and not one that can be dismissed or tokenised by those serious about a more equal world.

Finding new centres

Chapter 4:
'Not for us':
The privileged
bias of 'more
like machines'
organisations

Prejudice and privilege are invariably messy subjects because they make us look more deeply at the parts of ourselves that have been shaped by some of the same social forces we actively oppose. The kind of defensiveness I've experienced when I've raised some of these questions with broadly progressive people online and in person is unparalleled in my experience. These things make us *really* uncomfortable! Which is usually a sign that there's something there we need to address and re-centring our work, to ground it in the realities of a wider range of people, is an important step we can take to do so.

Making sure our organisations are truly open to a wider range of people, like everything in this book, will involve personal as well as organisational change. The 'more like people' principles of humanity, autonomy, and complexity can offer some direction as to the kinds of change required, whether in relation to our hiring practices, the kinds of meetings we hold, or to how we become more conscious of our own subtle prejudices.

In this context, *autonomy* is about adapting to the people not currently engaged with our work, but also those within an organisation, like Maurice, or the people in Veena's Runnymede report, who felt they had to hide or change parts of who they are to be accepted in their jobs. Open-ended, perspective-based application and interview questions can be a good way of encouraging people to apply in the ways they feel most comfortable doing so, rather than pigeonholing applicants into demonstrating niche experiences that will invariably favour people with particular privileges. Formal qualification requirements, on the other hand, are a good way to exclude people.

'more like people' re-centring

Humanity: Empathy and self-awareness help us see both how our actions and behaviours might alienate others, as well as appreciate how different peoples' experiences will vary from our own, leading to very different assumptions about the world and how we organise within it.

Autonomy: Those within and outside our organisations should not have to change who they are to engage with us; our organisations should find out what we can do to adapt for them.

Complexity: Diversity increases complexity and without diversity, our organisations are ill-equipped to deal with a range of other complex problems that are a part of our work.

The *humanity* principle means consciously building empathy with the experiences of others, even if it means putting our own advantages under the microscope. It is also in the self-awareness of thinking about how our own actions and comments might be read by people of different backgrounds. *Complexity*, meanwhile, *is* diversity. Promoting a range of experiences, opinions, and perspectives will always help us to navigate a complex world better than a lack of them will.

While organisations have been having these conversations for decades, my experience has been that all but a few remain at a 'check-box' level of depth. Rarely do they involve the perspectives of those they are aiming to involve. As best I can tell, this is due to a) discomfort with the issues, b) lack of understanding of what can be done to move beyond superficial indicators of change, and c) the fact that many people who aren't directly affected by discriminatory professionalism aren't aware that it's a problem. I hope Chapter 4 has addressed the final problem, offered some insights on the second one, and helped provide some motivation to explore that discomfort.

While there is a major need for most of our organisations to get better at embracing differences, we can't just force this kind of change from above. The development of particular projects or outreach materials can come from a range of people and teams. And each of us can think more specifically about how we might engage in more open ways at the office, our events, and on the web, modelling 're-centered' behaviours wherever we find ourselves. Let's push ourselves to make sure our practices can live up to their intent and encourage the widest range of people to get involved, even if it means shifting some of our own underpinning assumptions.

Chapter 4:
'Not for us':
The privileged
bias of 'more
like machines'
organisations

[i] Tim Wise, 'Membership has its privileges: Seeing and challenging the benefits of whiteness,' TimWise.org, 22 June 2000. http://www.timwise.org/2000/06/membership-has-its-privileges-seeing-and-challenging-the-benefits-of-whiteness/

[ii] Andrea Smith, 'Without Bureaucracy, Beyond Inclusion: Re-centering Feminism,' *Left Turn*, 1 June 2006. http://www.leftturn.org/without-bureaucracy-beyond-inclusion-re-centering-feminism

[iii] Ibid.

[iv] Interview with the author, initially appeared in 'Being Human,' *Engage Magazine*, June 2010.

[v] Veena Vasista, 'Snowy Peaks': Ethnic diversity at the top,' The Runnymede Trust, 2010, p. 11. http://www.runnymedetrust.org/uploads/publications/pdfs/SnowyPeaks-2010.pdf

[vi] Pew Internet, 'Twitter Update 2011,' 1 June 2011. http://www.pewinternet.org/Reports/2011/Twitter-Update-2011/Main-Report/Main-Report.aspx

[vii] Frederic Dubois, 'The #OSJUBA event stresses early moves by net activists in South Sudan,' *South Sudan Info*, 13 August 2012. http://southsudaninfo.net/2012/08/the-osjuba-event-stresses-early-moves-by-net-activists-in-south-sudan/

[viii] Jon Evans, 'In five years, most Africans will have smartphones,' *TechCrunch*, 9 June, 2012. http://techcrunch.com/2012/06/09/feature-phones-are-not-the-future/

[ix] Interview with the author, 2 October 2012.

Innovation, failure, and hip hop genius

'Hip hop didn't invent anything. Hip hop RE-invented
EVERYTHING!'
– Grandmaster Caz

'If you're not prepared to be wrong, you'll never come up with
anything original.'
– Sir Ken Robinson

'Chance favours the connected mind.' – Steven Johnson

5

New ideas are elusive. You can search and search for them, eventually give up, and then find them right under your nose, back where your journey began. Or not. While it may be en vogue for our organisations to create 'innovation forums' and the like, we might be better off to start looking further afield for inspiration, and to start understanding how things we do in other parts of our lives might be 'remixed' to the benefit of our jobs, our work, and our cause. As much as anything, maybe we need a bit of space to try things out, and to accept that they'll inevitably go wrong along the way.

The Tuttle Club brings Enlightenment café culture to the 21ˢᵗ Century

In late 2007, Lloyd Davis (@LloydDavis), a former civil servant, musician, and active member of the London blogging community, wrote a blog post called 'Wouldn't it be cool to have a space where we could get together?' The inspiration behind the unremarkable title was little more than a recurrent frustration amongst London bloggers with their lack of non-virtual space to chat without being talked at, put to work, or compelled to buy things.

Feedback on the blog post was enthusiastic, with suggestions from Lloyd's readers to open a dedicated building, combining an open space and areas for co-working and informal learning to take place. He was encouraged to write up a business plan, approach potential funders, and take the steps necessary to create a new physical meeting place for those involved in sharing ideas online.

Which all made Lloyd a bit uncomfortable. The financial cost to set up and maintain such a space, but more importantly, the compromise he knew from his civil service background would inevitably be required to produce something on that scale, just didn't seem to fit the need.

'I don't want to play that game!' he decided. '[I'd rather] make it a bit more like you'd make a piece of software. Prototype it, try it out, we get some feedback, we make it better... and then we keep doing that... and there's no distinction between developers and users, because we're all going to turn up and use this thing.'[i]

So in November 2007, Lloyd booked a church hall in Bloomsbury for £50 and invited people to create their own 'social media café,' bringing cushions, cookies, tea, and a small donation for the space. Twenty or so people showed up, thoroughly enjoyed themselves, and encouraged Lloyd to make a regular thing of it.

But Lloyd was less keen. It seemed like a lot more work than he had bargained for.

A couple of months passed, and with a bit of badgering, he conceded to a 'flashmob version' of the get-together, simply announcing, 'We'll be somewhere in Soho; you decide where we'll be, and put it on the wiki.' The offer on the table was conversation. Nothing more.

When the selected date arrived, about twenty or so hackers, bloggers, and fringe geeks in black t-shirts descended upon the Breakfast Club on D'arblay Street and sipped about a dozen cups of tea and coffee between them over the course of several hours. This was a big hit with those who showed up, but was less popular with the café, whose business model, after all, depended on people spending money if they were going to hangout there. By lunchtime they were asked to move along.

Not wanting to piss off any more of their hosts, Lloyd sought out an alternative space for this impromptu conversation. A timely introduction to the landlord of the Coach & Horses pub on Greek Street, who had recently renovated an upstairs room and installed wifi, provided the answer. From there, he set up another wiki and let people figure out the cost and logistics themselves. At 10am, a couple of Fridays after the Breakfast Club engagement, the Tuttle Club was born.

The name 'Tuttle' was borrowed from Terry Gilliam's dystopic fantasy flick, *Brazil*. In the film, Robert DeNiro plays a guerrilla repairman, working only under the cover of darkness to subvert the bureaucratic nightmare in which the film is set. His work involves fixing unsuspecting citizens' air conditioners when the state had buried their request for service in a mountain of paperwork. Harry Tuttle was the clandestine alternative to 'the way things are done': a hack solution to a problem that should never have been.

'This is a place for people who would be friends of Harry Tuttle,' Lloyd is often heard telling newcomers to the gathering, on the days when he happens to be around for it.

What began as a casual conversation within a niche community of geeks has continued ten-til-twelve every Friday morning in Central London for years, moving between at least a half dozen different venues. It has swelled to sixty or seventy people some weeks and dipped to as few as five or ten in others. The demographics have been equally variable, partly depending on current venue and location, moving from techies, to PR types, to education theorists, with regular infusions of new blood gradually shifting the weekly conversation with whatever it is they might bring to the table.

Beyond the clear enjoyment that keeps bringing people back, however regularly or irregularly, these conversations have paid off in ways Lloyd and his early co-conspirators never would have imagined. In 2010, Lloyd and several of the group's early regulars were asked by the British Council to form a consultancy, bringing whatever mix of knowledge and experience they had – particularly, but not exclusively, in relation to social technology – to the staff at their London offices.

Others who met at Tuttle and became acquainted through its objective-free conversations have gone on to make collaborative films, develop software, and work together on a remarkable array of paid and voluntary projects. In fact, several of the people who have offered critical feedback on this book throughout the process have been people I personally met at Tuttle. We didn't know we'd end up here when we first started talking, which is probably why it has been able to happen so naturally – we each followed the conversations that were of interest to us, until we decided to stop and focus a little more on an idea or relationship which seemed to resonate. This is the kind of space that innovation needs in order to thrive: a space without formal objectives, where participants can be free to exist in the 'now' and see where it takes them.

Speaking at the Royal Society for the Arts (RSA/@theRSAorg), Steven Johnson (@stevenbjohnson), author of *Where Good Ideas Come From*, asserted, 'Good ideas normally come from the collision of smaller hunches, so that they form something bigger than themselves.' The difference between the hunches that come and go in our minds, and the real breakthroughs is often 'another hunch that's lurking in somebody else's mind. And you have to figure out a way to create systems that allow those hunches to come together to turn into something bigger than the sum of their parts.'[iii] Tuttle, in its near-total absence of structure, and its absolute lack of particular focus or direction, has created just such a system, demonstrating what can emerge when we make the effort to release ourselves from the responsibility of aims, goals, and targets.

Johnson attributes the wealth of emergent ideas prevalent during the European Enlightenment, in significant part to the popularity of café culture around the continent at the time. In 17th-century France, for example, the leisure and aristocratic classes, having nothing in the way of 'real work' to distract them, would often spend their days sipping coffee and discussing whatever interested them in the countless Parisian sidewalk cafés of the time. While by no means an egalitarian model of idea generation, it goes to show what a culture that promotes the value of free time is able to produce. It also stands in stark contrast to the growing importance of 'work ethic,' which has since come to dominate so many cultures, supposedly in the name of productivity.

Tuttle is part of a broader revival of establishing dedicated free time and space in our lives. Without open, non-directed opportunities, we may well look back and realise we were driving in neutral this whole time, becoming needlessly stressed, while going nowhere.

Another part of this unstructured space revival, which has emerged from the software world Lloyd borrowed Tuttle's organising approach from, is 'Hack Days.' Hack Days are a 24-hour period in which a group of software engineers at an event or within a company or organisation (Twitter, as one notable example), form their own teams and spend the day creating something new to share with the wider group. There is a sense of friendly competition, but the 'what,' 'who' and 'how' of the day are entirely up to the participants.

And while software lends itself to this kind of hands-on, practical collaboration, there's nothing that makes the method exclusive to software development. You could just as easily run an 'Invent a new project or campaign' Hack Day, or a 'Propose something better for the organisation' Hack Day. The point is that Hack Days offer the free space to explore ideas we don't normally make the time for, amongst those who may not normally work together.

Before Tuttle began, Lloyd had experienced the pain of so many contrived networking events, and knew they were not what this community needed. Too often these kinds of efforts are setup by organisations with very clear aims and objectives attached to them, usually to help leverage a bit of someone's budget to cover the cost of biscuits or cheap wine. Spaces are setup to 'support innovative practices across the organisation,' 'enable a culture of open information sharing,' or 'encourage cross-departmental collaboration amongst staff.' However, these objectives are exactly the problem; they sound like good ideas on paper, but there's something about how our brains work that changes as soon as we've got a specific task in mind. We become focused, and with that focus, we become restrained, unable to see beyond what we've always told ourselves is the correct path to the identified goal. This makes perfect sense in plenty of working situations, but encouraging new ideas is not one of them.

Online conversations that create 'offline' change

My friend David Pinto (@happyseaurchin) – another semi-regular 'Tuttlista' – has described the gathering in *small book BIG THINK* as 'Twitter in the real world': a wide-open conversation, without any particular direction or boundary, where serendipitous things are free to emerge.[iii] Like Steven Johnson's descriptions of European café culture during the Enlightenment, Twitter and other social media are increasingly opening up the kinds of non-directed spaces in which our minds are free to collectively wander, until we bump into something new worth pursuing.

In the office, Twitter can be a welcome diversion from so many goal-orientated tasks. It can also be a way to learn from the activities of others doing similar work, as some of our braver organisational counterparts begin to open their processes up to external critique, letting staff share their learning from different campaigns or projects online. An idea that has been tried elsewhere – even at another charity or NGO – can still be 'new' in the context of your work!

More and more creatives, thinkers, organisers and activists relate to Twitter and other social media, not simply as either a broadcast channel or newsfeed, but as a place to engage in a conversation amongst those who care enough to involve themselves and offer different points of view on the things they are experimenting with. If we are serious about new ideas, making the time for unstructured conversation – online and in the flesh – is a crucial first step.

Free software: The collaborative nature of new ideas

Conversations are interactions – ideas coming together from different places and creating something that wasn't there before. Rarely do eureka moments emerge completely out of nowhere, but more often through their interplay with other opinions and alternatives. To put it another way, ideas are collaborative.

The global free software community is one network that has embraced this notion. Free software is inherently collaborative, as developers work together, mostly on their own time, to improve on each other's programmes, fixes, and adaptations. Their work, by its nature, is made available in its entirety for anyone else to adapt or improve on as they see fit. Not only is the final product made public; so is the source code, the building blocks upon which the software was developed.

And their work is hardly just the hobby or pet project of a tiny number of technically gifted social outcasts that many imagine it to be. Free software has created systems that run major governmental and corporate websites around the world, regularly ousting their private sector 'competitors' in a range of institutions. Free software has regularly proven itself to provide better technical solutions than those patented by its corporate counterparts. This is in significant part because it is built very differently than the products we've come to know from Microsoft or Adobe.

To highlight the process difference, which Lloyd Davis described and reapplied to the collective prototyping that eventually birthed the Tuttle Club, the best free software usually comes from developers who are also users of the product they are creating, adapting it as they experience the existing flaws for themselves. In the corporate world, this is unlikely to be the case, as IT is generally outsourced and developed by specialists who rarely have to put their own work into practice. Further, the concept of intellectual property at the core of so much of the private sector would prevent the open sharing and adaptation of other peoples' work, as is central to the success of open source and free software communities. If someone builds a new graphic editing program and someone else thinks of something better, rather than create a competitor, they are free to build on the existing software, collaborating and improving, rather than competing for better results.

When the free software movement emerged in 1983, it was based on four 'freedoms' that separated it from its proprietary counterparts. These were published by the Free Software Foundation in 1986, beginning with 'Freedom 0' (which referred to the zero-based numbering at the core of most computer systems, and was the kind of geek-speak that probably scared off much of the technology-illiterate public until the last decade or so). The four freedoms set out by FSF were:

- Freedom 0: The freedom to run the program for any purpose.
- Freedom 1: The freedom to study how the program works, and change it to make it do what you wish.
- Freedom 2: The freedom to redistribute copies so you can help your neighbour.
- Freedom 3: The freedom to improve the program, and release your improvements (and modified versions in general) to the public, so that the whole community benefits.[iv]

These are the kinds of simple guidelines that allow innovation to flourish. Rather than the closed, protective systems our organisations so often house their 'intellectual property' within, these systems open up what we've got, allowing us to connect with others who've done the same, enabling new possibilities when our work and ideas can join more freely with one another. But like so much else in this book, they require us to let go of the organisational control that is becoming so untenable in the digital age.

'The time has come,' wrote Phillip Smith (@phillipadsmith) and Dmytri Kleiner (@dmytri), in relation to free software, way back in 2004, 'for more organizations to explore a movement that not only parallels the philosophical foundations of the not-for-profit sector but can empower these organizations to achieve more with less.'^vAnd while both the philosophical and practical arguments for free software in social change organisations make perfect sense, there remains the deeper question: how can our organisations work more like the open and free software communities that we share so much with, if we want to develop better, more collaborative solutions for the world around us?

What if we pledged to freely share a range of our organisational resources, encouraging other organisations to do the same? We would already have much of the Creative Commons library of software, images, music, and ideas to add to and use freely (search.creativecommons.org). Could our internal resources; from financial management systems, to the cleaned (impersonalised) data from our engagement with supporters, find a home where other open-minded organisations could put it to use on their own projects or campaigns?

Governments around the world are reluctantly beginning to open up their vast quantities of data to the public in the name of democratic accountability. What if we shared the information that told us what worked and what didn't with our campaign emails, our public events, our internal management systems, with the same motivation in mind?

Platform (@PlatformLondon), a small environmental NGO challenging oil industry sponsorship of arts and culture, regularly opens their organisation up to the world through their blog. When their team is stumped, they may well tweet the question they're trying to answer. When they've figured out a new way of doing something, or have undertaken an experiment, they may well blog it. Their doors are open for others to see and learn from, as well as for people beyond their offices to contribute to, should they have an answer or idea themselves. They are contributing to the commons, while reaping its benefits in the process.

Another example comes from community and organisational consultants Creating the Future (@CreatingTFuture), who broadcast their board meetings live on the web, inviting anyone who's interested to join in. Doing so builds trust through transparency (critical for those of us dabbling on the fringes of management consultancy!) and offers learning from a far wider pool of knowledge and perspective than most meetings can boast. While not ideal for discussions of confidential personal details, or the particulars of a direct action, there may be a range of meetings in all of our organisations that could benefit from this approach. I often suggest that organisations start from an assumption of total transparency, and only limit this when there are specific reasons to curtail it.

Mozilla (@Mozilla), the non-profit that built the Firefox web browser (consistently one of the most popular browsers, globally, with Google Chrome and Internet Explorer), is one of an increasing number of open-source organisations that have applied the principles of open and free software to their operations. Much of their governance practices take place on an open GoogleGroup,[vi] and their 'global community of people creating a better Internet' describes itself as:

> an open source project governed as a meritocracy... structured as a virtual organization where authority is distributed to both volunteer and employed community members as they show their abilities through contributions to the project.[vii]

The values they describe on their website would probably feel at home in any of our organisations, though the ways in which they choose to apply them are probably very different. The most notable difference relates to their stated view of being a part of something bigger (the Internet) and thus not claiming their community's collective work as their own, but actively ensuring that it is available to anyone looking to 'create a better Internet.'

Open-source and free software represent ways of working that apply beyond the realms of software development. Through their non-proprietary approach, the Mozilla community harnesses the goodwill, commitment and creativity of thousands of independent coders, developers, and software engineers, to work (usually for free) towards their shared mission. Then lets *anyone, anywhere* build upon the fruits of their labour, as they see fit.

This second part is what separates Mozilla from most of our organisational relationships with volunteers and wider movements. We too often hold on to what we do, limiting its wider power to shape and influence change with our protectionist attitudes around property, investment, and branding. Mozilla, like many of its partners in the free and open software communities, knows that innovation is a collaborative process and thus anything that makes it harder for people to work together and share ideas is going to get in the way of new products and practices.

> *What components of what you do could be shared openly with the world?*
>
> *What would we have to change to make everything we do available to anyone who 'wants to create a better world for human rights/sustainable energy/global equality/etc?'*

Searching for that lightbulb moment

After the Enlightenment, and before the online conversations of social media, few individuals stand out in the history of innovation like Thomas Edison. The American inventor held over 1,000 patents in his name before his death at the age of 84 in 1931.

While credited with the first phonograph and film camera, Edison's most famous achievement was the 'incandescent lamp,' more commonly known in these modern times as the light bulb.

One in a long line of inventors who looked to discover a safer and more efficient candle, Edison managed to capture the public imagination and went down in history as the light bulb's 'inventor,' even if much of what he did was simply tweak the efforts of many dozens before him.

The same could be said about most new ideas; to whom they get attributed is almost always a combination of luck, timing and relatively minor innovations.

Yet we continue to follow the unrepentant urge to tack someone's name to some significant happening, good or bad.

Whether the superhero CEO (Jack Welch 'singlehandedly' saving General Electric) or the extremist super villain (Osama bin Laden somehow masterminding all the wrong Al Qaeda has done in the world), we like to pretend it is specific individuals who are at the core of why the universe is as we know it to be. The rest of us are just the extras in the grand drama of a tiny minority of exceptional people.

This probably helps us make sense of a world that is inherently beyond our personal comprehension. Particularly in light of the ever-present machine metaphor that underpins our understanding of organisations, it makes a certain sense to think that an exceptional person made everyone else do what they did so effectively – that they were the sparkplug or the engine that allowed the other components to kick into gear.

But it's not true. Just as Edison built on the successes of so many before him when he 'invented' the light bulb, so too do the rest of us stand on the shoulders of the giants that are our collective history, rarely giving credit to the chain of 'almost inventors' to which each innovation is inevitably due.

Dmytri Kleiner, a post-Marxist free software and anti-copyright activist, argues that trying to credit something as fluid as an idea to a particular individual is impossible. 'Unlike a material object, which can exist in only one place at a given time, ideas are infinite and non-exclusive.' He goes on, 'Every expression is an extension of a previous perception. Ideas are not original, they are built upon layers of knowledge accumulated throughout history.'[viii] Kleiner makes an interesting philosophical point, but more importantly, underscores the fact that if we view individuals as the sources of innovation and achievement, we feed into a cult of personality that only serves to distract us from the factors that actually fuel new ideas.

Our organisations are almost universally guilty of this, whether by always deferring to the traditional leader figure for press and public speaking opportunities (even when someone else has done the work), or by publishing reports for which only the lead author is appropriately credited. All of which reinforces a pattern of recognition and resource distribution that is unlikely to encourage new ideas, over-emphasising the contributions of a few select individuals and largely ignoring the daily innovations that emerge everywhere that people are trying to do things better.

In *The Wisdom of Crowds,* James Surowiecki puts forward the thesis that 'under the right circumstances, groups are remarkably intelligent, and are often smarter than the smartest people in them.'[ix] He describes the critical circumstances that allow for a group to be greater than any of its component parts as: 'Diversity, independence, and a particular kind of decentralization.'[x] Group achievements are not primarily the results of the individual expertise present, but of the interplay that takes place when different perspectives are free to constructively challenge one another in a purpose-driven but self-directed environment.

Just as Edison would have been unlikely to create the light bulb without the wealth of knowledge that preceded and surrounded him at the time, so to would each of us have failed on countless occasions if left entirely to our own devices. So as much as we might like to celebrate the hero who achieves something new, we perhaps need to put that recognition into perspective and better investigate the role of the collective in making new things possible.

But attribution is not the only culprit in stunting our collective understanding of innovation. The demonisation of failure is perhaps even more damaging.

Failure as the foundation of success

When most of us think about innovation, failure is not the first thing that comes to mind. In fact, our culture has come to regard the notions of success and failure as opposites, rather than the interdependent cousins that a different take on history demonstrates them to be.

While Thomas Edison may be known for the light bulb, few remember his 10,000 or so *attempts* at a light bulb that preceded it: 'If I find 10,000 ways something won't work, I haven't failed. I am not discouraged, because every wrong attempt discarded is another step forward,' he said.

In his 2011 book, *Adapt: Why success always starts with failure*, economist Tim Harford (@TimHarford) argues that there are three critical steps to becoming an adaptive and innovative organisation. They are 'to try new things, in the expectation that some will fail; to make failure survivable; and to make sure that you know when you've failed.'[xi]

Many a great mind has been dismissed in their own time for experimenting with ideas that seemed crazy or impossible to their contemporaries. Only once those ideas finally achieved results (and sometimes well after) were these people recognised for their work.

AdmittingFailure.com and the development community's elephant in the room

Risk-adverse funders and a management culture that treats failure as a character blemish on whomever it is associated with, are major barriers to innovation in social change work. The world of international development – perhaps because both its stakes and its level of investment are so high relative to other social ventures – is especially plagued by the systemic demonisation of failure.

In 2011's *Walk Out Walk On*, Deborah Frieze (@dfrieze) and Margaret Wheatley write that in spite of massive international investment in aid over several decades, the aid project has by and large failed: 'Stories of intervention gone awry abound with laughable absurdity– were it not for the deadly serious suffering they inflict on peoples' lives and livelihoods.'[xii]

A pattern of constant espoused success remains the norm at most NGOs, due to a combination of funding pressures, organisational structures, and fear of slipping public perception. But in 2011, Canadian NGO Engineers Without Borders (@ewb) decided to acknowledge the international development community's 'elephant in the room': that most of what they do doesn't work... at least the first time round.

Given a widespread culture of denying, de-emphasising, or glossing over things that didn't go to plan, this was a major challenge, but Engineers Without Borders decided it was one that needed addressing. When they launched *AdmittingFailure.com* (along with their own first annual 'Failure Report'), they politely told their colleagues that they could all learn much more, and make a more meaningful difference in the world, if they were honest about all the things that go wrong with such invariably complex work:

> Imagine field staff who have the freedom to publicly share results, good and bad, in order to ensure subsequent efforts are not simply repetitions of ideas that have already been proven ineffective.

> Imagine project managers who create space for field staff to innovate, rewarding learning as much as success.

> Imagine NGOs that adapt and adjust constantly to the stream of information coming from the field – always looking for ways to improve the effectiveness of their work and making real-time adjustments when possible.

> Imagine donors who are willing to support intelligent innovation and experimentation, accepting the possibility of failure as a necessary step on the path to success.[xiii]

Reading those words for the first time, many NGO staff breathed a sigh of relief.

AdmittingFailure.com (@admitfailure) has opened an international conversation that is no longer only relegated to the cynics sitting in the back of the auditorium at so many organisational AGMs, or the people on the ground living through the mistakes our organisations have imposed on them and so consistently ignored. People from NGOs around the world have submitted their own stories to the website of projects and initiatives that have gone terribly wrong, as well as the learning that they walked away from the experiences with. Perhaps more importantly though, they have started to make it easier for others to admit their own failures, opening up more opportunities for people and organisations trying out new ideas which might just work out better than their predecessors... but with the explicit acceptance that they might not.

By opening up to failure, we open up to innovation, and with it, new possibilities of success, previously hidden behind our attempts to paint a perfect picture of the work we do. If we can't admit when things go wrong – to ourselves and more widely – we are unlikely to discover the new ideas and methods that will help them go right in the future.

Learning to think differently

While funders, management, and traditional organisational structures may discourage innovation, the problem goes back further than that. In fact, most of us have innovation, and its lesser-known parent, 'divergent thinking,' purged from our thought processes during our school years.

Our systems of public education still operate on principles inherited from the Industrial Revolution, which sought to turn undisciplined children into work-ready adults, much as a car can be produced along an assembly line. Students who know the right answer get good grades, go on to the better universities, and often end up in the better jobs. This sounds like meritocracy in a nutshell, but leaves us with the unaddressed truth at the forefront of our understandings of complexity, and that is at the core of new ideas: *there is always more than one right answer.*

Sir Ken Robinson (@SirKenRobinson) has written extensively about the ways public education has been based on creating new generations of factory workers, who can follow orders, learn rote tasks, and keep to others' schedules. Unfortunately, the skills required for a simple, repetitive factory job are almost exactly opposite to the ones needed to develop new ideas, in a factory or elsewhere.

Robinson describes 'divergent thinking' as 'the ability to see lots of possible answers to a question,' making it a fundamental threat to Frederick Winslow Taylor's 'one best way' logic. Divergent thinking allows us to see beyond the status quo, imagining new solutions that have the potential to improve our current practices. It's an essential quality for navigating a world in flux, but one we're doing far too little to foster.

In the late 1960s, George Land carried out an experiment to test the divergent thinking abilities of the same 1,600 school kids between the ages of three and five, eight and ten and finally thirteen and fifteen. Initially, 98 percent of the group ranked as divergent thinking geniuses. By age ten, 30 percent of the same group of students qualified to such a level. By fifteen, only ten percent of the kids were thinking at a 'genius' level of divergence.

Since our schools grade us on our ability to see a single, pre-defined answer to a question, it is no wonder so few of us are able to see beyond the answers we've been told are correct, be they out-of-date management practices, or international development efforts that do more harm than good. Needless to say, this kind of environment is not good for innovation. New ideas are too often dismissed as 'wrong' simply because they are not what we have always done, or how we have always done it. If we can't allow ourselves to think differently, we can't innovate. The choice is as simple as that. But the ideas sprinkled throughout this chapter can help us to unlearn the Taylorist notion of singular correctness that we have likely absorbed in our education and working lives.

When was the last time you actively pursued an idea that others dismissed or ignored, because you felt it was worth pursuing?

When do you feel your most creative?

From necessity to innovation: Flippin' something outta nothing

Sam Seidel (@husslington) is one of a few teachers and community organisers in the United States and abroad in the last ten or fifteen years to bring hip hop music and culture into the classroom. At a time when poor urban neighbourhoods in otherwise 'developed' countries have been frequently described as warzones, the fact that educators would look to the largest manifestation of urban youth culture for solutions is not surprising. But what Sam and others have done and are doing is very different from much of what has become more commonplace in classrooms and youth clubs since the early

2000s. Critically, they treat hip hop not simply as a music form, but a culture, with divergent thinking embedded in its very DNA.

Hip hop emerged in the South Bronx in the 1960s and '70s as a culture of necessity. Gentrification, systemic racism, and a slumping economy were among the trends responsible for turning much of the Bronx into no-go zones for anyone with better options. Drugs, violence, and corrupt policing were the backdrops that gave rise to a now global culture and art form. 'If the hip hop generation was the first to enjoy the freedoms of a post-civil rights world,' writes hip hop historian Jeff Chang (@zentronix), 'they were also the first to recognize the hollowness of those promises and to bear witness to the effects of the repeal of many of those same freedoms.'[xiv] If you were a young person of colour in the South Bronx in the 1970s, options were limited, to say the least. But you also likely had a fair bit of non-directed free time to experiment with new ways of doing things.

Hip hop culture is fabled to have begun when a young Jamaican immigrant calling himself 'Kool Herc' spliced the wiring of a local street light to power two turntables, an amp, and a pair of speaker stacks, reigniting the feeling of the street parties he had grown up with in Jamaica. Not only that, but the music – usually some combination of reggae, soul, and funk records, which Herc and his contemporaries nicked from their parents' collections – was rarely played in full, instead being chopped and mixed with other songs, creating new arrangements that had never been heard before. A kick or a snare drum looped here, a trumpet blast there, a bass line layered underneath it all, and 'scratching,' the phenomenon in which a DJ does something their parents invariably told them *not* to do with their record collections: sliding a piece of vinyl back and forth under the needle to create new sonic possibilities.

These were some of the early manifestations of what Sam Șiedel describes as 'Hip Hop Genius'; or as it's often referred to in hip hop communities around the globe, 'flippin' something outta nothing.' Siedel writes:

> Faced with racism, classism, ageism, and other forms of structural subjugation, many young people have developed

the courage to break rules, the audacity to believe they can do things that have never been done, and the creativity to imagine how. This is hip hop.[xv]

In essence, 'hip hop genius' is creative rule breaking, applied to the oppressive elements of the status quo, opening up vast possibilities where none had previously been imagined. 'Sampling' breaks both the legal rules of copyright law (which controlled the free-flow of ideas), as well as a range of old cultural norms around 'what constitutes music,' (given its lack of traditional instrumentation, and its birth in communities where instruments were prohibitively expensive).

To be clear, there is a thread of this phenomenon that can be found in poor communities everywhere – necessity often spawns new ideas – but there is also something distinct in hip hop. 'Hip hop artists have not just created a new kind of music,' writes Siedel, 'they have integrated how music is made and linked with other commodities, and altered systems of ownership and distribution in ways not previously considered possible.'[xvi]

Remixing your office

Besides creative rule breaking, another core part of hip hop genius is the concept of the remix. It is central to hip hop music – sampling and adapting old funk and soul songs into completely new arrangements. It is part of hip hop dance (break-dancing) – drawing on Brazilian Capoeira, Asian kung-fu films, and a blend of popular American dances of the time. It is found in hip hop lyrics – reviving the words and styles of African griot poets, black power leaders, and innumerable pop culture figures. It is even ingrained in the nuts and bolts of the culture, whether 'remixing' electricity from a streetlight to power a street party, or remixing a thrown-out piece of linoleum flooring to create an urban dance floor in a park or on a sidewalk. Adam Mansbach (@adammansbach), a US author who publishes novels in the little known genre of 'Lit Hop,' describes remix culture as 'intellectual democracy through collage... a free-ranging, studious, and critical-minded approach to source material and, by extension, life.'[xvii]

Hip hop has made an art and a culture from turning old things

7 'remixed' principles for innovation

- Free, unstructured time and space
- Diversity of perspective
- Breaking the rules
- 'Remixing' the old
- Necessity
- Prototyping
- Supporting failure

into new things, a practice I'm sure a few of our organisations could benefit from more of, given the abundance of 'old' we often have permeating the systems that shape our work! To start, what could we do with our meeting formats, our office plans, our annual reports, or our communications policies, (as a few random examples) to remix them into something more effective or meaningful than they so often are? Where could we be fostering and practicing divergent thinking? One could argue, for example, that Lloyd Davis 'remixed' the free software development process in the way the Tuttle Club was created. Where in our workplaces could we introduce innovations like these?

'I think a lot of times it's the people with more to lose that have trouble being more innovative,'[xviii] Sam tells me over Skype one February evening, echoing the flipside of the 'necessity breeds innovation' truism. Like the social movements visited throughout this book, 'Hip hop genius' requires tossing out a range of our organisational assumptions. Namely, if we are serious about doing something new, rules can and must be broken, and there is no shame in taking something that has been done before, elsewhere, and refitting it for your own purposes. We can seed a 'remix culture' in our workplaces, laying the groundwork for new ideas by introducing a range of old ones from unexpected places.

The Centre for Creative Collaboration in London is an excellent model of this idea: if you put a bunch of people in a space together who care about what they do, but would normally never cross paths, interesting things can emerge. In essence, they will all remix each other's work, by default. The architect will influence the playwright's staging choices; the playwright will influence the new web start-up's promotional language; the new web start-up will offer guidance to the photographer on making the most of their online presence, or an infinite number of other, less-expected connections that are free to emerge when you share a space together.

It has also been central to the Hub (@HubWorld), a loosely grouped network of several dozen socially minded co-working spaces around the world, which, via a more traditional open-plan office hot-desking arrangement, aims to give freelancers and start-up companies (whose work happens mostly at desks) a chance to cross paths with those who might inadvertently inject a new perspective into their current project. This obviously still limits the kinds of people who will end up talking to each other, but goes well beyond the structures and layouts of most organisational settings, where the water cooler is often the only place that offers any semblance of something that could encourage remixing. It also varies from Hub to Hub, with some adopting a more structured approach and others providing more open space, which can be used more liberally, encouraging different people to get involved. One thing the Hub has absolutely understood is that one size will never fit all if you aim to encourage innovative working in many different settings.

While countless corporations have played with office configurations and layouts, few seem to have moved beyond the surface level. Nurturing a remix culture means changing relationships, not just furniture, so success in this realm is as much, or more, a question of individual behaviours as it is design.

This is why hip hop, like innovation itself, is hard to teach. 'The technical know-how [to re-wire a streetlamp or mix between two turntables],' Sam reminds us, 'is only valuable if you have the imagination, desire, and confidence to do something that's never been done.'[xix]

'more like people' innovation

Humanity: Giving space for people to chat, as it gives us space to think more freely than if we have specific aims.

Autonomy: Not trying to control how people do what they do, accepting that every person works differently, and letting them follow paths that make sense to them will reveal new possibilities.

Complexity: Allowing for emergent, rather than predetermined outcomes, as new ideas are rarely predetermined!

*What might fostering imagination, desire, and
confidence mean where you are?*

*What rules would you like to start breaking (and
encouraging others to break) in your workplace?*

*What are some of the unexpected places you might
draw on to make your organisation 'more like people'?*

From reading about new ideas to applying them

But all of this is only a starting point. Innovation is everywhere, all
around us. We innovate when we can't find a bottle opener, run
out of paper clips, or when a ride home falls through at the last
minute. What's unique is having developed systems so effective
at rooting out something so ingrained in all of us.

While the sense of necessity that helped birth hip hop was
primarily a combination of economic and social oppression, most
of our organisations have their own pressing need to change
based on the tyranny of established practices that can so easily
drive a sane member of staff to the point of either rebellion or
apathy. Rather than simply bemoaning the lack of progress we
see around us, can organisational inertia inspire a 'hack' (making
a system or structure do something it wasn't originally created to
do) or a remix (putting old tools or ideas to work in a new setting
or for a new purpose) that might enable innovation to begin in
our own seemingly insignificant corner of the office, below the
radar of official protocols?

In complex systems, isolated and small-scale actions can in fact
have wide-ranging implications. 'The butterfly effect,' if taken
to heart, can empower even the most junior of staff in the most
entrenched of bureaucracies to try new things. The concept
provides the opportunity for good ideas to come from and go to
any part of the system they are discovered in or needed, giving
the hack or the remix vast potential when embraced by those
hoping to try new things, wherever they sit in the pyramid.

There will always be arguments against breaking established
norms. There will always be voices within our organisations that
fight tooth-and-nail against anything that poses any risk to the

comfortable continuation of what we've done before. But we too often ignore the risk inherent to *not* taking risks – of stagnation, missed opportunity, and eventually, irrelevance – until it's too late.

Once again, the 'more like people' principles of humanity, autonomy and complexity play themselves out as we discover new approaches to making space for new ideas. The Tuttle Club's lack-of-direction is a prime example of complexity at work, allowing for emergent, rather than pre-determined outcomes to come to life through unknown and ever-changing processes.

Humanity is also central to the open-conversations idea championed throughout this chapter – engaging in the most basic of human interactions, without a chair or agenda to control the process. Also, as the old saying goes, 'to err is human,' so to provide the space and encouragement for people to make mistakes is fundamental to a 'more like people' way of working. Finally, innovation needs autonomy, because if we are all thinking and working in the same ways, within the same systems, it is unlikely any of us will come up with anything new. Letting each of us be ourselves and see each other as creative collaborators, rather than other cogs in a machine, opens the possibility of relationships that can create new possibilities. The free software community would not have created Linux, Firefox, or so many other innovations, had someone been telling each of the countless individual programmers what to do.

A 'remixed' collection of principles for innovation, drawn from the thinking, writing, and experiences of those highlighted throughout this chapter might include:

- Providing everyone with free, unstructured time and space without predetermined outcomes
- Enabling staff who wouldn't normally cross paths to share ideas together
- Breaking established rules, even when they seem sensible
- Applying old ideas in new places, remixing existing content and practices for new purposes
- Responding to pressing needs however makes sense (rather than 'as we always have')

- Experimenting with and prototyping far more ideas than you expect to implement
- Supporting those who courageously fail, as they are taking a necessary step towards success

The examples I've discussed in this chapter come from an array of places, because we need to be looking further afield for inspiration if we are serious about pushing the boundaries in what our organisations currently do. As we've seen, innovation often means seeing how existing ideas, processes, and practices might work in a different context. Part of your job, as someone wanting to change how we organise ourselves, is to find those practices and to try them out. Hopefully these pages have begun to whet your appetite for the task ahead, as we create, remix, or redefine the tools, structures, and systems that will help us thrive in a complex world.

Chapter 5: Innovation, failure, and hip hop genius

[i] Interview with the author, 30 April 2012.

[ii] Steven Johnson, 'Where good ideas come from,' *Riverhead Books*, 17 September 2010. http://www.youtube.com/watch?v=NugRZGDbPFU

[iii] David Pinto, *small book BIG THINK*, self-published, 2010, p. 134-135.

[iv] Wikipedia contributors, "Free software," *Wikipedia, The Free Encyclopedia* http://en.wikipedia.org/w/index.php?title=Free_software&oldid=564645195

[v] Phillip Smith & Dmytri Kleiner, 'What not-for-profit organizations need to know about free software,' 2 December 2004. http://www.phillipadsmith.com/2004/12/what-not-for-profit-organizations-need-to-know-about-free-software.html

[vi] https://groups.google.com/forum/?fromgroups#!forum/mozilla.governance

[vii] http://www.mozilla.org/about/governance.html

[viii] Dmytri Kleiner, *The Telekommunist Manifesto*, Institute of Network Cultures, 2010, p. 30.

[ix] James Surowiecki, *The Wisdom of Crowds*, Abacus, 2004, p. xiii.

[x] Ibid. p. xviii.

[xi] Tim Harford, *Adapt: Why success always starts with failure*, Little Brown, 2011, p. 36.

[xii] Margaret Wheatley & Deborah Frieze, *Walk Out Walk On*, Berrett-Koehler, 2011, p. 171.

[xiii] http://www.admittingfailure.com/about/

[xiv] Jeff Chang, ed. *Total Chaos*, BasicCivitas Books, 2006, p. xi.

[xv] Sam Seidel, *Hip Hop Genius*, Rowman & Littlefield Education, 2011, p. 6.

[xvi] Ibid. p. 7.

[xvii] Adam Mansbach, 'On Lit Hop,' from *Total Chaos*, BasicCivitas Books, 2006, p. 93.

[xviii] Interview with the author, 24 February 2012.

[xix] Sam Seidel, 'Hip Hop Genius,' Rowman & Littlefield Education, 2011, pp. 3.

The kind of ownership that can't be bought or sold

'Tell me and I'll forget; show me and I may remember; involve me and I'll understand.' – Chinese proverb

'Employee ownership turns a company into a community.' – Richard Wilkinson

'People who participate in decisions tend to stick to them.' – Carne Ross

6

Bureaucracy is antithetical to most of what this book is advocating. Its divisions and specialisations work against our sense of ownership, motivation, and notions of collective responsibility and trust. In short, it kills our passion and our sense of purpose, making for far less satisfying working lives than most of us would expect from charities, NGOs or unions.

And while bureaucracy has become synonymous with most organisations, it is becoming increasingly clear that it doesn't work, even on its own terms. If we can foster a shared sense of ownership, motivation, and shared responsibility, we can begin to enjoy more of our working lives, and concurrently start to accomplish things our old organisations could never have imagined.

'Doing good has never felt so bad': How our structures kill our passion and purpose

Remember the story I began the book with? The deeply disillusioning job at a national charity that left me feeling so frustrated and powerless to bring about change? The one that shook my youthful faith in what 'working for social change' was all about, so filled with disputes, grievances, and an atmosphere so thick with tension you could cut it with a knife? You've probably got your own story like this.

When I look back at my work there through the lens of the 'more like people' principles of humanity, autonomy and complexity, I see the incongruity at every level of the organisation's practices. Complexity was everywhere, yet nowhere to be discussed. Linear cause-and-effect systems permeated every organisational crack and crevice, starting with a policy binder as deep as your forearm.

Humanity was signed away in every job contract, then squashed at any sign of re-emergence through soul-destroying jargon, characterless dress, fake smiles, and a calm 'professionalism' that coated deeply dishonest and adversarial relationships. Management also treated conflict as a 'blame game,' making it that much harder for anyone working there to see the multiple dimensions of an interpersonal problem and understand their part in it.

Autonomy was constantly re-buried when it wormed its way back to the surface, with endless sign-off processes, strict rules for everything under the sun, and the frequent disciplining of staff for insubordination.

I've since come to appreciate how stressful such a dynamic would be to those in management, even if all I could see at the time was the wrong I felt they were inflicting against those of us who spoke up. This game is one that sucks the life out of those who play it, whatever their role. When you're inside it, it can feel like those progressively higher on the organisational ladder must be infinitely happier with their bigger paycheques and their prestigious job titles, but the truth is often much worse: they're not. Everyone's miserable in this kind of environment.

The 'more like people' lens goes some way to explaining and opening-up alternatives to this kind of 'organisational asshole-creating machine.' We can see how a lack of appreciation of humanity, autonomy and complexity, could have helped create such a mess, but what can we do about it? Can these principles help us regain a sense of pride and passion in our work, and foster organisations that will support this?

Ownership: Maybe the capitalists got this one right?

Chapter 6:
The kind of
ownership
that can't be
bought or sold

The free market has long told us that value is created by owning something. There is no value to a forest until it is desired for private land, or for lumber. There is no value in a lake until it is bottled and sold.

It is not hard to see how this notion of ownership is killing the world. It is market ownership and applies only to the cash value that something can be deemed to wield by making it scarce.

But there's another kind of ownership – not in deed or title – but in spirit. It's the feeling of knowing that you have created something, that something really is *yours*, but without becoming exclusively so (as market ownership dictates), as it does not have to be *only yours* for you to feel it. It is the feeling of making a contribution to the world that is uniquely your own. It is an ownership that can't be bought or sold – let's call it 'more like people' ownership.

In the process of stripping workers of the fruits of their labour, industrialism also took away much of this subtler form of ownership. Being the person who added seven wing nuts to an assembly line aluminium bed frame doesn't offer quite the same sense of accomplishment in the final product that designing and building a bed frame yourself might.

This kind of ownership requires autonomy. It also tends to require someone be free to be themselves, birthing ideas and ways of manifesting those ideas as only they could. The Taylorist notion of separating everything into its component parts, ranks, or functions is anathema to 'more like people' ownership.

The organisational lines we draw pretend that we get the best results when each person does a particular, specialised task, and then passes along the incomplete results to a different specialist to finish. There are clearly times when more specialised skills may be required, but we've gone to such lengths to make our organisations more efficient (though less resilient, as described in Chapter 1), that we've lost track of what this means for the people who are a part of them.

Taylorism flows deep in the blood of our organisations. Think about job descriptions and team divisions, and the others ways we allocate work. Who writes the grant application? The project plan? Who keeps track of it along the way? Who is doing the hands-on/frontline stuff? Who manages the partnerships? Who is communicating about it more widely? Who reports to funders or donors?

When we specialise to this degree, not only do we lose valuable critique and input from a wider range of perspectives along the way, we also make it harder for people to feel that elusive notion of 'ownership' that is so fundamental to people's abilities to achieve greatness.

In a machine-like world, specialisation is practical and efficient. In a complex world made up of people like you and me, too much specialisation gets in the way of our freedom to make unique and amazing things happen.

So how can you involve more people in different kinds of work?

At the smallest scale, GoogleDrive, DropBox, Twitter hashtags, and a range of other collaborative technologies make certain ways of working together very technically easy. A range of questions or pieces of work can be put to entire teams, organisations or communities to begin to find answers to, through simple collaborative processes.

More fundamentally, we could scrap the job descriptions that tend to keep people boxed in to a particular set of predefined tasks. Imagine advertising jobs without the standard list of bullet points, but rather just a description of the project or desired result. An ad hoc team might identify particular members who can address specific skills gaps, but that person wouldn't be limited to that specialisation – their responsibility would be as wide as anyone else in making sure that the work got done.

Ricardo Semler, whose Brazilian industrial company, *Semco*, has been modelling 'more like people' principles since before I was born, has been practicing this approach for years. Shop floor workers responsible for particular products organise themselves around the whole rather than the parts, with teams taking collective responsibility for the final product. At the same time, workers are informally training each other in the various stages of production, making them far less vulnerable to personal variables such as sickness, injuries, or holidays. Thus, when someone isn't there it doesn't cause things to grind to a halt, with one part of the team able to stop the work of the rest. It simply slows them down by one, while the team adjusts for the person who is absent. This shared responsibility has made them far more resilient to the inevitable fluctuations of human organisation.

Chapter 6:
The kind of
ownership
that can't be
bought or sold

On the more radical side, Michael Albert's Parecon (Participatory Economics) model, employed by independent publisher South End Press and at least a handful of other forward-thinking companies and non-profits, advocates a more formalised structure that seeks to address both overall team functionality, as well as individual job satisfaction. Parecon's model of 'balanced job complexes' acknowledge that 'not all tasks are equally desirable,' and so share all work amongst all staff. This ensures a distribution of dull, rote tasks, and more empowering, creative jobs, so no one is stuck cleaning toilets or inputting data every day, and everyone has a chance to regularly explore more exciting options. Personally, I would worry that over-formalising this looser model may create some of the same issues that any job description might create (inflexibility being the main one), but a Parecon structure would still be miles ahead of most current work regimes.

Taylor would surely describe all such systems as deeply inefficient, given the additional time required to make sure people can do a range of jobs. However, in many less-structured work environments this co-training happens naturally, as it offers people variety, and a chance to develop in their day-to-day roles.

One possible 'more like people' job advert

How much do you care about homelessness and young people?

We're putting together a two-year project team made up of current staff, community members that our organisation works with, and new prospective employees, to launch a campaign around public perceptions of young people sleeping rough.

Do you have experience with some combination of web design, campaigning, homelessness, project reporting, partnership working, data analysis, mental health issues, or work with young people? Do you have any other skills or strengths that you think could make a difference to the campaign?

We are not hiring for a specific role, but for a group of both paid and voluntary activists who can bring the necessary range of experiences to working together, as they see fit, to create a massive public impact.

If you are chosen as a part of the team you will not have a manager. And you will not be a manager. You will be a member of a team, working together and supporting each other to make this campaign amazing.

Your work will vary considerably day to day, with many new and emerging opportunities.

You will also be welcome to find other projects around the organisation to spend your time on, as long as you've discussed it with the project team.

Send us a cover letter, record us a YouTube video, or find another way to tell us why you should be joining us!

For any questions, feel free to drop us an email, Facebook message, or a Tweet, or give us a call.

As an organisation starts to operate this way and work becomes more fluid and project-based, teams or departments may dissipate. Rather than a 'Campaigns Team,' why not have a temporary group of folks who are working around a particular campaign? They will probably include people from what would have been 'Policy,' 'Communications,' maybe someone from frontline services, even an IT or HR person who happens to be particularly passionate about the campaign and who wants to contribute. When the campaign wraps up, members can move along to another project group where their skills are needed. They might even be involved in multiple groups at once, depending on the contributions they were making to each. Salaries could continue to be paid (ideally, more equally), trusting people to find the project where they were most useful at a particular time, but not letting that limit what they do, if their efforts could be spread more widely.

Chapter 6:
The kind of
ownership
that can't be
bought or sold

Alternatively, could the methods that helped the anarchic web of Climate Rush activists we met in Chapter 3, to break into a coal plant in England's West Midlands, through the self-organised system of 'buddies,' 'bricks,' and 'affinity groups,' help us organise our collective efforts better? These kinds of systems have been described as 'swarming' or 'clustering,' and their principles underscore much of what makes grassroots activism effective. We may even find that terms we use to describe our work like 'campaigns' or 'services' become increasingly less relevant, as projects organically take on elements of several different departments when no longer restrained by our old divisions.

From the perspective of 'more like people' ownership, these looser systems allow people to feel a part of the whole. This was the core of Marx's 'Theory of Alienation,' which described the capitalist system's tendency to separate workers from the fruits of their labour and thus their sense of ownership, making for a soulless, exploitative work experience. Joel Bakan explored the ethical dimensions of this tendency in *'The Corporation,'*[iii] explaining how individually decent people within massive corporations consistently fail to feel any sense of personal responsibility for the suffering that can result from the corporation's blind pursuit of profit. The disconnection between our specialised efforts and their cumulative results keeps us from experiencing both the pride of ownership and the responsibility for wrongdoing. Helping ourselves to reconnect with the whole of what we do can make us both happier, and more accountable.

There's also the 'hack' version (re-purposing parts of an old system for something it wasn't initially intended for, without permission from the owners), for those not in the position to re-wire organisational structures just yet. It happens when groups form around areas of mutual interest at lunch breaks or after hours, when they can be free to explore new ideas without job titles or the dead hand of management to get in the way. Such clandestine groups can still start to change working dynamics, as participants gradually bring successes back to their respective teams, subtly manifesting the case for new ways of organising. Via this method, the old systems continue to exist, they just become less relevant as more staff learn to subvert them through more appropriate working relationships.

Social media can also be a key tool for this kind of change. Through the online world, departmental lines that might impede looser networks at the office are pushed to the side as people find other ways of communicating and working together, regardless of team, specialisation or seniority. Groups might begin online, move offline, and then bring in official decision makers at the end to rubber-stamp the project.

The clandestine nature of this kind of collaboration offers strong assurance that it can't be adopted, co-opted, or reshaped along traditional organisational lines by less forward-thinking senior staff, as it is happening outside of the formal channels.

Office environmental groups often emerge this way, and are thus able to circumvent the dead-end systems that might have trapped them, had they been formed in response to a senior management decree rather than the beliefs and commitment of individual staff. Instead of replicating the hierarchy of departmental structure, they subvert it both through their mixed membership and their ability to go straight to the appropriate decision makers, or make practical changes themselves, rather than slowly making requests through a command chain.

This is the kind of self-organisation that is already happening within bureaucracies everywhere, and may well be the way forward for those who want to organise differently, but do not have the formal power in their job titles to push it through established systems.

> *How much of your work can you find ways to do outside of the formal processes dictated from above?*

> *What kind of groups could you suggest and create to allow work to happen more organically across divisions?*

> *Who are the 'allies' you know who are also keen to start trying new things in a particular area?*

*Chapter 6:
The kind of
ownership
that can't be
bought or sold*

From trust to ownership

There's a role for management in opening up space for more dispersed ownership, in terms of official restructuring, and there's a role for everyone else, in terms of finding our own ways to work together on the things we care about. When it happens horizontally, the power of hierarchy plays less of a role and everyone is equally accountable to everyone else who is a part of creating the change, but when managers attempt to facilitate this kind of change, they need to trust the practical actions of those they manage, if they hope to see their efforts bear fruit. When we are trusted, we are more likely to own what we do, knowing that there is no one else to blame – or to give credit – for the choices we have made ourselves.

As described previously, our current systems tend to lack trust. Fixed working hours and working locations, how annual leave is determined, how we measure success, and who answers to whom are just a few of the places our organisational mistrust discourages any sense of ownership in most staff. But it doesn't have to be this way.

Ricardo Selmer's approach, for example, has been to 'hire adults and ...treat them like adults.'[iii] Similarly, Netflix, the highly successful online video streaming site, has a paid holiday policy for all salaried staff of 'as much as you want.' The policy is based soundly in trusting their workforce to know best how to do their jobs, without being told how many days of the year they need to spend doing them. Netflix carries this attitude over to employment contracts without fixed hours per day or per week, encouraging employees to work wherever and however they are most comfortable, and assuming they will let the right people know when they are not at their desks. Meanwhile, BestBuy has pioneered a 'Results Only Working Environment' (ROWE) where everything besides their accomplishments is up to each member of staff, letting them figure out their own best ways to get things done.

These examples stand in stark contrast to the practices of most of our organisations, which imply mistrust and emphasise 'effort over result' through a series of costly and time-consuming record-keeping systems and sign-off procedures.

Semco, in the mid-1980s, went a step further and began to allow more and more staff to make collective decisions, and even to set their own individual salaries, knowing the company books were wide open and they would be accountable to their fellow colleagues (rather than 'the boss') if they gave themselves a raise they couldn't justify. Today, *Semco* staff continue to make most organisational decisions through democratic votes, including, on one notable occasion, deciding on a new factory location against the unified opinions of what remained of senior management.

When Semler encouraged workers to turn their shop floors into whatever they would like them to be, decisions were made collectively, and countless staff chose to show up at the factories on their days off to paint them the colours they had agreed. This is 'more like people' ownership.

Ricardo Semler has been described by a militant trade union leader as Brazil's 'only trustworthy boss,' while twice being named the country's Business Leader of the Year. This wide-ranging support demonstrates that a more human approach to organising can strike a chord in unexpected places, highlighting that the demand for organisational humanity can be found across the political spectrum. This approach is as good for business as it is for the people in it.

In a similar vein, Google trust their staff enough to give them 20percent of their paid time for projects they care about, but which aren't directly related to their work. As a company, they are confident they have hired good, responsible adults, so give them the chance to pursue their passions on company time for a full day each week. This has led to a significant range of Google products, including Gmail, which would have remained unrealised, or found itself in the hands of a competitor, in countless other companies.

In business terms, Google's managers know there are good ideas spread around the company, and they want systems that can capture them, rather than restrict them. Ironically, meanwhile, so many social change organisations, which are meant to have people at their core, have been much slower on the uptake, still pushing private-sector models that even the private sector is abandoning in droves.

'Want commitment? Get out of the way!' More lessons from worker-run factories

Remember the story of the Argentine *Unión y Fuerza* pipe factory from Chapter 3? Workers took over a bankrupt and shuttered factory, chose to organise along equal, participatory and democratic lines, and became the national leader in their industry. The commitment of those involved goes a long way to explaining what they've achieved. And the story is far from unique. Here are just a few other examples of Argentine workers organising to make their jobs their own:

- When police tried to shut down the Brukman textile factory, which had been reclaimed by the mostly women who worked there, workers from a range of factories came out and turned the police away.

- The story was the same in May 2002 at the worker-run print shop, Chilavert, when a small army of police and armoured vehicles tried, unsuccessfully, to kick-out the workers running the publishing house.

- The nurses, lab technicians, administrators, and cleaning staff at the private Israelite Hospital worked unpaid for almost a year providing much needed medical services to the community after the business was declared bankrupt. While staff numbers shrunk from over 400 to about 160 during that time, the remaining employees eventually turned the hospital into a cooperative and were able to re-employ nearly 250 staff, expanding services again while working for themselves at equal wages.

The stories could go on, but while the workplace reforms have varied from occupation to occupation, what has been shared is the sense of ownership that comes from working together with a mutual stake in whatever results. As Richard Wilkinson, co-author of *The Spirit Level*, has said, 'Employee ownership turns a company into a community.'[iv]

By 2007, the popularity of these quasi-legal structures had continued to grow, even as the Argentine economy improved. 'I could probably have found a job at another company, but I like this concept,' said Salvador Fernandez, a middle-aged worker at the *Cortidoros Unidos Limitada* leather factory. 'To be your own boss. That's nice.'[v]

Organised as co-operatives, Argentine reclaimed businesses have much in common with some of the more egalitarian co-ops that have long existed in so many other countries. While financial ownership played a significant role in each of these situations, there is no reason the horizontalism practiced in regards to waging and decision making should apply only to profit-making organisations.

Perhaps more importantly, if we want people to feel that the work they do in our organisations is *theirs* and is *meaningful*, perhaps senior managers, by their hierarchical nature, get in the way of the notion of such equality? Not to say that there isn't a place for the people who currently hold those jobs, but that place may have to change if we want organisations that are owned by everyone within them, financially or otherwise. In other words, if we believe in the kinds of ownership described here, let's stop getting in the way of people finding it for themselves.

> *Can we break down the barriers between our teams or departments, to allow people to gravitate more easily to the work they find most meaningful?*

Can we organise ourselves within our less-representative organisations to make decisions, should management not provide the space to do so?

Do I know what I would need to feel like I 'owned' my work, and what, specifically, is getting in the way?

Motivation: Best kept out of the hands of the professionals

Chapter 6:
The kind of
ownership
that can't be
bought or sold

When people feel a sense of ownership over their work, they tend to be more motivated to do it. Social change organisations seeking to motivate their employees by offering individual performance bonuses or executive salaries that can compete with the private sector would be warned to heed the advice of Dan Pink (@DanielPink). In his book, '*Drive: The surprising truth about what motivates us,*' Pink smashes one of capitalism's core tenets: that greater pay will lead to greater performance. One could argue that a chicken-and-egg relationship exists between ownership and motivation— which leads to the other? —but the lessons Pink offers to support greater motivation are very similar to the lessons about 'more like people' ownership discussed so far. Therefore, if we want to encourage 'more like people' ownership over our work, we need to understand the systems that support us to be motivated.

Pink says, 'the best use for money as a motivator is to pay people enough to take the issue of money off the table.'[vi] Basically, from a purely capitalist perspective, salaries should stop people from worrying about covering their basic needs if we want them to do their best work. This is clearly a variable figure, but provides an important guideline for organisational salary structures.

Bonuses may work for the most rote tasks where only physical improvement is needed to improve performance. However, Pink tells us, anything remotely cognitive (stuff that you need to actively think about) will be unaffected or even adversely affected by cash incentives. More specifically, incentives and punishments generally reduce intrinsic motivation, stifle creativity, and encourage cheating, shortcuts and short-term thinking. They can also turn things we naturally like into chores by impinging on the sense of autonomy we'd previously enjoyed, making them an imposed obligation, rather than something we do just because we want to.[vii]

Currently, big NGOs tend to base pay scales on market rates, just as a hedge fund company might. The underpinning assumption here is the same: Better salaries attract better talent. However, industries that reward performance through financial incentives are often also those most guilty of fostering anti-social tendencies amongst staff, from jealous dog-eat-dog competitiveness, to dishonest reporting, to emphasis on short-term goals at the expense of longer term ones. Such incentives breed toxic results.

As an alternative, Platform (@PlatformLondon), a small UK environmental and human rights NGO mentioned in Chapter 5, has developed the 'Social Justice Waging System,' a means of addressing staff needs while accepting the subjectivity of peoples' situations. The system is simple: everyone receives the same base wage, but people who have dependents or debt will receive extra to compensate for these additional costs. It takes the egalitarianism of the flat pay structures adopted by so many occupied Argentine factories and balances for people's individual circumstances and needs, so a single mother or someone saddled with student debt are not disadvantaged by 'objective' equality measures.

Pink suggests that 'mastery, autonomy, and purpose' will stimulate motivation better than any rewards-based system. 'Mastery' is captured by the *Semco* approach of encouraging people to learn different roles, and autonomy is central to the Netflix and BestBuy working models described earlier. 'Purpose' is what brings self-organised groups together. It is what pushes us to find better ways of doing things, and is why people put their names, their bodies and their lives on the line with activism. It's also why Google staff like having a day a week to follow their passions.

Like ownership, purpose can't be imposed from above. Each of us might have many senses of purpose in our lives; the best collective action for social change occurs when we find just enough common ground to feel comfortable being autonomous together.

Occupy's 'We are the 99%' slogan captures a sense of purpose – that we want the world to work in the interests of the vast majority, not a tiny minority – while leaving massive space for internal divergence and individual differences.

Organisations, political parties, and trade unions have all struggled with this. Collective purpose emerges from 'bare minimum structures' like the *Occupy* slogan, which offer us just enough common ground to commit, without having to sacrifice parts of ourselves in the process. Even our organisational mission statements are often too specific to allow for the juxtapositions of individual and shared notions of purpose to coexist.

Chapter 6:
The kind of
ownership
that can't be
bought or sold

If we want people to be motivated by what we do in a world of loose networks, we should present our organisations with doors as open as we can manage, accepting differences as a fundamental part of what we do, rather than trying to confine employees to a narrow vision of social change.

What are your deepest motivations for doing the work you do?

When have you felt your sense of purpose most aligned with a number of others?

Can our organisational mission be crowd-sourced, and then regularly refreshed to keep it aligned with those who are doing the work (paid or voluntarily)?

Self-defined roles: The thousands of ways the Occupy movement has flourished

A step further afield from the worker-run Argentine factories are the hundreds of thousands of activists around the world who took over parts of their city centres in the autumn of 2011.One of the critical things Occupy offered both new and seasoned activists was a clean slate as to what people could contribute to advancing their beliefs, should they be uninspired to follow someone else's pre-planned march route, or send a template letter to their elected representative. The Occupy concept became a new commons, ready and available not just for shared use, but for the generation of new ideas and practices, available for all to take and make their own. Whereas so much of the activism that had come before it had revolved around a relatively limited number of specific activities, Occupy opened the doors to the imaginations of those electrified by the movement's core values and simple messages.

So many social change organisations limit volunteer opportunities or calls to action to a few easily managed, lowest-common-denominator activities for people to choose from. Sadly, one of the hallmarks of these simple, focused actions is that they are always *additional* to whatever else people are doing in their lives. It's not easy to attend to all the other things you need to do in your life, while making time for a several-hour protest march.

Paula X. Rojas, who organises with black and Latino women in the US who have experienced domestic violence, describes an alternative inspired by the Zapatista movement. To give some context, since 1994, several indigenous communities in the Mexican state of Chiapas have lived without state government. These communities have made a conscious choice to reject encroaching neo-liberalism by actively living their lives according to different values, making each collective meal, or effort to keep the streets clean, a political challenge to outside authorities. Rojas writes:

> In these new movements, much of the political work happens close to home. It's not that mass demonstrations are no longer considered useful. But there is a growing understanding that such tactics... are largely, if not entirely alien to the reality of most people's lives... What if, as a tired overworked, underpaid or unpaid woman I do not have to add going to this march to my list of things to do? What if, instead, I could integrate my political participation into my daily life? What if there were a 'space' where I could build and learn politically with others, a space I could go that was part of how I take care of myself and others?[viii]

Occupy, drawing on the more integrated forms of activism found in Tahrir Square, Egypt, amongst the Spanish 'indignados,' and throughout a range of Latin American social movements, like the Zapatistas, have tossed our old models out the window. Unlike an organisation, which will seek to control these hands-on DIY approaches and thus provide very few specific options to those who'd like to get involved, a movement can grow from whatever people are inspired to offer it.

When Manhattan's Zuccotti Park filled with activists on September 17, 2011, the organisers from the New York City General Assembly had no plans for an encampment that would last several months. Many of the thousands present that day, however, decided they were going to stick around. When they chose to stay, a range of practicalities that many American activists weren't used to dealing with emerged – food, sanitation, accommodation, energy production –as well as a series of things that some may have had experience with: group decision making, publicity, education, facilitating group dynamics.

Chapter 6:
The kind of
ownership
that can't be
bought or sold

While traditional NGO organisers may well have walked away from the challenges that sprung up with the encampment that evening, these challenges offered countless new activists unique opportunities to contribute based on their own experiences, abilities, and enthusiasm. This meant cooking for two thousand people, finding tents and sleeping bags for those that didn't have them, generating energy for the camp, dealing with garbage and basic sanitation, and addressing simple medical needs.

So, if you were the 'tired overworked, underpaid or unpaid woman' that Paula X. Rojas describes, an Occupy camp might give you the chance to do some cooking you would have done at home anyway, but as part of a movement you support and that needs to be fed. Or staying the night might become a social experience that you would have made time for in another form anyway. Or you might find a group of people there who can support each other with childcare or a range of other basic needs that you would have otherwise had to pay someone for, thus embedding a practical reciprocity into activism.

This approach encouraged thousands of practical actions to emerge from the many encampments around the world (some of which have been explored elsewhere in the book). Most remarkably, in the days and weeks after Hurricane Sandy wreaked havoc on so many New York neighbourhoods in the autumn of 2012, Occupy Sandy (@OccupySandy) emerged from the OWS networks, as Sarah Berman wrote for *the Tyee* news site, to fill the 'early gaps in the relief industry, making disaster recovery a human experience rather than a bureaucratic one. . . Whereas institutions like the Red Cross encourage monetary donations, Occupy accepts all supplies and skill levels.'[ix] Within days, like at the Zuccotti Park camp a year before, thousands of volunteers were giving whatever that had to give, unrestrained by the older structures telling them what they could or couldn't do to help others in the city through the black-outs and water shortages that followed the storm. While the Red Cross relies on cash contributions from the public to fund its range of services, OccupySandy opened the doors to thousands of committed New Yorkers with so much more to give than just money, enabling far more to be achieved, by offering bare minimum structures for so many more to find their own ways to contribute to the relief effort.

This kind of self-directed involvement creates ownership.

While Occupy's 'We are the 99%' slogan lacks specificity (a regular cause for outside criticism), its broadness helped so many find their own reasons to adopt it, placing it in stark contrast to the niche taglines our organisations so often produce for our campaigns or services. Meanwhile, the vast majority of these organisations kept a significant distance from the camps, ignoring the countless lessons emerging on the streets and squares outside their offices.

Power to the People! Consensus decision-making in Oaxaca, 2006

In June 2006, the state police in the southern Mexican city of Oaxaca attacked hundreds of public school teachers who were camped out in the city's main square, protesting for better wages. This was far from the first time Mexico's most powerful trade union had occupied the square and public support for their cause was inevitably mixed, as the 'plantons' (public encampments) created significant inconveniences for many in the city centre.

But as mixed as public perceptions of the protest had been, very few Oaxacans expected or supported the violence faced by the teachers on June 14th.

In the weeks and months that followed the attack, hundreds of thousands of Oaxacans, from the city and its neighbouring towns converged on the historic urban centre, time-and-time again. They came both to protest the state government's corruption and violence, demanding the governor's resignation, as well as to collectively remove the vestiges of its political power (from the civil service, to the police), filling the gaps left in their wake themselves.

Chapter 6:
The kind of
ownership
that can't be
bought or sold

Diana Denham, in a collection of testimonies she edited from Oaxaca in 2006, entitled, *Teaching Rebellion*, describes how a population 'took over and ran an entire city for six months':

> Without relying on centralized organisation, neighbourhoods managed everything from public safety (crime rates actually went down dramatically during the course of the six months) to food distribution and transportation. People across the state began to question the established line of western thinking that says communities cannot survive, much less thrive, without the intervention of a separate hierarchy caring for its needs. Oaxaca sent a compelling message to the world in June 2006: The power we need is in our hands.[x]

Barricades were erected by neighbours around key entry points to the city to prevent plain-clothes paramilitaries from entering and attacking the emergent hubs of self-organising. These barricades became the main spaces for a new local participatory democracy during the city's months of self-government.

Many of the practices used at both the individual barricades, and the Popular Assembly of the People of Oaxaca (APPO), had emerged from the traditional practices of indigenous communities (who count for roughly half the state's population), many of whom shared a long history of self-government in their respective 'pueblos' (towns).

In hundreds of neighbourhoods, neighbours came together to defend their communities around makeshift roadblocks built with whatever was available at the time. From sunset to sunrise, neighbours took shifts keeping watch, bringing each other food and coordinating their activities with other 'barricaderos' (either directly, or via *Radio Planton* – the peoples' pirate radio station). In the process, they also got to know and trust each other as few ever had before.

Yeyo Beltran (@yeyoenoax), a community learning practitioner and activist, who was a host on *Radio Planton* during the uprising, described the decision-making process used at both the *APPO* and most of the more-than 250 local barricades:

> the voting model is only used to take minor decisions (the date or route of a demonstration, but never the strategic importance of doing it or not; the use of a word or another in a document, but never the content of it). The Assembly model has open spaces of participation for social groups never listened to before (like the women's movement, youth, etc.). It has enabled otherwise 'antagonistic' groups to discuss and struggle together. In a session of the Assembly, the Marxist/ Leninist Communist party can testify on one side, and on the other, the grassroots groups of the Catholic church. Both listen to the other side's arguments and express their own arguments and often, discover together that both are part of what has been notoriously recognized in Oaxaca in recent days as The People.[xi]

At its best, consensus processes provide the space for common ground to emerge from a seemingly disparate array of opinions and arguments. They also offer everyone present the power to stop a process if they feel it is fundamentally wrong for the group. This distribution of power offers a strong sense of shared ownership. Whereas 'majority rules' voting so often becomes a numbers game, to win over just enough people for one side to impose its will on the other, consensus gives everyone equal say. It encourages a more collaborative approach to decision-making.

In late November, the state government decided they'd had enough. The governor, with support from the federal army, unleashed a brutal new wave of violence that crushed the self-organised communities of the city and reinstated the old regime before Christmas.

Six years on, the remnants of the uprising are still present, in the graffiti (now a world famous case study in street art and social unrest), in the public spaces that housed the movement, and in the attitudes of so many people who learned during those traumatic, yet empowering months, that they didn't need government to organise their city or their lives on their behalf.

What makes consensus work?

The ultimate value of consensus-based decision making lies in equalising power within a group, shifting the lens through which decisions are made, from 'how do I convince you to agree with me?' to 'how can we work together in a way that works for everyone?' When you stand on equal footing to someone with whom you disagree, it is easier to see compromise as a shared victory, rather than a personal failure.

Consensus also has a range of issues which (in my experience) are inherent to the process (namely, lengthiness and inefficiency), which are simply *different* to the problems associated with more executive processes (such as lack of buy-in, lack of information, and lack of perspective).

What both approaches share is an inability to make the right decisions all the time, but in my experiences, what's lost in unilateral decisions, while often less-obvious, is costlier in terms of what the group can ultimately achieve. Consensus provides a piece of the 'ownership' puzzle, by distributing the sense of responsibility for whatever is decided.

A few questions to keep in mind when deciding if consensus is right for your situation include:

Do we need to achieve one decision, or would several different ones suffice?

- Is the decision at hand related to agreeing a broad framework for individual activities (i.e. – a 'We are the 99%' kind of slogan), or is it more operational?
- If we didn't take a single decision together, would it prevent others from being able to take action autonomously?

Are we all emotionally mature enough to put our egos to the side for a little while?

- Are we able to address challenging dynamics directly and non-judgmentally together?
- Are we more committed to 'being right' or 'being able to work together?'

Are our aims appropriate for the size and type of group we have?

- Are we a small group, making practical decisions for our own actions?
- Are we a large group looking to establish the broadest baseline from which to work together?

While consensus offers an ideal to aspire to in many situations, because it gives everyone an equal voice (though sometimes this needs to be encouraged, to compensate for louder and more dominant voices), it is not always possible if someone is not invested in the collaborative nature of the process.

In such situations, there are variations on the method that offer something like a middle ground from which group decisions can be made. 'Consensus minus 1,' and 'Consensus minus 2' provide an approach in which one or two individuals are unable to 'hijack' a process, holding everyone else at ransom with an unwillingness to compromise on a hardened stance.

Also, consensus shouldn't be seen as an elaborate group sign-off process, hampering individual action. As David Graber, in his thorough account of consensus processes used by Occupy Wall Street writes, 'One should not feel one needs authorization from anyone, even the General Assembly (which is everyone), unless it would be in some way harmful to proceed without it.'[xii]

The long tail of activism

At the core of our reluctance to engage with supporters and the public in the ways Occupy has, or the ways the people of Oaxaca did with each other in 2006, is the need for organisational control. The more choices we offer, the harder it is to be sure people will do what we want them to. But we shouldn't see this as a problem. Trying to control what people will do with a cause is, unsurprisingly, exactly what keeps most people from getting engaged.

Nearly a decade ago, Clay Shirky (@cshirky) and Chris Anderson (@chr1sa) identified the 'long tail' phenomenon – the idea that the future of business lies in targeting niche markets in the thin edges of a distribution curve rather than the mass bulge in the middle, a concept that businesses are finding easier to exploit in the age of the social web.

While Anderson looked at this phenomenon in relation to business models, Shirky then applied the notion to activity in the blogosphere, noting that the vast majority of links to individual blogs were distributed across a huge array of blogs, as compared to the proportion that linked to the most popular ones. Basically, while some blogs will always stand out above the others, the vast majority of blogging activity is actually taking place within niche communities, read by a relative few, but collectively comprising most blogging action.

Meanwhile, *Occupy* and countless more local self-organising movements are creating space for activism's long tail as we speak by offering countless individuals the space to create their own forms of activism, rather than slotting them into pre-planned actions, activities and events. Though the relatively few campaigning actions or volunteer opportunities we offer still have greater individual uptake than the self-organised opportunities within non-hierarchical movements, the cumulative involvement of so many self-created opportunities seem poised to account for the lion's share of stuff done for social and environmental causes. In other words, our handful of organisational engagement options are the bulge at the centre of the distribution curve, while the infinite involvement possibilities of the grassroots movements are increasingly the long tail, where more and more is going on.

What if our organisations opened up and embraced the long tail of activism? Instead of saying, 'you can do a, b, or c, if you want to contribute to this cause,' what if we opened our doors and our

'more like people' ownership

Humanity: 'more like people' ownership is about feeling a sense of purpose in your work. Humans have long-strived for purpose. It is as natural to us as anything, and thus should be a clear part of our working lives.

Autonomy: Having the space to determine your own best way of furthering your purpose is critical to ownership.

Complexity: 'more like people' ownership means too many different things to different people, and changes with each of our circumstances; therefore it has to be discovered uniquely by each person in a team or organisation.

resources to those who care enough to engage with the issues on which we're working? Rather than exclusively pitching generic mass actions, what if we opened our desks, our databases, our results, and our systems to those with a passion for advancing our causes? What if people used our organisations as a catalyst to find their own ways of contributing to a cause, blurring the lines between paid and unpaid activists and volunteers? What if we genuinely put our organisations into the service of the broader movements they are a part of, rather than trying to direct those movements?

Chapter 6:
The kind of
ownership
that can't be
bought or sold

We could create our own General Assemblies to decide where resources were most needed, with people from around the movement contributing ideas. Small projects that just required some desk space, some tools, or some broader participation could go ahead freely without specific approval or scrutiny. Most of our organisations would likely still need to take on the kinds of 're-centring' work described in Chapter 4 to ensure the doors were truly open to the breadth of the movement, but giving people the chance to engage as they are inspired to makes that kind of re-centring more likely to happen.

> *What does your organisation have that it could open up to those who support its cause?*

> *What aspects of your organisation could serve as testing grounds for opening up organisational resources to those outside your walls?*

> *What would you do if someone who chose to become involved with your organisation did something that your organisation didn't approve of because they felt it was the best way to advance the cause?*

Making our work our own

It's unsurprising how common stories of burnout and frustration have become in large social change organisations, when you start to unpack our individual relationships to those organisations and the work many of us do within them. With so little sense of real input, it can feel like we are simply cogs in a machine, working towards something abstract we may never experience ourselves and in which we have no investment.

Management, by its nature, separates each of us from both ownership and responsibility for what we do at work, watering down either the pride or the guilt we might otherwise experience as a result of our actions. The more manager oversight and distance that exists between us and the results of our actions, the less we are likely to feel anything, positively or negatively, about what we do.

The more control each of us has over our work, the more motivated we are likely to be to do it. The more motivated we are to do it, the greater our sense of ownership. And with a strong sense of ownership, we are more likely to make a meaningful difference in the world around us. The human desire to find purpose in what we do is universal, so systems that encourage and enable this desire will tap into our core humanity, whereas those that discourage it will invariably undermine it.

At the core of 'more like people' ownership is the notion of autonomy. Industrialism has stolen autonomy from so many of us, but more and more possibilities are emerging to take it back. The question for our organisations is whether or not we will be helping to open up these possibilities, or if people who might traditionally have supported us will be left to find them elsewhere, or to simply create them on their own.

'More like people' ownership is also complex because it will be different for everyone and thus cannot be imposed from above. As the lengths Argentine workers were willing to go for their reclaimed workplaces demonstrate, when we feel like the work is ours, we treat it very differently than the transactional systems of 'effort-for-pay' that are common in so many big organisations. When we can self-organise ourselves around what we believe in, we can achieve things senior managers could never have managed.

'more like people' organisations are owned – literally or in spirit – by those within and around them. They are defended with a commitment that could never be imposed, and they reap the immeasurable benefits of the creativity and sense of purpose they help to unleash amongst staff and supporters.

And while our organisations may feel a long way off from a grassroots social movement or a reclaimed factory, if we can get past relying on senior management approval to bring about change, we might be closer than we think. Chapter 7 will investigate the journey from individual change to culture change. As Chapter 1 outlined, there are several approaches to organisational change; Chapter 7 will explore how they can each help to mould the cultures we want to be a part of.

Chapter 6:
The kind of
ownership
that can't be
bought or sold

[i] Michael Albert, *Parecon,* Verso, 2003, Chapter 6. http://books.zcommunications.org/books/pareconv/Chapter6.htm#_VPID_45

[ii] Joel Bakan, *The Corporation,* Viking Canada, 2004.

[iii] Ricardo Semler, 'Managing without managers,' *Harvard Business Review,* September – October 1989.

[iv] Brooke Jarvis, 'Why everyone suffers in unequal societies,' *Yes Magazine,* 4 March 2010. http://www.yesmagazine.org/happiness/want-the-good-life-your-neighbors-need-it-too

[v] Rory Carroll, 'Here's the chocolate factory, but where has Willy Wonka gone?,' *Guardian,* 11 May 2007. http://www.guardian.co.uk/world/2007/may/11/argentina.rorycarroll

[vi] Daniel Pink, 'Drive: The surprising truth about what motivates us,' The Royal Society for the Arts, 2010. http://www.youtube.com/watch?v=u6XAPnuFjJc

[vii] Daniel Pink, *Drive,* Riverhead Books, 2009.

[viii] Paula X. Rojas, 'Are the cops in our heads and hearts?,' in *The Revolution Will Not Be Funded,* South End Press: Read. Write. Revolt. 2007, p. 211.

[ix] Sarah Berman, 'Occupy Wall Street's new job: disaster relief,' *TheTyee.ca,* 10 November 2012. http://thetyee.ca/News/2012/11/10/Occupy-Sandy/

[x] Diana Denham, ed. *Teaching Rebellion,* PM Press, 2007, p. 27.

[xi] Sergio Beltran, "The Case of Oaxacan Society Uprising" in *Reflections on Now Activism,* self-published, 2006, p. 134.

[xii] David Graeber, *The Democracy Project,* Allen Lane, 2013, p. 227.

It's up to us!: From individual change to culture change

"No culture can live if it attempts to be exclusive."
– Mahatma Gandhi

7

Most of us have experienced miserable workplaces cultures, yet exactly what makes them so bad can be hard to put a finger on. Many senior managers and boards have tried extensively to re-engineer their office cultures, generally with noble intent, but still with little or no effect.

Culture change cannot be masterminded from above, but can be encouraged from anywhere within an organisation. Even in the most hierarchical of bureaucracies, culture is still an emergent phenomenon, created and constantly changed by the countless relationships among people involved. We can change those relationships through awareness of our own behaviour, and through constructive one-to-one connections with others. This chapter looks at our experiences of working in less-than-ideal environments, and digs into the institutional and the personal innovations that can help to create something better.

Our remarkably human capacity to change

Before my wife, Jen (@GuerillaGrrl), and I left London for Oaxaca, Mexico, she had been working for a university involved in primary health research. She was a part of a team that had been built around a specific piece of funding, and didn't have any direct accountability channels into the rest of the organisation. It didn't take long to realise that the office culture there wasn't a good one. And as is often the case, most of the office felt strongly that they could point to the source of their problems: the boss.

In fairness, the woman who led this team made an easy villain of herself. She would yell at staff in the middle of an open-plan office, would micromanage to the point of forbidding the use of 'copy-and-paste' shortcuts, and would regularly demean those whose working preferences were different to hers. This environment took its toll on Jen each day, to the extent that she was often stressed at just the thought of going back to the office.

As is often the case in such situations, the rest of the team become each others' allies, taking any opportunity after the manager had left the office to vent and share stories of her latest abuses of power. Countless office conversations, while cathartic, seemed to build up the boss as the sole source of all of their shared unhappiness. 'Nothing can change as long as she's around,' became the black-and-white consensus.

Now, there seems little doubt that this particular manager had significant issues that needed resolving, but the collective energy that inadvertently built her up as so exclusively bad may have been part of the problem, too. As swathes of staff fled the office, none expressed any of their frustrations, directly or through HR, even as they walked out and away from day-to-day contact with her.

In the regular discussions that took place amongst the rest of the team, no one seemed to think there was any point raising these frustrations, as their manager was 'too messed up' to be able to do anything constructive with their criticism. Instead, each day they came back to work, feeling evermore resentful of their situation.

When Jen put in her notice, she struggled for a long time about how she was going to leave. She didn't need a reference, so was at some level happy to burn bridges with this workplace tyrant, but still wasn't sure if it was worth the stress of the confrontation.

She decided to share her experiences with HR, outlining the ways in which staff, herself included, had been mistreated and undermined during her time at the university. And when HR passed this information along to the manager, Jen heard about it. Not through the manager going ballistic at her insubordination, but through former colleagues emailing to tell her something far more surprising: they were being treated like people for the first time!

While still far from perfect, this manager had stopped some of her most destructive habits (physically grabbing telephone receivers from staff, mid-work conversation, and butting-in to tell her version of things to outside colleagues, for example). It wasn't quite a Jekyll-and-Hyde switch, but it made a difference.

I won't pretend that simply telling someone they've done something wrong is necessarily enough in many situations, but I would suggest that it might have more value to it than we can initially see from inside a difficult situation. As hard as it can be to believe this from within a culture of entrenched hostility, people have the ability to change in drastic and remarkable ways.

So what happened there? A dozen or so adults in professional jobs let one person shape a workplace culture that none of them liked, but that all of them likely helped perpetuate through silence and active resentment. All it took was one person for this to begin to change. There are two things that I took from this story:

1. We are all contributors to bad situations we are a part of, if we are not actively doing something to challenge that which we are criticising.

2. People can be unaware of behaviours that seem as clear as day to the casual observer, which means that bad actions are not necessarily the result of bad intentions, but often personal blind spots that need to be constructively addressed.

Both of these dynamics, while not immune to the powers of hierarchy outlined in Chapter 3, still give each of us a shot at creating change, even in systems where it can feel impossible. They also offer two ways that we, as individuals, can approach culture change:

1. Being aware of what we are bringing to any relationship in the workplace, and doing what we can to ensure that we are not perpetuating a problem through our own actions and behaviours;
2. Challenging others about specific actions in a way that is less likely to perpetuate the problems (i.e. – not in public, not through blame, and generally not while tensions are high).

Organisational culture as a 'field' we can all affect

Margaret Wheatley, in her book *Leadership and the New Science*, described organisational culture as a 'field.'[i] In science, a field is a force that is only visible through its impacts on the world around it – for instance, gravity. We see the apple drop from the tree to the ground, but we can't see what makes it happen. So it is with organisational culture: it affects us, it shapes our experiences and our behaviours, but we can't easily put a finger on what it is, beyond being confident that it clearly exists.

It is also not universal. Just as gravity acts differently in varied settings, so too with culture, even, sometimes, within the same organisation. Even in the worst organisations, there are often teams that have managed to forge their own subcultures, avoiding the toxicity that surrounds them by choosing to do things differently. IT teams are the classic example of this. Partly enabled by the fact that no one else in the organisation has a clue what they actually do, IT staff can often create a space (metaphorically, if not physically) in which they are free to be themselves.

In Chapter 2 we talked about the challenge of bad workplace relationships and the importance of not getting sucked into contributing to bad ways of doing things because those around you have – that even if a colleague tells you to piss off, it is still your responsibility to not respond with the same destructive attitude they chose to come at you with, no matter how tempting it might feel in the moment. When two young children get in a fight, they are known to run to the nearest adult and both declare that the other 'started it,' as though however they responded would then be forgiven. But like the thoughtful parent's response to those kids, when we are dealing with conflict at work, 'it's not about who started it, but who finished it.'

Organisational culture is the field that individual working relationships create, as they shape and are shaped by other individual relationships across an organisation. It is the collective sum of relationships of all those within a system.

When one person's insult becomes two people's fight, the impacts spread beyond the immediate participants. What might have been dismissed by colleagues within earshot as an 'asshole with a bad attitude,' may instead be perceived to be part of a broader pattern of animosity. If that two-person fight leads colleagues to take sides, this perception is further reinforced.

A subtle war may ensue, only rarely surfacing as open battles, but constantly permeating the attitudes and behaviours of those in the field where it is being fought. If you feel as though you are slinking into enemy territory when you enter a departmental meeting, you are unlikely to contribute anything positive to that meeting, even if you have good cause for feeling that way.

Organisational culture doesn't have to be negative, however, even though we rarely talk about it when it is constructive and enabling. When it's working, it just feels *like life should*, with people contributing to each other's achievements and developments, rather than undermining them. But this more positive kind of culture is also the result of individual relationships, shaped by many, over time. Positive workplace cultures allow us to achieve amazing things, because we don't spend so much time thinking about or stressing over them. They offer us the freedom to focus on the change we want to make in the wider world, rather than the change we want to make to our dysfunctional working relationships.

The Projection-Perception Loop

Another way of understanding organisational culture is as a series of relationship loops, which are always being made better or worse, depending on how we choose to engage with them. I find this approach can be helpful in identifying the places where each of us might be able to take practical action to change our part in a destructive pattern for something better.

I call these 'projection-perception loops': one person in a group takes an action (their projection onto the group's culture), another person internalises that action (their perception of the first person's action), and then responds, projecting something new into 'the field.' This second projection is inevitably perceived by others, leaving each of them with the choice of how to respond. The issue is always whether a destructive gesture (say, yelling at staff in the office), is answered by another destructive gesture (yelling back in middle of the office, or turning around and talking badly about them behind their backs), or if the loop is broken through a different choice. As natural as some of those responses can feel, they also don't help us, our situation, or the groups we are a part of. In fact, they actively contribute to making things worse.

Retrospectively, I can remember countless ways in which I made things worse for myself and others at my job at the large non-profit described previously. A combative attitude, mixed with an inability to confront my problems with more understanding of others' situations, meant that I was definitely contributing to the issues I had there. I often felt that if I fought hard enough, I would eventually win. But it never played out like that. I was mostly just prolonging the fight.

Popular culture has long promulgated the idea that somehow fighting fire with fire will eventually put an unwanted fire out. But as simple physics would tell us, the world, and more specifically, the people in it, don't work like this.

While we may have to spend some time understanding our own responses to conflict, it is within all of our reach to be sure our responses are not simply reinforcing the initial action that we had so much reason to dislike. 'The measure of success here is not that we stop getting provoked,' writes Margaret Wheatley, 'but that we notice when it happens sooner and we get over it faster.'[ii] As we get better at noticing when we're provoked, and checking our reflexive response, we can start to throw a spanner in the works of the negative 'projection-perception loops' which we have previously contributed to, unquestioningly, and start to reverse patterns of dysfunction in our organisations.

The biggest asset we have going for us is that when we are kinder, more direct, less combative, and more understanding of where others are coming from, our actions may well start to perpetuate those qualities. The default responses of those we work with may well change for the better, if we can give them a reason to. Most people, no matter how trapped they are in an institutional mindset, prefer to be treated well. If we are the ones willing to extend the olive branch, we might find our approach gradually begins to catch on more widely.

Culture is likely the part of organisational change that relies most heavily on the 'emergent change' described in Chapter 1. It cannot be orchestrated, from either above or below, but can be influenced from anywhere within the organisation, levelling the hierarchy in the process. Leaders, just like everyone else, can model certain ways of doing things, but no one can change others at this level.

> *When have you made a situation worse by perpetuating a negative loop between yourself and someone else?*

> *Were you able to break the loop in that situation, or other situations, and shift it towards something more positive?*

How Peter Wanless – and Twitter – opened the doors of the Big Lottery Fund

When culture change does come from the top, it looks the same as the changes coming from any other parts of the organisation. It's not about policies, statements, or declarations, but a different way of engaging with others, particularly in difficult dynamics. Social media gives all of us a chance to re-shape our working personas to be better aligned with who we are in the rest of our lives, which often gives others an implicit permission to do the same.

My first encounter with Peter Wanless, chief executive of the UK's Big Lottery Fund, was a single tweet in early 2009, wishing me luck on a grant application I had flippantly posted that I was struggling with. By late 2011, we were heading to a punk gig in Camden market, celebrating my birthday over a few pints with friends.

Peter sits at the helm of the largest grant-giving body in the UK, but his Twitter feed doesn't for a moment give the impression he holds the high-and-mighty position his business card says he does. A somewhat unpredictable combination of cricket commentary, Elvis Costello-laced music playlists, and random ALL CAPS bursts when his son gets hold of dad's phone, are interspersed with occasional updates about the latest grant programme BIG has announced or delivered on.

And he engages. Happy to have a chat or answer questions from people who want to talk to him on Twitter about his work, or otherwise. Peter first started using Twitter in late 2008 when, on a good day, it was viewed suspiciously by most of his counterparts in other large foundations and government.

Twitter has opened a door to Peter, and by extension BIG, for thousands of stakeholders, many of whom may previously have seen the funder as a bit of an ivory tower. In turn, Peter makes clear Twitter opened his own doors to the world beyond his office in the City of London. 'I really think of Twitter as a place to exchange views and learn a tremendous amount,'[iii] he tells me.

Through a relatively open and honest online presence – particularly given the pressures on someone in his position to toe a strict line on all issues political – Peter has found a regular opportunity to engage directly with those whose only previous connections to BIG were half a dozen or so rungs down the organisational command chain. In other words, he can learn directly from the frontline, subverting some of the inevitable shortcomings of an established hierarchy, without leaving the meetings that fill so much of his days.

That said, he was also keen to remind me that social media will only go so far in engaging staff or stakeholders in how the organisation is run: 'Only certain people will walk through your open door – for others, you need to leave your office if you want them to engage with what you do,' he says. Essentially, if not used carefully, Twitter can simply amplify the voices which are already shouting the loudest, while others become more marginalised. So Peter makes sure to get out of the office and meet the people who receive support from BIG.

He is also very conscious of who he follows, wanting to ensure that he is not creating an echo chamber for his own views of the world, but is learning from some of the diversity that Twitter enables him to so easily explore.

Peter admits that his first forays into the medium resembled the 'broadcasting' motives that have pushed so many organisations to create accounts, telling the stories of grant recipients when the media was broadly disinterested in picking them up. '[I had] this sense of wanting to alert the world to the fact that there were these incredible people doing amazing things which it was a great privilege for us to be funding.'

However in late 2009, when a British newspaper ran a hatchet-job on the funder, noting Peter had claimed £9,000 in travel expenses the previous year and had 'found the time' for over 3,000 Tweets, it was Twitter that came to his defence. 'Even before the press office had moved into position to develop a rebuttal,' Peter recounted, 'various people were Tweeting: "well thank goodness there's a chief executive who bothers to engage with us directly on social media and takes time to travel out and see what we're doing on the ground in our charities!"'

While our organisations go to great lengths to prepare themselves for the kinds of PR disasters that very occasionally pop up, thanks to an errant tweet or blog, we rarely think of social media as our first line of defence against a range of public attacks or criticisms.

Yet Peter's story demonstrates just that: the time he had spent on Twitter (and out on the road) had been more valuable in protecting the organisation's name than any number of disaster-response spin doctors the Lottery could have hired in to try and undo the reputational damage of a national paper's smear campaign.

It also blurred the organisational lines of the past, as unpaid supporters unofficially became a part of the organisational response to the smear, demonstrating that a culture of openness isn't confined to the organisation's walls, but influences a wide range of stakeholders.

As the support rolled in, Peter thought for the first time: 'Wow! This is *very* powerful!' It was at this point he started to use Twitter differently – engaging more, listening more, learning more – taking advantage of not only his steadily growing audience, but also the extensive learning pool of Twitter users that he was able to engage with.

Gradually, @PeterWanless and @BigLotteryFund both began 'creating space for people to tell their own stories' opening the medium to sharing direct testimonials of people and groups they had helped to fund, rather than trying to tell others' stories through a singular, organisational voice.

While social media is still a minority sport at the BIG offices, Peter believes the tone and personality of the organisation are much more open and engaged than they once were. Twitter's informality has meant that far more interactions, inside and outside of the organisation have begun to feel, in Peter's words, more like an 'exchange of equals', brushing traditionally professional behaviour aside, in the interests of nurturing better relationships. And while there are still people within BIG who feel organisational culture hasn't opened up as much as it could, the fact that Peter can hear those voices at all – and takes them seriously enough to tell me they exist – is an indication of how far things have come.

While he would likely deny that the growing openness at BIG was his own doing, Peter has clearly modelled a way of being and working that others have felt comfortable enough to adopt and run with themselves. In contrast to an infinite number of other institutions' change management exercises, which have likely produced a fraction of the results, Peter and so many other employees at BIG have just gotten more comfortable being themselves at work, and seen the effect spread, online and off.

Transformative leadership – wherever it comes from in an organisation – is so often about doing something differently for others to see, rather than telling others to do something differently themselves. This is the kind of culture change that happens when people are freer to be themselves and that freedom starts to catch on. It can come from anywhere in an organisation where someone has the nerve to shift the ways they relate to one another for the better.

Culture change comes from everywhere

Organisational culture change can feel elusive, wherever you sit in the hierarchy. As a field that everyone has potentially equal input into, it's no wonder that it takes more than a few shifts at the top to change it. It is also why this chapter is a little sparser in stories than many of the others, as very rarely do we get a meaningful glimpse of the many autonomous yet interdependent actions and relationships that have enabled a culture to shift. Actions can often be pointed to as significant, but can rarely be said to be 'the cause' of whatever came after.

Focussing your energies on one particular working relationship that causes you stress might begin to open up wider potential for change. If you can build a better dynamic with a former adversary, you are demonstrating the potential for culture change for the rest of the organisation to see. This is why waiting for others to change a toxic culture only tends to breed more of what's already there. When we look up the command chain for these answers, we perpetuate the power of someone else's behaviour to affect our working environment. Too much input from the top will only serve to reinforce hierarchy and acceptance of centralised organisational power, hindering the odds of individual changes by their very imposition.

If a CEO is indeed a significant instigator of toxic culture, what we need to challenge is the obedience of 'professionalism' that continues to offer him or her that power. Rather than expecting the boss to change, why not model an alternative ourselves and

'more like people' culture change

Humanity: When we share ourselves more openly, we are helping to give others permission to do the same. Many of us have long been restrained by workplace cultures that don't allow us to be ourselves, so when we can be, it frees us to explore our work and our working relationships as more whole people, enabling new possibilities to emerge.

Autonomy: When we are working together at our best, it is because we have found just enough common ground to be comfortable being autonomous with each other. A loose but shared sense of purpose allows us to each find our own best ways of getting where we all want to go. Autonomy, with shared purpose, allows our differences to become complementary, rather than contradictory, while giving each of us the chance to potentially set a broader culture change in motion.

Complexity: Culture is a 'field' that emerges from countless relationships within and beyond the organisation, thus is cannot be orchestrated from above, but can be sparked by people anywhere within the system choosing to engage with it differently. Behavioural change is the first step any of us can take toward culture change.

constructively challenge their specific behaviours – or the specific parallel behaviours of someone we engage more regularly – when they affect us, directly or indirectly? This can be scary, but is one of the risks that each of us has the power to take to improve things.

Telling someone – regardless of your hierarchical relationship to each other – to 'be more positive' or 'be less judgmental' is often a good way to get the opposite effect. Alternatively, challenging specific actions, in a non-antagonistic or public way, is far more likely to encourage deeper reflection. We can't help if someone gets defensive when challenged, but we can be conscious to shape our challenges in ways that are less likely to elicit defensive responses in those on the receiving end.

*Chapter 7:
It's up to
us!: From
individual
change to
culture change*

Humanity, autonomy and complexity can offer us some guidance as to the steps each of us might take to influence better working cultures. Complexity tells us that culture change cannot be orchestrated, given the number of interdependent relationships it would have to shift, but that cultures move based on any of those individual relationships changing themselves in a way that resonates more widely.

By acting autonomously within each of our working relationships, we have the potential to set this kind of emergent change in motion. At its best, organisational culture offers everyone involved the space to be themselves, but with a sense of shared purpose that doesn't subsume individual differences.

Finally, humanity is what allowed Peter Wanless and so many of his colleagues at the Big Lottery Fund to open their doors and connect via Twitter, one-to-one, with people they would have remained isolated from in so many other organisations. As humans, we seek out new connections and relationships, and technology is, somewhat ironically, helping us reconnect with this dormant impulse. As culture change can spread around an organisation as organically as a cold or a YouTube video, new connections will only help to make it happen.

The upshot of all this is the equalising effect such an outlook has on our understandings of power and change. Organisations have traditionally told us that the power rests solely at the top of the organisational chart, and thus that this is where changes must emerge from. Neither assumption, however, is true, unless we surrender our individuality to the whims of those who tell us they are steering the ship.

While we have likely spent much of our working lives giving up some element of our individuality (and with it our power to affect change), it doesn't have to be this way. Simply by rethinking how we choose to engage with those we work with, we may begin to set a new direction into motion.

While we may previously have been unable to see the roles we've played in shaping our organisational cultures, now is our chance to bring a level of consciousness to our efforts, and see if they can start to break the less constructive cycles we often engage in.

While this approach to culture change is neither sure-fire nor necessarily speedy, it offers real possibility to transform an organisation for the better, where previously we have suffered from either a sense of total impotence, or the allusion of being able to control the uncontrollable. Since neither has brought us organisational cultures we'd like to find ourselves in, why not try believing in our own ability to manifest the first shoots of the systemic change we want to experience?

i Margaret Wheatley, *Leadership and the New Science*, Berrett-Koehler, 1992.

ii Margaret Wheatley, *So far from home*, Berrett-Koehler, 2012, p. 135.

iii Interview with the author, 4 April 2012.

Complexity doesn't strategise: Learning to embrace unforeseen circumstances

'I went out drinking with Thomas Paine
He said that all revolutions are not the same
They are as different as the cultures
That gave them birth
For no one idea
Can solve every problem on Earth'
– Billy Bragg, 'North Sea Bubble'

8

We really like the idea that if we are well enough informed about the past, we can use this knowledge to predict the future. From strategic planning to scaling-up (the re-application of a blueprint for local success in a vast array of new locations, with the expectation of the same result), we assume we can know what's best without experiencing the current context of time and place, without understanding the unique relationships that will make any situation, at any given time, fundamentally different to any other. But our emerging understanding of complexity tells us that context and relationships are the greatest determinants of result. When we ignore context and relationship by trying to replicate the same steps taken elsewhere, we can succeed only by chance.

However, there is another way to shape and organise our work, which doesn't fall afoul of the core principles of complexity. When our purpose is clear and we stay with the moment, we can follow that purpose where our efforts are most needed, freeing ourselves from predetermined plans that are no longer serving our cause. Further, we can learn from the experiences of others (as is meant to be the point of scaling-up), but to do so we must be free to choose whatever course of action we feel is appropriate in a given context, rather than having a script imposed based on what may have worked elsewhere, or what was decided should work everywhere.

If we pay attention to what we're doing and accept that single solutions cannot be applied universally, rather than always trying to predict what should come next and assuming it will be replicable, we may well find we are our own best compasses in navigating a complex and changing world.

Stumbling my way into the anti-globalisation movement

I got involved in the anti-globalisation movement because I'd left my house keys at high school one day and found myself wandering the snowy streets of Toronto's Parkdale neighbourhood, waiting for my parents to get home and let me in. But the story gets better.

On that cold January evening in 2001, I happened across a group of activists at the corners of Queen and Lansdowne, flyering for a screening of *This is what democracy looks like*, a just-released documentary about the World Trade Organization protests in Seattle in November 1999. I can trace innumerable life changing experiences and events, even up to deciding to write this book, back to the conversation that happened on that street corner that evening.

I initially only chatted with the folks handing out flyers to distract myself from the cold, but was convinced enough by what I heard to check out the screening a few days later. By the time the closing credits were rolling, I had decided to throw myself, full-tilt, behind the organising efforts against the upcoming Summit of the Americas in Quebec City that April.

I tell this story because of the friends I made that day, and in the weeks and months that followed, and how those new friendships linked me into a network of grassroots activism that would come to shape a range of my choices and work for many years to come. Some of these new friends were in organisations, many were not. I'm fairly certain none of them were paid to be there flyering that evening. While mobilising towards the Summit, most had other social justice activities they were involved in; tenant organising, Palestinian solidarity, defence of political prisoners, anti-police brutality, and local anti-fascist campaigning, to name a few.

Seattle, Quebec City and a handful of other global summits around that time served as flashpoints for much of the left. People involved in a range of causes, linked by shared opposition to the human and environmental costs of unbridled free market economics, gravitated together, putting a range of differences aside to make sure the global meetings in each of these cities didn't pass unchallenged.

In the time leading up to Quebec City, I came to realise how many of the activists – for all their disparate activities beyond Summit organising – had worked together on a range of issues before. In the time since, I have crossed paths with many of them again. They have informed me of important issues, offering me a chance to get involved, and I have in turn done the same for them. I have also met people who – like I was in 2001 – were becoming active for the first time, but have since become familiar faces.

In 2001, there was a lot of talk about the wonders of email in the anti-globalisation movement's organising processes. Through non-hierarchical groups and forums, people organising around one summit or the next, from one city or country to another, were able to share lessons and tactics and coordinate actions together, as had never been done on that kind of scale before.

*Chapter 8:
Complexity
doesn't
strategise:
Learning
to embrace
unforeseen
circumstances*

When the immediate focus subsided, the forums and email lists remained. The relationships between people definitely did too, and in the years between Quebec City and Occupy Wall Street, media became all the more social, strengthening the connections among activists through regular online contact.

The Twitter feed I flick over to every so often while writing this, offers me updates from Canadian peace activists I worked with nearly a decade ago, UK students I campaigned with in the last couple of years against the Alberta tar sands, and Mexican community organisers I have come to know in Oaxaca just lately. The time passed since our most recent practical collaborations has done little to erode our connections, maintained by the simple contact of an occasional Tweet and semi-regular updates from our current respective activities.

Just as the business world has long-embraced 'networking for networking's sake,' activists have done this through active partnerships. Once the connection is formed, it may be put to use whenever the time is right and either party feels drawn to reconnect.

Contrary to popular opinion, networks *do* provide lasting structures. But not in the ways our organisations tend to think of them. When the event or issue that brought them into being has passed, the relationships behind them remain. They later re-appear with a reinvigorated sense of purpose, involving

Thinking Strategically

I'm walking blindfolded, backwards into traffic at night, with a map to show me the way.
Each step is written before it is taken,
I am the author of a destiny that will never be.
I play at 'playing God,' which isn't as much fun as the real thing,
But the real thing is confined to a seemingly innocuous pair of words in the fine print:
"Unforeseen circumstances."
We don't talk about them.
Those two words are a rabbit-hole deep enough to render our countless metrics obsolete.
We go down it, we may never come back up again.
We have found a way to freeze time... or at least our place in it.
Through Perpetual Prediction we ensure tomorrow will never come, held at bay by the never ending 'today' we maintain through the magic of our denial:
"If tomorrow isn't what we've said it will be, then it is still today."
We fear the future, and so we try to predict it,
Finding comfort in the illusion of control it offers us;
Solace in the familiar wallpaper it applies to the unknown.

To be continued

new people from countless peripheral networks when they do, expanding the relationships the web can call upon to respond to what's needed each time round. With each new iteration, fresh ideas, perspectives and approaches are introduced, helping the group stay dynamic and preventing more established participants from getting stuck in fixed ways of doing things.

'We scaled up in, like, 24 hours,' reported one Occupy Wall Street participant after helping launch Occupy Sandy, a spontaneous effort sparked by the Occupy network, in which autonomous individuals were among the first on the scene providing support to those affected by Hurricane Sandy in October 2012.'The old networks were moving within a couple of hours.'[i]

This is the pattern of emergence and dispersal that brought us from anti-globalisation to Occupy. While side-lined by the criminalisation of protest that followed 9/11, the networks reformed around resistance to the Iraq War, regularly resurfacing in more local forms over the coming decade before finding their next global manifestation in Zuccotti Park in September 2011, following on the heels of uprisings in Europe and the Middle East earlier that year. During that time it broadened its reach considerably and moved from primarily challenging the status quo, to collectively experimenting with alternatives to it.

In Toronto, considerable parts of the same networks that were involved in the Quebec City protests went on to mobilise against the wars in Iraq and Afghanistan, as well as a range of more local causes. When I moved to the UK in 2006, I realised how many of the people who had been active in the British versions of each of those movements were within a few degrees of separation from the people I'd been organising with across the Atlantic before my move. As I became more acquainted with London activism, the relationships among radical environmentalists, student activists and anti-austerity protestors started to reveal similar patterns.

Some might describe this as a case of 'the usual suspects' (which it at some level definitely is), but the breadth of the movements described also tell us that those we call 'the usual suspects' are also a less fixed or static group than they might sometimes feel. People come and go, but rarely do they disconnect entirely from a network they have chosen to enter into. No one will engage

Thinking Strategically (continued)

The obsession with a hypothetical 'tomorrow' leaves me neither here, nor there,
Disconnected from both the oneness of now, and the possibility of what's to follow.
Schedules, agendas, lists, plans, targets, strategies...
We micromanage our precious time on this planet, aiming to maximise it, but instead whittling it down to the odd 'in-between' space that has narrowly escaped the ruthless chopping block of our calendars.
We trade 'purpose' for the closest objective we can find, moving from one to the next in a constant linear path, on a circular treadmill, finding ourselves no closer to the sense of meaning we so deeply desire.
We've been learning this futile dance for so long, many of us radiate disbelief at even the suggestion of 'another way.'
But it's there.
It's here.
It is ever-present, sitting invisibly just below the surface of the plans and projections we make, becoming ever-so-briefly visible in the moments when 'Life' sneaks up through the cracks and claims a bit of space for itself.
I'm tempted to grab it and hold on, but doing so would involve letting go of that map I'm stumbling backwards into traffic with.
That map feels like it's all I've got, but really, all that I've got is the possibility of letting go of it, and finding Life in the places it used to be...

every time someone they know puts a protest or an organising meeting onto their radar, but the doors remain open for them when they do choose to re-connect, remaining receptive to the relevant information, while, critically, knowing whom to approach if the relevant information about a particular issue doesn't come to them directly. Whereas old organisational communications are based on being able to directly reach as many people as possible with a polished message, when you choose to, the emergent paradigm places far greater emphasis on making sure people know where to find you when *they* want to engage, rather than when *you* want to reach them.

The emerging networks of social media work on the same principles to those of activist networks. They rebalance communications to fit recipients' choices of what information they want to receive, rather than primarily what those distributing information want to tell them. And these parallels are not coincidental; social media and social movements grow through self-organisation, via individual autonomy (choosing the info you take in and share for yourself) and purpose (connecting with others with whom you have something in common). These are the reasons why grassroots activism has been able to do so much more with social technologies than NGOs and charities, even though many of those organisations are allocating considerably more resources to these platforms.

Social media – like social movements – offer those who are a part of them the freedom to connect with countless others in countless ways. They provide a constant stream of self-selected possibilities, any or none of which may be pursued, leaving engagement entirely in the hands of the individual. There is no 'broadcaster' in the dynamics of a distributed network; only equals, giving and receiving on each of their own terms, as they feel inspired to do so.

When I locked my teenage self out of the house in 2001, I stumbled into an emergent network that has since guided me through much of the last twelve years of my life. And we're only beginning to appreciate the power of such emergent networks as forces for social change. No mission statement could have captured the breadth of activity these networks made possible, and no strategy could have projected the paths of these emergent and adaptive networks in advance. They went where they were needed, without anyone telling them to. They self-organised and are continuing to do so, in ways none of us could have planned, but all of us could have shaped and contributed to.

So what can the networks of global grassroots activism tell us about how we organise at a more human level? And how could clearer notions of autonomy and purpose shape each of our individual actions to create wider change?

Complexity doesn't strategise

I first sat down with Pamela McLean (@Pamela_McLean), co-founder of *Dadamac* (@DadamacN), a small UK-Nigerian development partnership, after she read some of my blogs and asked me to write some web content for the organisation. Pam is a former school teacher, an online learning-and-collaboration explorer and a tireless activist. She began working in Africa in 2001, and in 2008 co-founded *Dadamac* with a Nigerian organiser named John Dada. John's *Fantsuam Foundation*, with which Pam became acquainted and by which she was inspired, facilitated a wide range of community development-related projects around Kaduna State, in the north of the country, where he lives.

Explaining *Fantsuam's* work, Pam described a naturally messy process of a man purposefully ambling his way from one social cause to the next, in an area where the silos between 'disease prevention,' 'education,' 'economic development,' and 'nutrition' were academic distinctions in the lives of the people affected. As someone committed to working with communities to help improve people's lives, John went where he was needed, learning, adapting, and figuring things out along the way. From microcredit loans, to AIDS prevention, agriculture to local IT service provision, John's work could not be easily pinned down. If he were to try and explain it in a CV, you'd probably just feel more confused by the time you got to the end.

My first meeting with Pam took place at the *McDonald's* in London's Victoria Station (described by some on the fringes as their 'London office' because of a relaxed long-term seating policy), and for me was one of those conversations where everything seemed to click. She told me a piece of her story, which flowed effortlessly into a piece of mine, and then back again, joining-the-dots between our respective life journeys to this unspectacular fast food joint in a Southwest London train station. Without missing a beat, we moved from the abstract – 'a trusting society,' 'open-source everything,' the importance of 'possibility' – to the concrete – knife crime, funding regimes, AIDS in Africa. The ground we were walking felt common, though we hadn't spoken before.

So when she asked me to do some writing for her, it seemed a natural fit. I offered to start with a blog about *Dadamac*, *Fantsuam*, and their particular approaches to development, communications, and relationships among equals, and we agreed to discuss paid work from there.

We went our separate ways, thanking each other for the conversation, and I got to work on the blog.

This is where the collaboration got unexpectedly difficult. I think my first mistake was using bullet points to describe the journeys John and Pam had taken in doing the work they each do. In trying to convey the messy core of the on-the-ground, unscripted, do-what-needs-doing development work that Pam had described to me, I had inadvertently turned the story into a retrospective project plan. I had linearised something that could only have happened through its lack of linearity. And she wasn't happy about it.

That blog never saw the light of day and Pam and I didn't end up working together.

While my own experiences of the messiness of community-based projects had made her stories immediately resonate, my writing had remained trapped in the cause-and-effect narrative that would have explained nothing of the amazing successes that had occurred. I had fallen into the trap of so much planning-and-evaluation, making it all sound far more inevitable and concerted than it could ever have been, devaluing the kind of active thinking-and-doing that makes that kind of work possible.

Chapter 8: Complexity doesn't strategise: Learning to embrace unforeseen circumstances

It was more than a year later that I discovered the phrase 'Start anywhere, follow it everywhere,' and finally had a lens to understand the alternative that Pam, John, and so many who had moved seamlessly between various progressive social movements had been living.

'Start anywhere, follow it everywhere': practically addressing complex situations

Several years ago I came across a bit of social change jargon you may well be familiar with: *mission drift*. For those unfamiliar with the term, it is generally used to describe the state of desperation in which an organisation pushes its *raison d'être* to the side in the name of a particular piece of funding, or to curry favour with those in power.

The usual lesson associated with 'mission drift' is: stick to what you know, never veer too far off course, don't let outside forces shape your work. There's of course some wisdom to this, as having your efforts determined by funders or politicians is a recipe for irrelevance and resentment. But there are also remnants of Frederick Winslow Taylor buried within this seemingly sound advice: Specialise and become an expert in one thing, leave the rest to others.

The problem is that complexity doesn't always respond well to such stratagems, because they ignore the centrality of relationships and context. In their deeply inspirational book *Walk Out Walk On*, Deborah Frieze and Margaret Wheatley tell the story of Joubert Park in Johannesburg, South Africa, a place left in ruins by a combination of crime, drugs and violence, and the steps through which a community began to reclaim it. The complexity of trying to address so many interdependent and cross-cutting concerns in Jo-burg could not happen through a narrow focus on one or another symptom of the wider social decline. Such situations require a more intuitive and adaptive approach, one that gradually comes to understand the ways in which so many interrelated issues can come to reinforce one another, thus addressing them through an equally interdependent web of solutions that don't remain limited to one or another siloed definition.

Many established NGOs would have dug in on their particular area of expertise (child poverty, HIV prevention, sex worker safety) and likely plodded away for years, minimising certain symptoms, but without ever getting to the core of the problem.

More forward-thinking NGOs might have formed a consortium filled with experts in each of the social ills identified, developed strategies and tracked their progress against a pre-determined set of milestones and outcomes. Doing so may have improved things a little more than the former approach, but would probably have missed the forest for the trees, as the focus remained on 'fixing the component parts,' rather than appreciating the dynamic relationships among them.

Chapter 8:
Complexity
doesn't
strategise:
Learning
to embrace
unforeseen
circumstances

But what happened in this particular instance was that a range of groups – not just organisations – jumped in where they felt they could help, gradually coming to support each other's efforts as they intersected, working together in ways that none would have expected when they first decided to intervene. Wheatley and Frieze described the approach, borrowing a phrase from Myron Kellner-Rogers, as 'Start anywhere, follow it everywhere.' 'If we were to proceed in Joubert Park in the conventional way,' they wrote, 'we'd be debating which problem to tackle first. Prepare to be surprised, for the starting place was simply the moment when a few people stepped forward to act, to create a better future.'[ii]

In practice this meant finding the particular aspect of the complex situation that spoke to different individuals' passions and abilities, and each of them running with it, staying open to how their efforts were affecting the wider situation and those involved. The change process began with a group of photographers who worked in the park, organising themselves with whistles and cameras to prevent crime and capture images of the petty criminals that regularly mugged the park's visitors. A deeply pragmatic observation, that 'people won't come to have their pictures taken if the park doesn't feel safe,'[iii] led to this critical first step in the process of reclaiming the space.

It was paralleled by the Lapeng Family and Childhood Centre, which started by taking care of poorer children, gradually moved on to providing classes for their parents, continued by helping

Why an NGO funded a cock-fighting ring in Honduras

So the story goes like this:

An NGO wanted to build a school in a rural community in Honduras. Educational attainment was low there and the opportunities for schooling were minimal, so the choice seemed to make sense.

But when it was proposed to the community, the women of the pueblo came out against it.

The NGO staffers asked the women what they would prefer. Their answer? A cock-fighting ring.

The staff got uncomfortable, but asked why a cock-fighting ring would be of more benefit than a school.

Apparently, the next village over had a cock-fighting ring. On Fridays, after work, all the men in the village would take their pay and head to the neighbouring town and gamble away their income, often returning home empty-handed.

Because of this the children had to work, otherwise the families often wouldn't eat.

So what would a school do, besides sit empty as the children made up for their fathers' gambling habits?

The women proposed they could run the local cock-fighting ring cooperatively, so their husband's losses could be reincorporated into the community. With a bit more money staying locally, their children would not have to work, thus paving the way for education, once hunger was no longer an issue.

Reluctantly, the brave NGO agreed, financing the new cock-fighting ring, and trusting the wisdom of the community, against their own – or their donors' – best judgments from afar.

spawn creative arts programming for the park's marginalised youth, and eventually helped launch a greenhouse so locals could begin to grow their own food together... A serious case of 'mission drift' by traditional organisational standards!

While some level of planning is clearly a part of everything we do, our organisations have made a religion of it. And the Taylorist assumptions of 'One Best Way' predictability, expertise and specialisation have become hallmarks of the new faith, dismissing and undermining the old fundamentals of intuition, presence and responsiveness (all with their flaws, but also with profound benefits not found in many organisations today).

Henry Mintzberg has written extensively about the pitfalls of our organisational planning efforts. His book *The Rise and Fall of Strategic Planning*, published in 1994, is considered by many the gold standard for pulling the rug out from under a process that is still at the core of most organisational practices.

'Strategies are not tablets conceived atop mountains, to be carried down for execution;' Mintzberg wrote in 1987:

> They are learned on the ground by anyone who has the experience and capacity to see the general beyond the specifics. Remaining in the stratosphere of the conceptual is no better than having one's feet firmly planted in concrete.

> Add all this up and it appears that managers may be most effective as strategists by letting a thousand strategic flowers bloom in their organizational gardens, rather than trying to raise their strategies in a hothouse.[iv]

While clearly honed for a more corporate audience than *Walk Out Walk On*, Mintzberg was advocating the essence of *start anywhere, follow it everywhere*, more than twenty-five years ago.

Technologist and NYU professor Clay Shirky (@cshirky) followed this train of thought in his 2010 book, *Cognitive Surplus*, arguing, 'Anyone creating a new opportunity for social action has to understand the limits of planning.' He goes on, 'As a general rule, it is more important to try something new, and work on the problems as they arise, than to figure out a way to do something new without having any problems.'[v] Further, if we want to take advantage of the massive untapped potential of our shared 'cognitive surplus,' we need not just one, but a lot of 'new somethings' and 'the only group that can try everything is everybody.'[vi]

Shirky's approach was embodied during the people's uprising in Oaxaca in 2006 (described in Chapter 6). Of the 250 local barricades erected to keep paramilitaries from entering the city, many didn't follow the decisions set out by the APPO – the movement's primary organising body – if they didn't feel the decision made sense for their neighbourhood. 'We eventually started discussing agreements and decisions made by the APPO Council and the teachers' union,' wrote one activist of his experience with the barricades. 'There were a number of occasions when the barricade chose actions that were against those agreements, which in my view, only strengthened our capacity for organized resistance.'[vii]

Another activist, reflecting on the autonomy on the barricades, saw this divergence as a fundamentally different approach to change:

> The diversity of cultures on this globe will make our struggles look different. We have to learn from all the different paths towards transformation, but if we try to come to some agreement, I don't think we'll ever be successful. Each of us has to do what we can in our communities. That's how broad transformation will take place.[viii]

Activist Yeyo Beltran's (@yeyoenoax) perspective on the primary organising shift that took place in Oaxaca in 2006 related to a practical acceptance of diversity, the idea that good ideas could come from a range of places, and that one didn't have to trump another, even if they might seem ideologically or practically incompatible.

Indigenous traditions in one place could sit alongside more modern and formalised processes in another place. The APPO could come to a decision, and several of the individual barricades would decide to put that decision into practice, while others could ignore it, or opt for something completely different. Different people and groups could 'start anywhere, and follow it everywhere,' while still contributing to a broader movement, simply by aligning themselves with the same overall mission.

The organisational argument for unity is intended to avoid the 'divide-and-conquer' strategies used by those being challenged. However, if we each have the freedom to challenge a policy or politician in whatever ways make sense to each of us, no single counter-strategy can break the movement. Our disproportionate focus on 'unity' may well be where many organisations have set themselves up for defeat. Relying on agreement in many situations makes us sitting ducks, easily tripped up by a single counter-strategy.

Discussions in which everyone has a chance to be heard are always an important piece of movement building, but we should not assume the need to agree on everything. (See Chapter 6 for more on when you might opt for consensus-based decision-making processes).

'Scaling across' with the Occupy movement

A close cousin of our faith in the wisdom of strategic planning, is the belief that good ideas can be infinitely 'scaled-up.' But thinking we can copy-and-paste a good idea from one place to another, ignores the same principles that regularly doom our efforts to create useful strategies, namely, the importance of contexts and relationships. Whether it's a programme that succeeded in curbing youth violence in one neighbourhood, or a way of reducing the spread of AIDS in a particular country, we are constantly searching for 'best practices' that can then be applied to countless other locations, like a formula, expecting the same results.

But because context and relationships are always emerging, taking a model that works in one place and imposing it elsewhere will only work through some combination of chance and disruption. Yet we keep trying, telling ourselves that if we can just find each of the silver bullets for each of our compartmentally understood social problems, we can apply them to the rest of the world and no one will ever have to worry about them again, like a disease for which a vaccine has been found.

Sadly, we have yet to find even one such silver bullet (or 'One Best Way'), but continue 'scaling up,' convinced that doing so is the only way to affect change across a broader system. However, there are more grassroots ways in which good ideas can be shared, person-to-person and community-to-community, rather than via an imposed formula, applied by those lacking the local experience to know which pieces of the previously successful approach to take, and which to ignore. Margaret Wheatley and Deborah Frieze describe this process as 'scaling across,' putting it at the heart of a broader approach called 'trans-localism.'

> Suppose that the kind of large-scale systems change that many of us have been yearning for emerges when local actions get connected globally –while preserving their deeply local culture, flavor, and form.[ix]

Trans-localism argues that in our increasingly interconnected world, a relevant idea that is given the freedom to spread independently will grow stronger and more resilient, adapting to its local surroundings better than any pre-planned, top-down intervention.

In January 2012 I found myself wandering around the modest 'Occupy Wellington' encampment in New Zealand's capital city. A half-dozen or so camping tents, a 'living room' space with chairs and a couch, and an enclosed kitchen, provided facades for an extensive display of political slogans and artwork. Homemade 'The people are too big to fail,' 'Lost my job, found an occupation,' and of course, 'We are the 99%' posters, grounded this tiny camp in a global movement of millions. The strength of this particular action was clearly more than its numbers of participants might have suggested.

Having spent a fair bit of time kicking around London's various Occupy experiments in the preceding months, I was keen to see what the slogan had become here, so many thousands of miles away.

I was quickly welcomed by the campers when it became clear I wasn't simply gawking at this unexpected use of public space. I met a man there named Trevor, who made me a cup of tea and invited me to sit down for a chat.

Trevor was not a seasoned activist, though had devoted much of his life in the recent months to keeping the Occupy vision, as he perceived it, alive in Wellington. He had taken on a security role, to ensure the camp —while very much open to homeless Wellingtonians – wouldn't simply become an ill-equipped crash pad for those struggling with addictions.

Recently out of prison, with a missing eye and a face that told the kind of story most of us hope we'll never have to experience, Trevor explained to me a proposal he was making to the City Council the following week.

His idea? Teach homeless people how to snorkel.

I probably chuckled a bit when he first said it, but managed to bottle my initial response and ask him to tell me more.

His reasoning? Wellington harbour is full of seafood. Snorkelling would provide a means for the city's most marginalised to feed themselves for free, rather than going hungry. But knowing enough about the world of homelessness, he knew food was only a stepping stone to addressing a wider range of problems. The classes would include a cooking component – how to prepare your catch – offering both practical, employable skills, as well as a chance to build up the participants' social support bases by spending constructive time together.

While I'm not an expert in either homelessness or fishing, I saw that Trevor brought a certain experiential understanding of both to the table, and was doing his best to share that understanding with others.

I'm not qualified to weigh the merits of his idea, but it certainly captured the kind of divergent thinking that is needed, when so many organisations tend to start by dissecting new ideas from the conservative perspective of 'what will go wrong?' rather than 'how can we make this work?'

(A simple organisational tool for addressing this, when a colleague presents a new idea in a meeting, is to encourage everyone present to start by trying to improve the idea, rather than simply highlighting its potential flaws. I've heard this called 'yes/and' over 'no/but.' It is about contributing more constructively to seeing if an idea *could* work, rather than proving why it *might not*.)

It is possible that Trevor's idea *might* have worked in Wellington. I wasn't about to take it back to London and start encouraging homeless people to eat eels out of the Thames, but with so many other Occupy camps, there would inevitably have been other port or coastal cities that might have learned something from Trevor's thinking. This is not to say these other Occupy camps would each take a blueprint, and apply the same steps themselves, but that through a more organic, peer-to-peer sharing process, they might have found a core of an idea that they felt inspired to make their own.

Just as many of the tools discovered or adopted by the Zuccotti Park encampment in New York have since found their ways to camps around the world, those other camps have also offered-up their own learning and innovations and let them spread through the online and offline word-of-mouth channels that connect one Occupy camp to another.

A plethora of knowledge and ideas can be found on *interoccupy. net*, as well as a range of Twitter hashtags (#OWS, #Occupy, #O15, #GlobalNoise and others) and individual accounts of different encampments or spin-off projects (which include Occupy Debt, Occupy Our Homes, Occupy the Marines, and Occupy the Economy, to name but a few). None of these resources are ever imposed on other camps, but anyone from any camp that comes across, say, a better way of providing electricity, based on someone else's bike-powered systems, can propose it to their own General Assembly, and members can decide together if they'd like to adopt or adapt such an idea together.

Occupy is far from the only example of 'scaling' across, though may be the biggest experiment to date. It also parallels the open sharing and adaptation at the core of the free software communities described in Chapter 5, which created much of the technical backbone for the Occupy movement.

Scaling across cannot guarantee the uniformity of outcome that most of our organisations futility pursue, but if we give it the space, we might find the important stuff finds its way to where it needs to be.

Getting over organisational fortune-telling

Imagine the fluorescent lights fully dimmed, as flickering candles cast ominous shadows across the boardroom's high-back orthopaedic chairs. Incense smoke clouds the light beaming from the overhead projector announcing next year's budget predictions, while a crystal ball sits before your Chief Executive Officer, perched mightily at the end of the long, daunting table.

'I'm seeing something!' he suddenly proclaims. Everyone leans in a little closer, keen to find out which jobs will survive the impending budget cuts, and whose programmes will be deemed part of the strategic vision that is just coming into focus.

A scribe sits by the guru's side, eager to minute the predictive insights that the crowd of directors has gathered there to witness.

Then, in a rapid-fire succession, the pronouncements are made. Everyone is free to leave, safe in the security of knowing all that will befall their organisation in the next five years. A document is produced laying out the steps for all others to follow, illustrating a clear path between 'a challenging now' and 'a successful five-years-later.'

Now take a step back, remove the crystal ball, incense and candles, and ask yourself how often, in your experience, that planning document, whatever the ritual that creates it, has lived up to its promise? Or how often the parallel processes of rolling out a good local idea to countless other locations, inhabited by different people, in different situations, end up looking anything like the results in the place the idea emerged from? The two-word suggestion coming out of this chapter in relation to how we plan what we do is simple: 'pay attention.'

'more like people' planning

Humanity: Top-down planning processes reduce people to numbers, stripping away individual nuances. If we acknowledge each other's humanity, we come to understand the bigger picture much better than if we imagined everyone involved as cogs in a machine, with particular, fixed roles to play.

Autonomy: People give their best when they can set their own direction. If we tell them what to do, we will only impede their sense of purpose. We should always make sure our work feels like 'options,' not 'impositions.'

Complexity: There is always more going on than we can see. If we plan based on what we know, we will make it harder to see what we don't. Alternatively, if we clarify our purpose and act with both feet firmly rooted in our immediate realities, we can respond and adapt to the inevitable changes in the world that we are trying to affect.

Complexity is antithetical both to strategic planning, and to attempts to scale an idea beyond its place of birth. Context and relationships are everything, and thus approaches that don't keep both factors at their core and aren't able to change, as context and relationships do, are unlikely to create anything like their intended results.

'Paying attention' is about recognising the humanity of all the people involved in a project, inside or outside the organisation. Strategy, scaling-up and other top-down planning approaches, tend to turn people into numbers, and contexts into the limited traits any large group of people have in common, dismissing anything else that they might have to offer.

So by focusing on the now and addressing the realities of those involved, as they come up, we can help to reconnect the humanity principle with our planning processes. As long as we are clear on the purpose of our work, we can be freer with the practicalities of it. Autonomy means avoiding the outside imposition of structures or methods, putting a range of options on the table, and letting people find what works for them, when it works for them.

Grassroots activism succeeds when people with an individual sense of purpose are free to connect with other people and activities that align with that purpose, on their own terms. If we try to take away the autonomy of committed individuals by telling them the steps they should take, or imposing a model that worked somewhere else on them, we are confining them to what we've decided they can or should be doing, limiting their (and our) potential in the process.

If you are still committed to the notion of 'strategy,' perhaps you could manifest it as an on-going process of collective, short-term decisions, grounded in some general principles that all involved have been a part of developing and are keen to get behind?

If you are still committed to the notion of taking a good idea and scaling it up, perhaps that good idea should simply be made available to others (maybe making it 'open source,' sharing stories and principles publically?), so others can take it and make it what they will, without any obligation to follow the steps taken by others before?

While I realise that a lot of this chapter has been fairly abstract, I hope it has helped to paint a picture of how change often happens, in spite of the plans we make for it.

Should you be looking for the potted version, I'll conclude with a tweetable (140 character or less) summary:

Stay flexible, don't expect to end up where you think you will, and respect context and relationships. #morelikepeople

[i] Sarah Jaffe, 'Occupy's afterlife — a dispatch from New York's dark zones,' Jacobin Magazine, 3 November 2012. http://jacobinmag.com/2012/11/power-to-the-people/

[ii] Margaret Wheatley and Deborah Frieze, *Walk Out Walk On*, Berrett-Koehler, 2011, p. 84.

[iii] Margaret Wheatley and Deborah Frieze, *Walk Out Walk On*, Berrett-Koehler, 2011, p. 85.

[iv] Henry Mintzberg, 'Crafting Strategy,' in *Management? It's not what you think!* Prentice Hall, 2010, p. 110.

[v] Clay Shirky, *Cognitive Surplus*, Penguin, 2010, p. 204, 205.

[vi] Ibid. p. 207.

[vii] Diane Denham, ed. "David," in *Teaching Rebellion*, PM Press, 2007, p. 291.

[viii] Diane Denham, ed. "Adan," in *Teaching Rebellion*, PM Press, 2007, p. 325.

[ix] Margaret Wheatley and Deborah Frieze, *Walk Out Walk On*, Berrett-Koehler, 2011, p. 28.

Accountability: From 'compliance' to 'trust'

9

'Not everything that counts can be counted, and not everything that can be counted counts.' – William Bruce Cameron

'If it can be measured, it can be managed.' – Unknown Taylorist

Any professional will tell you the importance of accountability, but often what they actually mean by accountability is a much more hierarchical and coercive notion: compliance. How many of those same professionals will argue for the importance of trust, which is actually the core of a more effective and meaningful form of accountability?

Compliance is usually enforced through an obsessive use of number and check box-based systems, grown from a deep mistrust of what people have done and are meant to be doing, whether as staff or as grant recipients. Trust, on the other hand, fosters a kind of accountability that can't be 'gamed' through clever fiddling. As we allow and encourage people to connect with each other beyond the rigid parameters of their job titles and departments, we may find they develop stronger relationships that don't require any of the mistrusting, time-consuming systems of compliance on which we've long built up our organisational illusions of accountability.

Accountability and compliance

A few years ago, Paul Barasi, Veena Vasista and I wrangled a meeting with a national director of a large funding body. The three of us wanted to talk with them about developing funding systems that encouraged more equal relationships between funders and funded groups, opening up opportunities for learning and innovation in the process.

The director nodded along to our presentation, even occasionally finishing our sentences for us; he was clearly well versed in the pitfalls of the current system, having been a part of it for many years. But when it came to discussing alternatives – how we could develop more trust-based systems, reliant not on outside imposition to do the right thing, but on the intrinsic motivation that characterises strong relationships – things went cold.

There was a clear acknowledgement that the current system was filled to the gills with problems, but still a belief that that system was also, somehow, critical to maintaining accountability. Or at least the appearance of it.

This is one the first obstacles that comes up with organisations and funders any time I begin to discuss 'more like people' ideas: the ever-important question of 'accountability' – whether between funders and funded groups, staff and managers, or organisations and the people they serve.

Every group needs accountability, though I reckon we wouldn't have such negative associations with the concept if it weren't used so frequently to describe manipulative, top-down compliance measures, rather than relationships rooted in trust.

Compliance = accountability without responsibility, via control.

Trust = accountability with responsibility, via autonomy.

Compliance is *one approach* to accountability; it is typically imposed through targets, outputs, checkboxes and other requirements imposed by one group on another. It enshrines an unequal relationship in its very DNA. It is the practical essence of Douglas McGregor's description of a 'Type X' view of humanity, where a small number of 'good guys' spend much of their time and energy policing the much larger number of 'bad guys,' assuming it is the only way to get anything accomplished, but inadvertently spawning the very kinds of negative behaviours they wanted to avoid. As many others, including Clay Shirky, have explored, *when we create systems that assume mistrust, we are more likely to provoke it than if we start from the assumption of trust and address the challenges as needed.*

Accountability is a much broader concept than compliance. It doesn't have to be a means of reinforcing existing power dynamics. It can instead mean fostering a mutual sense of responsibility among people with shared interests. Compliance is an attempt to subvert the most critical component of accountability: responsibility. Through control systems, we offer ourselves the illusion of accountability, some truly believing that all the requisite paperwork is really a sign of people doing what they're supposed to, others more cynically knowing that as long as the right boxes are ticked, their heads won't be next on the chopping block.

The book *Getting to Maybe: How the world is changed* summarises the costs and realities of compliance-focused accountability, contrasting the typical funder's emphasis on learning and innovation with an underlying demand to produce results. 'This tension ... is seldom recognised, much less openly discussed. *Accountability messages trump learning messages every time.* As sure as night follows day, this attitude leads those who receive funds to exaggerate results and hide failures.'[i]

On the other hand, there is the kind of accountability that exists amongst friends, family, communities, and even large social movements. This is the unspoken accountability that emerges from equal relationships, which says 'I am going to do the best I can, because I don't want to let down others I respect and believe in.'

This accountability is enforced by each individual, on themselves, while their commitment encourages it in others.

When our systems impose compliance measures, they encourage a flight from trust, and ultimately from responsibility: people gaming them to get what they need, with no sense of accountability to those making the impositions. Sometimes this is malicious, more often it is practical. Like so many of the 'more like machines' systems of the Old World, their assumptions of mistrust and dishonesty tend to breed it where it wouldn't otherwise be found. And these systems run deep in our organisations, inside and outside their walls.

We can't have true accountability without responsibility, but responsibility can't be imposed through compliance. A different approach is desperately required; the impacts of the old ways are all around us, should we choose to see them for what they are.

The Accountability Spectrum

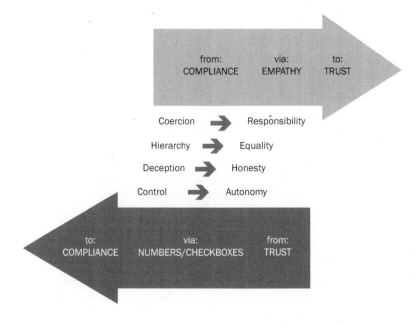

Teaching social workers to miss the forest for the trees

Children's social services in England, like those of many other countries, don't always have a sparkling public reputation when it comes to face-to-face relations. Like police, social workers who tackle state-mandated child protection cases spend their days witnessing and intervening in many of society's darkest moments. From paedophilia to domestic violence, a social worker often observes the worst of what human beings are capable of in a typical working day. It takes a special kind of person to avoid becoming jaded by a constant barrage of such experiences.

Combine those experiences with cumulative decades of government policies legislating ever-more-extensive reporting requirements in the name of 'greater accountability,' to the point where frontline staff are expected to spend, on average, 60 percent of their working week filling out paperwork.[ii] For instance, when a child on your caseload goes missing, you may not be able to escalate the investigation until you have received proper sign-off on a range of time-consuming process documents. Without these documents, you, personally, could be found liable for whatever becomes of the missing kid. Sometimes these processes are hardwired into computer systems and cannot be easily overridden, meaning that reporting undermines the ability to, say, involve the appropriate specialist, or a parallel agency, on short notice, in the critical moments when a child's safety is at risk.

Indeed, the professional accountability systems of child protection agencies in the UK (and elsewhere) often *undermine* the work of those who are meant to be ensuring child protection.

As we've discussed before, when a Taylorist sees a problem, they aim to fix the part they perceive to be 'broken' – in these cases, the 'parts' are the individual workers, and the 'fix' is more complicated compliance measures for each of them to complete.

Conversely, when someone who understands complex systems sees that something is not working as intended, they will aim to shift the relationship dynamics, rather than the people themselves. In practice, this might mean starting to better understand the relationship dynamics among individual social workers; among social workers and senior practitioners, doctors, lawyers, probation officers, etc.

From there, working to improve these relationships becomes key, but doing so inevitably involves acknowledging that power and hierarchy distort the sharing and flow of information. In the investigations that have followed several high-profile child welfare scandals, poor relationships among professionals have been identified as a central factor in the gaps that appeared, yet have remained largely unaddressed, as the application of their conclusions would challenge the underpinning mythology of compliance-based accountability.

Creating 'failure modes'

As the number of oversight policies grows, they often start to work against their stated aims, running afoul of one another as they cross paths in the real world in ways their architects hadn't planned for. The social worker, so preoccupied with the paperwork their job requires of them, misses a more obvious problem in a child's home because their attention was absorbed by their clipboard, or the stresses of another case for which they haven't been able to receive the necessary support. These are the kinds of policies that gradually produce an inability to see the forest for the trees; the 'abuse' from the 'three-page list of signs of abuse.'

An engineer would describe these policies as new 'failure modes': solutions to particular problems that unexpectedly create new problems in their wake. But engineering isn't the only place where proposed solutions have unintended consequences. For example, a classic 'failure mode' in urban planning might emerge when a traffic light is installed at a local intersection following a car accident there. Seems sensible, right? Then at another intersection a few blocks away, another is installed following a separate accident. And then again, in the same vicinity, after a third tragic crash...

Eventually, the lights are so numerous, that frustrated motorists and pedestrians either start running reds or jaywalking out of frustration at their inability to get around, or stop paying as much attention because the traffic lights have let them absolve their sense of personal responsibility for road safety. In both cases, the result is the same: accidents once again begin to rise.

Alternatively, Bohmte, Germany, and Drachten, Holland, removed *all* traffic regulation, forcing motorists to pay closer attention to what they are doing behind the wheel. This system is called 'Shared Space' and was envisaged by the late Dutch traffic specialist Hans Monderman. The European Union has since part-funded its continued implementation around the continent, as it has proven so successful in reducing accidents *and* improving traffic flow in several sizable cities.[iii] When everyone is paying attention and knows they are responsible to each other for their choices on the road or sidewalk, everyone benefits. This is trust-based, mutual accountability in action.

Numbers as replacement for trust

No method of compliance can effectively replace the kind of accountability that mutual trust provides in a relationship. The work created in attempts to do so is immense. Numbers have traditionally been seen as a substitute for trust, providing a way of measuring whether someone has done what they said they would. Or so we tell ourselves.

Too often we see numbers as an end point – the holy grail of research, evaluation, analysis, planning – rather than a step along the journey towards better understanding. But, as Margaret Wheatley says so unequivocally, 'nothing alive, in all its rich complexity, can be understood using only numbers. Nothing.'[iv]

When numbers become the end game, the pressure to manipulate their journey, fiddling, adjusting and otherwise reconfiguring them is immense. This is the essence of Goodhart's Law, named for Charles Goodhart, a former director of the Bank of England. Goodhart's Law declares that if numbers are used to control people (as with any numeric report requirements, as well as bonuses or penalties based on achieving or avoiding certain figures or numeric standards), they will not create the intended results. They may even undermine them.

Evaluating our work, without undermining it in the process

Program evaluation consultant Michael Quinn Patton has gone some way to addressing some of the accountability challenges that have dogged the non-profit sector; namely that fixed, linear, cause-and-effect processes are ill equipped to map how change happens in the real world. The 'developmental evaluation' method that he has pioneered is 'an approach to evaluation especially appropriate for situations of high uncertainty where what may and does emerge is relatively unpredictable and uncontrollable.'[v]

Its primary practical difference from most traditional evaluation methods is in the scrapping of what we would think of as the baseline – acknowledging that judging the present by the standards of a narrowly defined past will inevitably limit our understandings of what has actually taken place. When we ask – or more often *require* – this of others, it is no surprise that we don't end up with the quality of information we had hoped for. It simply wouldn't fit the frame we had offered to explain the project or campaign.

Instead, Patton talks about 'situation recognition' and creating a 'baseline' from what people recognise as their context at the start, the end, and at various stages throughout the project, gradually observing the differences between situations, based on understanding how the patterns at play may have changed, rather than predetermined outputs or outcomes.

Developmental evaluation is an iterative process, embedded in the first stages of planning, and continuing throughout the entire project or campaign. It does not simply look back at the end and ask 'did this work?,' it perpetually asks 'is this working?' and when it isn't, makes adjustments to both the project plan and the evaluation and project designs. This 'double-loop learning' approach doesn't simply respond to problems and correct them (single-loop learning), but looks at the sources of the problem and changes the system along the way. For example, a thermostat offers single-loop learning, adjusting the temperature when it gets too hot or cold; a double-loop system also addresses the insulation or ventilation in the building. Similarly, the Shared Spaces traffic system doesn't simply put up new stop signs to address dangerous intersections; it seeks to completely change the dynamics that lead to road accidents.

Addressing complexity in our evaluations requires more trust than we tend to offer, whether as funders, organisations, or managers. It requires the kinds of first-hand, real-time, on-the-ground updates that our traditional systems don't often notice. It recognises that a subtle observation by an outreach worker in a homeless shelter may be far more valuable and timely in understanding what has gone wrong with a service than an entire box of intake forms, questionnaires, or monitoring data. Rather than trying to establish proof, developmental evaluation trusts the observations of many participants along the way, adjusting as it goes based on real-time feedback.

While Patton describes a range of specific conditions in which developmental evaluation is most appropriate, many of its principles can apply not only to a wider range of evaluations, but to a wider range of accountability questions, from how staff supervisions and appraisals are handled, to how organisations work in partnership with one another.

Banking on trust

Can we imagine a banking system founded on trust rather than compliance? The idea may seem far-fetched, but in fact, the celebrated Grameen Bank, the 'bank of the poor,' founded in Bangladesh by Nobel Prize winner Muhammad Yunus, has achieved just that, and boasts a repayment rate on its microloans of nearly 97 percent – and trust-based relationships are a key reason why.

Grameen began by offering low-interest 'microloans' to groups of craftswomen in rural Bangladesh. The bank's approach has helped millions of women to break the poverty cycle perpetuated by loan sharks who kept women borrowing at rates that would never allow them to earn more than a daily subsistence for their work. While the Grameen approach has been adopted all over the world since its founding in 1983, very few of its spin-offs have taken to heart one of its most critical elements: the trust among the women who come together in small groups to receive loans from the bank, and the trust the bank offers these groups of women to be accountable with their loans. As Paul Sinclair writes:

> There is no legal instrument between the lender and the borrower. Grameen considers its relationship to be with people, not with papers. They build up a human relationship based on trust. Grameen succeeds or fails depending on how strong their personal relationship is with the borrowers.
>
> Their experience with bad debt is just 3.47%. Even then Grameen does not conclude that a defaulting borrower is a bad person. Rather that their personal circumstances were so hard that they could not pay back their tiny loan. Bad loans of 3.47% is seen by Grameen as the cost of doing business and it also represents to them a constant reminder that they need to improve in order to succeed.[vi]

The key lesson here? When we give trust, we get trust back. Not every time, but in most situations, most of the time.

The Grameen approach doesn't need contracts — it has something far more effective (and cheaper to manage!) to make sure its loans are doing what they are meant to be doing.

When we take the same assumption from the granting of the loan, and apply it to the reporting process, we don't need all the monitoring forms we once did, either.

When we ask for numbers — whether from staff, or funded groups, or those we support — we undermine their judgments. If we give them the chance, without the pressure to produce figures (not stopping them if they feel numbers *do* help to tell their story), we may find that we have encouraged a more honest understanding of the issues.

This approach shifts the power dynamics by offering trust; giving them the chance to provide a narrative that makes sense within people's experience, rather than the frameworks we have created for our own convenience or preference. Those who are trusted are more likely to be trust-worthy. When people you fund, research, employ, support or evaluate are trust-worthy, you're more likely to hear the important stuff from them, rather than a finely tuned propaganda piece, invariably filled with the kinds of selective numbers which succeed only in giving us the false impression of knowing what's going on.

Trust grows from the seeds of empathy

To rebuild accountability requires a sense of responsibility. When we are trusted, we feel more responsible for what we do, and in order to build trust, we need to share a sense of empathy with one another. When we can empathise with each other, we lay the foundations for trust. Thus, systems that create superficial distinctions between staff from different departments, or of different ranks, or between 'professionals' and 'non-professionals,' make it harder to find empathy and establish trust.

Think about how rarely in our traditional 'more like machines' workplaces, friendships cross over the divides of 'team' and 'rank,' compared to how often they remain isolated by one or both divisions?

The first key to supporting an empathic working environment is to provide the unstructured space for non-pragmatic relationships to emerge. Think back to Chapter 5's descriptions of 'The Tuttle Club' as a hub for innovation and new ideas. Just like the organisational pursuit of innovation, if we are serious about fostering the kinds of relationships that enable trust-based accountability, more often than not, we just need to get out of the way.

This is why the pub (cultural barriers discussed in Chapter 4 aside, for the moment) is so crucial – it lets people hang out on their own terms and connect with one another, beyond their titles and the assumptions those titles instil in others.

Unstructured spaces are also part of the significance of smoke breaks, where smokers are able to talk to each other without any objectives, and with a degree of candour that the office denies.

'more like people' accountability

Humanity: When we connect with one another, beyond our professional roles, we make space for empathy, which opens the possibility of trust, offering a stronger accountability than any compliance measure can ensure.

Autonomy: When accountability is discovered by each person involved, rather than imposed by some, on others, it allows each of us to find our own sense of responsibility, which compliance measures cannot instil in others.

Complexity: The complexity of the kinds of situations we face in our work mean that attribution is rarely a question of the simple cause-and-effect linearity that organisations judge themselves and each other on; it requires trust for those involved to make subjective judgments, based on their experiences and understandings of the situations they are experiencing.

And it is one of the strongest arguments for the use of social media in the workplace, offering a similarly unstructured setting for the kinds of interactions we crave, and which help us connect with each other as fellow human beings, rather than simply as colleagues with particular roles to play.

And social media does this without the culturally exclusionary effects of the pub, or the health impacts of either the pub or the cigarette break!

When these kinds of spaces open up – online or in person – they might need a bit of priming. People who are used to sitting at a desk for eight hours straight may not jump immediately at a looser, more flexible way of working. When you suggest a group of staff go to the park at 2pm on a sunny Wednesday afternoon, it is unlikely that those who most need the space will immediately embrace the opportunity. But as more people decide to take the freedom to create free spaces – within or beyond office hours – to get to know each other without a pre-set agenda, the bug often spreads.

These are the kinds of steps outlined in Chapter 7, from which an individual's actions can gradually come to affect broader culture change.

If we start to open the spaces for non-professional relationships to grow, we sow the seeds of empathy, which enables the possibility of trust and with it a very different, less bureaucratic and time-consuming way of maintaining accountability for what you do.

When Croydon Council cracked the 'Cult of Professionalism'

Sometimes though, the divisions run deep, and a slightly more focussed approach is needed.

In Croydon, officially the southernmost Borough of London, a forward-thinking local council Chief Executive broke long-established tradition in 2007, recognising the very real human consequences of what he called 'the cult of professionalism' on the Council's social services. By helping reconnect managers with the human experiences at the other end of their policies, Jon Rouse found the approach of those same managers changed significantly, as policy making became less of a bureaucratic, and more of an empathic, experience.

When I had a chance to ask him about the cult of professionalism, Jon Rouse described it as 'a tendency for professional institutes to use professional training to embed a set of norms, a way of doing things that makes it more difficult than it should be thereafter to inculcate cross-professional working and shared accountability to the service user.'[vii] More colloquially, the behaviours of the cult make it harder for people in professional roles to connect and communicate with one another, inside and outside of their organisations, creating a range of problems for those they work with. Accountability to the public is their most serious cost.

Rouse, unlike many of his counterparts in local government, was unwilling to concede that families who felt they had been torn apart by ill-conceived social service provision were simply an inevitable cost of his particular line of work. Rather than ordering a review of local children's services, or sacking a director and allowing the cult to continue its rituals, Rouse trusted a hunch and went straight to what he felt was the core of the issue: the professional environment that had been gradually built up over decades in the council had buried the sense of empathy of those at the top of the social services command chain.

Following this hunch, Rouse involved staff in a process called 'emotional moment mapping,' 'where you actually follow the customer's experience of using your services in terms of the emotions that are evoked by the experience.' The results helped to rekindle a largely dormant sense of empathy between senior staff and service users, highlighting the human experiences of those who were receiving a range of social services from the council.

Following the mapping exercise, Rouse arranged for several of his senior staff in the Council's social services department to see video testimonials from some of the local people who felt wronged by social services in the borough. Before doing so, he made clear to his colleagues: 'your role is not to defend the Council's actions, it is simply to listen and to hear. 'Specifically, Rouse recounts, 'this was not to make them feel bad about themselves or each other but as a motivation to improve the design of those services and therefore the future experience.'

When I asked why he hadn't encouraged face-to-face meetings, instead arranging private video viewings, he said, 'It needed to be a private experience in order to allow the staff members the freedom to have a natural emotional response.' When the sessions took place, several Council staff, often decades into their careers in local government, were profoundly affected. Some were brought to tears by the stories they heard. People hardened by years of the cool, professional disconnect that came from being told they were 'the experts' on child protection were deeply shaken by the experience. The human stories, unmediated by the broken telephone of hierarchical communication, cut through the usual justifications that had allowed them to maintain their distance from the frontlines.

Andrea Smith is a community organizer in Brooklyn, New York, working against the growing tide of professionalisation and its corresponding emotional disconnect between staff and service users of domestic violence organisations. 'While some boundaries are healthy,' Smith writes, 'the particular kind of distancing within anti-violence organizations is counterproductive to any goal of creating connection.' She goes on, 'Eliminating this difference increases the potential... to allow survivors to create the kind of relationship they want between themselves and the organization.'[viii]

While the work of a Council Chief Executive and a grassroots domestic violence activist in certain ways couldn't be more different, they have both seen the pitfalls of the emotional distance created by moves to professionalise their work on either side of the Atlantic. The disconnected professionalism that is increasingly taught in so many social work programs reduces the space for individual judgment, and stronger relationships, turning a role that traditionally relied on a range of highly developed interpersonal and subjective decision-making skills into an increasingly administrative function. And the increased distance of senior management from the issues has the tendency to reinforce the logic of this professional objectivity.

Shortly before his death (from non-traffic-related causes) in 2008, Hans Monderman, the inventor of the 'Shared Space' method of urban traffic regulation, opined that the reason for his approach's success was that it encouraged basic interaction between drivers, pedestrians, and cyclists.

Shared Space works, Monderman said, because it forced everyone 'to look each other in the eye, to judge body language and learn to take responsibility — to function as normal human beings.'[ix]

With his mapping exercise and his video testimonies, Rouse forced some of his staff into an uncomfortable place – 'unprofessional' as it was – but in doing so, did for his senior managers what Hans Monderman's traffic system has done for so many European urbanites. He helped them 'to function as normal human beings,' reigniting some of the empathy that years in the system had buried.

'In the next three to four months,' he observed, 'there was a definite loosening up of some of the professional boundaries,' Rouse told me. While admittedly, some of the old tendencies began to creep back into working habits, 'we were able... to use the window to start the process of change in our early intervention and family support services, and we now have a much improved service as a result.'

By helping a small group of senior staff to reconnect with a dormant sense of empathy, Rouse opened the doors to critical learning from previously ignored places. This kick-started a process that actively included the perspectives of those most affected in the development of social care and service policies across the borough, making those services more responsive to the people receiving them.

> *How can you connect – and help others connect – with the people who you support or advocate for and with?*

> *What are the barriers that get in the way of face-to-face contact and more meaningful interactions with those you support?*

Can you focus on making empathy a stronger part of your work? For instance, sharing a part of yourself with those you support, or putting yourself in their shoes when they tell you something that is personal to them?

We can't build trust without taking risks

To bring home the potential of trust-as-accountability, I want to tell you about a man named Paul Story.

I briefly met Paul in Edinburgh in the summer of 2009. Anyone familiar with Edinburgh will know that the sheer quantity of creative types that flood the city for its various overlapping festivals each August can make it hard to distinguish any particular actor, street performer, poet, or comedian from another. But Paul stuck out.

He's an author and former physicist; middle-aged with grey hair. He had setup shop in the city centre with a pop-up banner and a table, stacked high with copies of his new book, *Dreamwords*.

But he wasn't selling it; he was giving it away. He called it 'the Honesty Edition.' Paul's business model, after writing the book and maxing out his credit card to print ten thousand copies, was this:

- Go to public places
- Give out copies of the book to people who are interested in reading it
- Ask them to make a pledge:
    - 'If I like it, I will pay for it on the website'
    - 'If I don't like it, I will pass it along to someone who I think might.'

Paul experimented with a range of distribution channels, several involving tables at events or high-pedestrian traffic public places, but also simply placing books around town centres in Scotland, with flyers explaining the experiment.

Marketing experts had told him he could expect a maximum 3 percent return on this business model, but he still believed in a basic honesty amongst people that could make this seemingly crazy approach viable.

When I met him, it was early days still. I took a copy of his book, read it, enjoyed it, and sent him £8 through his website.

When I emailed him, two years later, he was coming to the end of the experiment, having distributed the full print run of the novel and just published the second instalment of the *Dreamwords* series.

When it was all said and done, over 800 people had done what I did and had chosen to pay Paul for his novel. This meant the printing costs were covered by peoples' voluntary payments. Paul was also left with an email list that would be considered solid gold by any marketer – over 800 contacts who clearly liked the first book in a three part series!

'Taking no account of genre, sex, age or even if an individual is really a reader, 8 percent of the public enjoyed the book enough to go out of their way to pay,' Paul wrote to me. 'When better targeted, that figure rose to 30 percent.'[x]

Should a future writing project manage to maintain anything like that targeted '30 percent' figure, Paul would be doing far better than most published authors, who themselves see 7.5 to 15 percent on a book's cover price (though obviously without shouldering the printing costs themselves).

Clearly Paul's time had not been accounted for, but his brave steps (or 'barmy' steps as they were described by *The Sun*) into the realms of a trust-based economy offer some important insights.

When we get bureaucratic accountability systems out of the way, we open up room for true accountability to emerge from a shared sense of responsibility and trust, grown from mutual empathy. Empathy is at the core of the humanity principle, having often been lost in the institutional assumptions of their respective opposites: coercion, compliance and professional distance.

Trust fosters autonomy; it encourages all of us to 'get on and do what we need to do.' No longer will we be compelled to 'game' the number-based systems that get in the way of our work.

And since complexity assures that we can't predict the future, trying to hold someone to account for not living up to the future results they've predicted is impossible, unfair, and a massive waste of our collective time.

So let's look elsewhere for accountability. We might start by asking ourselves when we've achieved our best, and see what kinds of requirements were made of us when we did. We might find, as with much of this book, that less is indeed more.

Chapter 9:
Accountability:
From
'compliance'
to 'trust'

[i] Frances Westley et al, *Getting to Maybe*, Vintage Canada, 2006, p. 182.

[ii] I dated a social worker for three years; this was the accepted rule-of-thumb presented during inductions.

[iii] Catherine Bosley, 'Town ditches traffic lights to cut accidents,' *Reuters*, 11 September 2007. http://www.reuters.com/article/2007/09/11/us-germany-traffic-odd-idUSGOR14512420070911

[iv] Margaret Wheatley, *So far from home*, Berrett-Koehler, 2012, p. 110.

[v] Ibid, p. 7.

[vi] Paul Sinclair, 'Grameen Micro-Credit & How to End Poverty from the Roots Up,' OneWorldOnePeople.org, 24 October 2011. http://www.oneworldonepeople.org/articles/World%20Poverty/Grameen.htm

[vii] Interview with the author, 19 July 2012.

[viii] Andrea Smith, quoted in Alisa Bierria, 'Pursuing a radical antiviolence agenda inside/outside a non-profit structure,' in *The Revolution Will Not Be Funded*, 2007, South End Press, p. 161.

[ix] Michael Brunton, 'Signal Failure,' *Time Magazine*, 30 January 2008. http://www.time.com/time/magazine/article/0,9171,1708116,00.html

[x] From an email from Paul Story; the more complete analysis can be found at http://www.dreamwords.com/honesty/

The time for change is now... and if you don't do it, we will!

"Once social change begins it cannot be reversed. You cannot un-educate the person who has learned to read. You cannot humiliate the person who feels pride. You cannot oppress the people who are not afraid anymore."
– Cesar Chavez

"People have decided not to wait for the revolution to start living differently."
– Manuel Castells

"Think of anarchism as an individual orientation to yourself and others, as a personal approach to life."
– CrimethInc. Ex-Workers Collective

10

Very few of the lessons in this book can be learned exclusively from reading. Most of the organisational changes described involve personal changes, and most meaningful personal changes require adaptation and practice. Many organisations, companies and governments have superficially embraced the transitions brought about by social media, but then reasserted their rigid hierarchies at the first signs of trouble. Sometimes they totally miss the point, at other times they just get cold feet in the face of unknown change.

The biggest stumbling block is often in becoming conscious of the need to align our values in a range of different parts of our lives. 'more like people' is not just a way of organising, but about working towards coherence of values in all realms of life, including politics, education, marriage, parenting, and many other interrelated areas. Work is just one possible starting point. Where we take it is up to us.

And while many of these ideas require significant personal reflection, via the web we also have the tremendous opportunity of being able to share those reflections with others who are taking similar journeys. It's up to all of us what this book can become; the Internet provides the space for an on-going sequel, for which these pages are only a starting point.

Fighting the claw-back instinct

When David Cameron's coalition government came to power in the UK in 2010, it went to great lengths to appear to be keeping up with the technological and social trends of the day. Digitally enabled consultations, 'listening exercises' and crowd-sourcing activities regularly asked the public to feed into everything from healthcare reforms, to public sector spending cuts, and foreign policy priorities.

Unfortunately, these initiatives proved more show than substance, used to promote and legitimise a pre-existing conservative agenda, with no real openness to taking direction from below. As the ultimate insult in the process, the government decision to slash the Education Maintenance Allowance (EMA), a move that triggered massive student protests in late 2010, was attributed to a crowd-sourcing activity, a move clearly at odds with a massive section of the population, even if someone outside government initially proposed it.

These were, it soon became clear, exercises in advancing the interests of a party, rather than a country, while giving the illusion of doing something more meaningful. If participation, openness, and democracy mean anything at all, they mean a willingness to listen to one's critics as well as one's supporters.

Anyone remotely familiar with the world of government won't be surprised to hear the Cameron consultations were stage managed and tightly controlled. 'Why would the government – conservative or liberal – implement a policy they disagreed with?,' I hear some of you muttering. This is symptomatic of our cynicism with government; we assume democracy will always be trumped by party politics. But this is not the assumption at the core of effective crowd-sourcing or online self-organisation; if people contribute, and are then ignored, they will become disillusioned. You don't get to violate this kind of trust too many times.

Institutions across all sectors have gone to great lengths to figure out how to use social media to their own advantage. Businesses ask their customers to help them design new products; government departments search for public sector innovation from the crowd; charities let their members vote on the next steps of a campaign.

But few take it to the point of listening to their critics or using this blurring of roles to enable more participatory governance and decision-making. In my more cynical moments I write off any 'crowd-sourcing' initiative I see coming from an Old World institution, but then remember the many people I've met, even in the most rigid of government departments, who are pushing hard to really make this stuff work the way it's meant to work.

The real challenge is this: the crowd doesn't always do what we want it to. When an organisation opens up, whether in the form of a staff consultation, or a collective planning or budgeting process, it will almost inevitably hear things that senior managers or the board don't want to hear. What separates a 'more like people' organisation, from a 'more like machines' organisation, is how it deals with the inevitable disagreements that arise from openness. Does it simply ignore the comments or suggestions that don't fit with its predetermined narrative, as the UK Government did? Or does it open up a further debate, putting the Board position forward, but not assuming it will necessarily prevail if it encounters widespread opposition? More pointedly, during such exercises, do those with traditional organisational authority actually concede and let others move forward with ideas that fly in the face of management preference?

Ricardo Semler has spoken a lot about the challenges of participatory democracy in the workplace, particularly for those still holding some semblance of traditional power. "Democracy is a lot of hard work, I kept telling myself and anyone who would listen," he wrote in 1992. "It needs to be exercised with conviction and without subterfuge or exception."[i]

When employees of Semler's company, Semco, voted to move into a factory that management was deeply wary of, the company still went ahead with the move. "We never considered overriding our workers' decision. Our credibility would have gone to hell,"[ii] Semler recounted years later.

There is nothing easy about letting go of control. For all I have written about it, it is still something I struggle with, in a range of settings – just ask Paul Barasi what it's like to get me to post his blog posts on our website! Most of what this book advocates involves exercises – individually and collectively – in letting go of control. While some of our organisations may be paying lip service to the democratic possibilities of social media, much like the UK Government has, I'm sure there are many more that enter into an experiment with the right intentions, but still reassert control at the first sign of trouble. This is a natural part of the process. We don't let go of habits collectively learned over many lifetimes after simply reading a book.

When we are used to taking a certain decision, we tend to be sure we know best, but when others, equally used to taking other decisions, don't involve us, we can be frustrated by the lack of opportunity to contribute. In other words, we see the shortcomings in the power of others, but it can be much harder to see it in ourselves.

Yet we must. Even when it doesn't seem to make sense to do so. In fact, *especially* when it doesn't seem to make sense to do so, as it is often our own judgments of 'what makes sense' that prevent change.

People will suggest things we can't possibly imagine happening as part of our organisation's work. The results may sometimes be poor ones, but a group of highly invested individuals may well surprise expert sensibilities. Only by assuming that we always have the right answers, can we be sure that we won't. As is hopefully obvious by now, no one does.

Opening things up *will* lead to mistakes, missteps, and misunderstandings – at times in terms of some of the results it creates, but more importantly, in terms of the times we don't actually share whatever power we have to share. When this happens, don't beat yourself up over it and don't give up at the first hurdle. Apologise. Correct it if you can. Be humble. Ask how you can make amends. Think about what you might do differently next time. If you're struggling, go on vacation for a while and leave others the free rein to make collective decisions in your absence. If necessary, physically remove yourself from exercising the controlling urge to get in the way of democracy.

It will always be a work in progress, but feel free to start where you feel comfortable, and expand from there. Ricardo Semler entered the world of participatory workplace democracy by letting workers pick their uniforms and shop floor paint colours, before gradually working up to the most fundamental decisions of how the business was run. Even many of the most 'more like people' examples throughout this book progressed through stages, as people throughout the groups or organisations became more comfortable with a more equal share of power, whatever roles they had played before.

Embracing our own autonomy can initially feel as challenging for some as not getting in the way of it can feel for others. But these are interconnected steps we can learn to take together. As we become more open about the challenges we face, whichever side of the coin we find ourselves on, we can support each other to take on more equal freedoms in the work we do together. We are not alone in defining our changing roles.

'more like people' beyond the office

I recently watched *The Iron Lady*, the cinematic portrayal of the life and times of former British Prime Minister Margaret Thatcher. What struck me most was the film's depiction of Thatcher's underlying character, honed and crafted to fit the political culture she ploughed her way into. If the portrayal is an honest one, Thatcher came to embody a way of being that challenged 'more like people' in every part of her life. As a politician, she was ruthless – unconcerned by the consequences of her top-level decisions on the people of the country she ruled. As a manager of a government, she was rigid, dictatorial and condescending to those who worked with her. As a wife and mother she was distant and dismissive to even her closest of kin.

Carried through these roles was a disinterest in – verging on repulsion from – 'feeling.' She presented a calloused intellectualism that suppressed any upwelling of tenderness, while actively ridiculing any perceived weakness in others.

In one notable scene, while teaching her teenage daughter to drive, Thatcher states, "the only thing you should remember is that everyone else is either reckless or inept," perfectly capturing the 'Type X' view of humanity described in Chapter 1. Thatcher voiced the dominant institutional belief about human nature with an honesty that few since Frederick Winslow Taylor have captured so succinctly.

Just as her ways of managing her Cabinet represented the organising tide this book is swimming against, so too were her approaches in both her family life, and her broader political persuasion, antithetical to 'more like people' at the micro and macro scales.

But just as Thatcher embodied the full breadth of opposition to the ideas of this book, 'more like people' is not simply a way of looking at management; it is a way of being, as the stories that have filled these pages have hopefully shown.

As Paul Barasi Tweeted during our first 'more like people action week': *"Work becomes more human -> then so do communities -> leaders -> world."*

While abridged and linearised for the medium, his point is crucial: every group of people, from families to societies, organise around particular principles, and the same principles that create fearful, abusive households, also create rigid, hierarchical 'Type X' organisations, assembly-line classroom settings, and even tyrannical governments. Our patterns in one set of relationships influence, and are influenced by, our patterns in other sets of relationships. This goes someway to explaining why police officers and soldiers – two professions generally built on top-down control and coercion – have among the highest rates of domestic violence of any profession.[iii] As one report on police-inflicted domestic violence described, "being the wife or girlfriend of a police officer means abiding by that culture's rules: What happens in the family stays in the family, and what happens in the police family stays in the police family,"[iv] highlighting the ways these seemingly separate spaces perpetuate each other's violent and secretive cultures.

Our Taylorist worldviews have allowed us to pretend that the divisions we have created between parts of our human and natural systems are far more real or permanent than they actually are. But our workplaces and our schools, our families and our communities, and our local and global ecosystems are all deeply interconnected. This is why 'the butterfly effect' described in Chapter 7 has the potential to bring about changes far more wide-ranging than shifting one workplace culture or another. We can't control outcomes, but we can continue to take the kinds of actions that we'd like to see spread like wildfire. This is why, as Gandhi said, we must 'be the change we want to see in the world.' The workplace is one part of a much broader system, which is influenced by and influences its many interdependent parts – from the families of those who work there, to the countries they operate in, and the ecosystems they are a part of. The consequences of what we do in one part of a broader system aren't necessarily confined to the walls we have erected around it.

Chapter 10:
The time for
change is
now... and if
you don't do
it, we will!

Understanding the complex relationships among seemingly separate systems can help us to be a part of a more positive kind of system change. You can help to change a broader system by reimagining your own contributions to it, whether at an office, or in your family, school, or neighbourhood. The basic process goes something like this:

- Find a core value that you believe in – let's say, 'trust.'
- Think about what it means for your actions, at every level – for example, how you treat neighbours, colleagues, children, strangers.
- Figure out where your current actions are out-of-line with that value – do you cross the street when you see someone in a hoodie walking in your direction? Do you insist on vetting everything your assistant writes? Do you assume a homeless person asking you for change will spend it on something you wouldn't approve of?
- Adjust accordingly.
- Keep adjusting when you inevitably fall back into old patterns.
- Adjust again. It gradually gets easier.

My friend Veena Vasista describes this process as "translating causes into ways of being."[v]

Change what you can!

It is easy to get stuck in the 'I'm only one person' trap, particularly when you start to think on a scale beyond a few people. If thinking of your influence beyond a few people feels too daunting, don't! Focus on the level of you and your relationships. You might start to see changes happening at that level and want to think beyond, but manifesting 'more like people' at the most personal level may still have wider ripples, regardless of if you consciously act beyond your immediate sphere of influence. At the very least, you've likely made your life and those of the people immediately around you a bit better in the process, which is definitely an improvement on not having done so.

At a more practical level, many of the changes advocated throughout this book can be adapted to a range of other settings.

- What would consensus decision-making mean in a family? Or a Cabinet meeting?
- What would the 'remix culture' of hip-hop – repurposing old things for unintended new uses – mean in a classroom? Or at the United Nations?
- What would 'scaling across' – the natural sharing and adaptation of good ideas, among practitioners, without external imposition – mean for healthcare provision? Or for parenting?

I have no idea what the answers might be, but you're welcome to experiment with them and see if you can figure some out!

Beyond pure profit: If we change *how* we organise, we change *what* we organise

We can also think about the broader significance of the 'more like people' principles in the practical terms of all of us connecting more deeply with the whole of our work:

- How many Lockheed Martin machinists would keep going to work each day, if they were also a part of the teams who had to clean up the bodies their bombs had helped to explode?

- How many Shell execs would continue extracting tar sands oil, if it was their family members developing rare cancers linked to the industry, or their own drinking water being poisoned?
- Or how many *Susan G. Komen Race for the Cure* staff would stick around if they saw the money that was being taken from cancer research and support by millions of dollars in annual legal fees spent suing smaller organisations for using the phrase 'for the cure' or the colour pink in their promotional materials?[vi]

I believe that if people at each of these work places – from the coalface to the executive suite – were in more direct contact with the broader implications of their work, very few would continue doing what they do for a living. If enough employees start seeing the whole of their work, it may be enough to push the companies to ask the deep questions that don't seem to get asked as long as stock prices remain high, or donations remain steady.

As Marx explained so long ago, our organisational divisions alienate us from our work, externalising their costs and enabling a cultural sociopathy in which our sense of responsibility for our actions is reduced by increasing our individual distance from its consequences. While social change organisations are a good place to start implementing the 'more like people' principles, because the contradictions of our current organising systems are so stark, most of the problems addressed throughout this book affect all large institutions, and the people that form them, to varying degrees. Thus, the potential applications for the 'more like people' principles are as varied as our workplace circumstances – from banks to food banks, publishing houses to housing co-ops – and have the power to affect far wider social change.

While 'more like people' is a mosaic of many ideas that have come before, I hope more of us will start to find our own ways of putting these ideas to use, wherever we are, and in various parts of our lives.

If there is one theme that stands out in this book, I hope it is the importance of doing our best to live our values in everything we do. It makes our relationships better, our communities better, our organisations better and our societies better when we choose to do so. Living our values is not the 'extra frill' we've often made it out to be; it is the only positive difference we can be sure we are making in the world, and our best bet to avoid inadvertently making some part of it worse.

The internet is amplifying small action in ways we could never have imagined. Seemingly insignificant acts are proving their value far beyond the scope we could have expected. We are better connected to one another than we've ever been, giving us the opportunity to raise our collective voices in ways only our institutions could have done in the past.

It's time to give ourselves the credit we deserve as change-makers, and to do so in a way that respects our individual actions – from a Tweet to a handful of followers, to a conversation with a colleague – for the potential they carry to make the world a better place.

A few things to keep in mind...

Hopefully by this stage the principles of humanity, autonomy, and complexity have started to sink in. These are like the seeds from which 'more like people' organisations grow. But there are a few more themes I wanted to make sure I'd pulled together, in case you haven't read the whole book, or weren't drawn to these particular ideas through your own reading.

1. *Be what you want to see.*

    In a complex world, small actions don't necessarily have small reactions. How we engage with each other can easily set broader patterns in motion, as one better or worse interaction spawns another in its wake. Our ways of relating to colleagues are the ingredients of our organisational culture. Our contributions to our working dynamics have the potential to build the kind of culture all of us want to be a part of.

2. *Wisdom is everywhere.*

    Many are better than few. The diversity of opinion, perspective and experience that invariably grows with numbers can help us tap into a collective resource we are just beginning to see exists. Wikipedia and the free software movement demonstrate what lots of people, making various bigger and smaller contributions to a shared sense of purpose, can achieve, that no experts or individual leaders could have before. Let's free ourselves from the ego that tells us we – or anyone we've chosen to put up on a pedestal – automatically knows best, and embrace what James Surowiecki called 'the wisdom of the crowd.'

3. **Focus on the NOW.**

    We spend the vast majority of our time trying to understand the past, and trying to predict the future. Complexity explains why we'll never be very good at either. With all the time we spend evaluating what we've done, and strategising for what we will do, we could be better resourcing ourselves to pay attention to the present, with a guiding sense of purpose and keen openness to change. Our strategies create blinders; our evaluations turn complex stories into linear cause-and-effect fantasies. If we pay attention and ask ourselves and others the right questions along the way, we might be able to help create the kinds of changes that we'd otherwise have missed.

4. **Accountability grows from trust.**

    When we treat each other with the assumption of basic decency and goodness, we're often surprised at how often we see these assumptions manifested. From Paul Story's 'honesty edition' book to Grameen's circles of mutual accountability, honesty begets honesty, trust begets trust.

5. **DIY organisational change.**

    In the anarchist tradition of 'Do It Yourself,' start with the places where power hasn't permeated. Organise in the cafeteria, the pub, the hallway, just as social movements so often begin, wresting power from the state or big business only after claiming or reclaiming virtual and physical spaces to establish themselves first.

    And don't ask for permission. "A touch of civil disobedience is necessary to alert the organization that all is not right," wrote Ricardo Semler. "Rather than fear our Thoreaus and

Bakunins, we do our best to let them speak their minds even though they often become thorns in our sides."[vii]

Bulldozers in the boardroom?

In the course of writing this book, the big debate that has gradually come to fill my thoughts is this: 'Can organisations be more like people, or do we have to abandon them to create something new if we want to organise in a way that maintains our humanity, addresses the world's complexity, and gives us the autonomous space to realise our individual and collective potential?'

My answer? I'm still not entirely sure.

On my darker days, I feel like the organisational form is a lost cause — that our hierarchical systems, as they stand, are too entrenched to turn around in a more than piecemeal way, and thus focusing our energies on them, (rather than quitting and creating or joining something new) is a waste of much well-meaning energy.

On these days I feel like I'm selling snake oil — that I'm suggesting we don't need to move beyond the 'Non-profit Industrial Complex' entirely to make the world a better place. That I'm offering a way to address some of our more urgent concerns, but without dealing with the fundamental problems that underpin them. That we can get away with making small changes, trusting that the big ones we need will necessarily follow suit.

On my more optimistic days, though, I remember that people are in different places. People will read this book with different assumptions, experiences, and levels of willingness or ability to change.

Fundamentally, I don't think organisations, as we know them, can be the way of a sustainable future, for people or the planet. But only time will tell what kind of countdown they've got left and if a full evolution from 'old' to 'new' is indeed possible. I also can't pretend that everyone will want to 'Walk out, walk on' to something better (as the title of one of the books that inspired this one encourages[viii]).

Some of you may read this and decide that the efforts to change your organisations are not worth the investment; if this encourages you to leave a job and go on to something new, with the 'more like people' principles in mind, I will be happy.

Some of you may feel there is too much that will be lost if we don't make every effort to turn our 'more like machines' organisations into something more human. If this book inspires you to take those steps to change your own behaviours, encouraging wider system changes, that is also amazing.

Some of you, like me, may find yourselves somewhere in the middle, continuing to make the most of the organisations you've got, while experimenting in something beyond, and allowing these parallel processes to continuously feed into one another. This excites me as well.

Continuing the conversation – an online experiment in organisational development

In the spirit of the complexity principle, I don't want to try to predetermine what this book will achieve, or where the world of organising for social change is headed. But on the whole, I feel there's a good starting point here. If you have ideas for applying, refining or replacing concepts I've discussed, let the rest of us know!

As I wrote in the introduction, the wealth of information that we could bring together through the online manifestations of this book will invariably dwarf what I've been able to write in the pages you've already read. Some of you have already been Tweeting links, observations, critiques and expansions of the text along the way, using the #morelikepeople hashtag to organise your thoughts with those of others. Some of you have been blogging more detailed responses, maybe recording videos, or having conversations with others about the things you've been reading here. For the rest of you, now's your opportunity! *morelikepeople.com* offers a space to expand on the ideas of this book, through the experiences of a significant pool of readers, all with your own valuable insights on what these ideas mean to you, your work, and your life.

No longer is reading a book necessarily a solitary activity. Give yourself whatever space you need to reflect on your own, but don't feel restricted in your ability to contribute to a much greater body of knowledge on organising for a better world. This body of knowledge is emerging right now, but still lacking the unique insights or anecdotes that only you could bring to the fore.

Online experiments are never guaranteed to succeed, but among us we have the opportunity to take the next steps together to grow an emergent 'hive brain' thinking through the challenges and opportunities of 'more like people' organising.

Think of this as one of an infinite number of on-going experiments in crowd-sourcing our collective future. We could leave it to the management consultants, but look where that's gotten us? As insignificant as we've often been made to feel about our power as individuals to affect change, I hope this book has demonstrated that even the most seemingly insignificant of actions can have enormous ripples in the pond of collective possibility.

So, join the conversation! Disgruntled social change workers of the world, unite! You have nothing to lose but your chains of command!

@hackofalltrades, #morelikepeople

Chapter 10:
The time for
change is
now... and if
you don't do
it, we will!

[i] Ricardo Semler, *Maverick!*, Century, 1993, p. 58.

[ii] Ibid., pp. 101.

[iii] International Association of Chiefs of Police, 'Discussion Paper on IACPs, Policy on Domestic Violence by Police Officers,' July 2003. http://www.vaw.umn.edu/documents/policedv/policedvpdf.pdf

[iv] Diane Wetendorf, 'When the Batterer Is a Law Enforcement Officer: A Guide for Advocates,' Battered Women's Justice Project, February 2004, p. 4. http://www.vaw.umn.edu/documents/battererlawenf/battererlawenf.pdf

[v] Veena Vasista, 'Dear Gandhi, you've got me in a muddle...', *See & Connect*, 8 February 2012. http://seeandconnect.com/2012/02/08/be-the-change-really/

[vi] Laura Bassett, 'Susan G. Komen Foundation Elbows Out Charities Over Use Of The Word "Cure",' *Huffington Post*, 25 May 2011. http://www.huffingtonpost.com/2010/12/07/komen-foundation-charities-cure_n_793176.html

[vii] Ricardo Semler, *Maverick!*, Century, 1993, p. 134.

[viii] Margaret Wheatley and Deborah Frieze, *Walk Out Walk On*, Berrett-Koehler, 2011.

Your more like people legend

1. Simple Starters

a. Tell someone that you appreciate something they did because *it might improve their day and they might pass the positive feelings along to someone else.*

b. Stop using jargon (and tell others you're doing so) *because it is likely confusing people inside and outside your walls, even if they haven't told you.*

c. Get to know someone new, somewhere else in the organisation, whenever you can *because you might like them, you might learn something new, and you might start to see how different parts of the organisation fit together.*

d. Dress as you'd like to dress at work, not as others do *because you'll feel more comfortable and there are probably others who hate coming to work in a golf shirt everyday.*

e. Send fewer internal emails; try to talk to people in person *because a lot gets lost in text-only communications, and the conversation might lead in unexpected and useful directions.*

f. Have chats with colleagues when you've got a question, issue or idea, rather than always scheduling meetings *because you might not need more than a few minutes, and a meeting too often unnecessarily becomes something more formal and stuffy than a chat* (Chapter 5 has more on the importance of unstructured conversations).

g. Try more ideas than you expect will succeed *because failure is a natural part of innovation and should not be avoided if we want to make things better* (Chapter 5 discusses the importance of accepting failure).

h. Talk to the colleague who can answer your question directly, don't use the official command chain *because command chains inevitably distort information and take far longer than just wandering over to IT and asking to install a new piece of software.*

i. Bake cookies or make a meal for those you work with *because it's a nice thing to do that breaks down the barriers between 'who you are at work' and 'who you are the rest of the time,' which can help everyone else feel more comfortable being themselves as well.*

2. Personal Development

a. Understand your role in difficult relationships *because no conflict is ever 100% one-sided and the longer we treat it as such, the longer it will be before we can address it and move on* (more in Chapters 2 and 7 on how we all contribute to organisational cultures with our own behaviours).

b. Admit your problems and mistakes, trusting others not to take advantage of you, particularly if you're more senior than them *because it helps others feel that you trust them not to take advantage of you, and when you do that most people will trust you, too* (Chapters 2 and 7 explore 'conscious vulnerability').

c. Speak up about things that are wrong, without simply blaming or attacking someone else for them *because when we don't speak up about a colleague being bullied, we become part of the problem that allows it to continue* (more in Chapters 2 and 7).

d. Work when you are happiest and most productive *because you are wasting your time and the organisation's resources if you're not.*

e. Address your own privilege and prejudice and the ways they might be inadvertently shaping your contributions to the organisation *because unspoken privilege keeps doors closed to people who should have the same opportunities as you to walk through them* (more on privilege in Chapter 4).

3. Social Media

a. Blog or Tweet about your organisational learning *because other people out there could learn from it and it costs you nothing to share* (Chapters 3 and 5 look at 'Open Source Organisations' and sharing learning publically).

b. Share your opinions and feelings about the issues you're involved in *because your views are invariably more interesting than what the organisation can get away with saying through corporate channels* (more in Chapter 2).

c. Connect with others around your organisation who want to make the workplace more human *because they may well be online and when you find others you can compare notes, brainstorm new ideas, and test things out with other forward-thinking individuals* (more in Chapters 4 and 6 about social media for internal communications).

Your 'more like people' legend

d. Use social media for staff learning and development *because for a small investment of time each day, you can learn more about your field or area of work than you would likely get through many, more costly and time-consuming L&D strategies.*

e. Use social media channels to regularly ask communities about their opinions on a range of questions *because they are the reason you have a job, and social media offers you an extra way to involve them in the decisions and processes that affect them* (more in Chapter 5 on using social media to test new ideas).

4. System Hacks

a. Set up a lunch time/post-work discussion group for those who are interested in doing things differently *because when you connect with others thinking similar thoughts, you might spark something far bigger and may even manage to surpass official organisational processes* (Chapters 5 and 7 explore informal groups within organisations).

b. Announce a 'more like people action week' at your office to encourage colleagues to do one thing to make the organisation more human *because it will help you to find the others who are not only frustrated, but want to try new things themselves, and it might spread...*

c. Start a project, semi-related to your work, with interested others around the organisation *because bureaucracy is slow and unresponsive, so you may well be better-off getting on with things until you're told otherwise* (more on just getting on with it in Chapters 6 and 7).

5. Holding Meetings

a. Scrap your next meeting agenda and let the conversation go where participants need it to go *because too often meeting structures don't provide opportunities for real discussion, they simply encourage us to follow pre-determined steps and avoid creative thought processes* (more on the problems with agendas in Chapters 1 and 2).

b. Alternately, start meetings by developing agendas together, *because doing so maintains some structure but remains more responsive to what everyone involved needs at the time, and can feel like less of an imposition on the conversation.*

c. Make everyone a chairperson so everyone is responsible for staying focused, intervening when necessary, and making decisions together *because the chair is too often the dictator of a meeting, but also everyone has to be more aware if they are responsible for keeping things moving.*

d. Hold meetings in parks, pubs, or someone's living room *because different environments – especially those less associated with 'work,' can help us to think and contribute differently.*

e. Ask yourself before planning a meeting, 'does this meeting really need to happen? Would a chat by the stairwell work fine?' *because too many meetings seem to happen 'by default,' wasting time that could be better spent.*

f. 'Livestream' your meetings, broadcasting them online via Ustream or Bambuser, giving others who are interested the chance to feed into the process, *because it offers both a sense of transparency (which builds trust) and taps into the diversity of experience and perspective that exist beyond your walls.* 'Creating the Future' does this with all of their board meetings, though it ~viously won't work in situations where confidential personal `~ or direct action plans are being shared (more in Chapter 5).

~ and Decision Making

'ecision making process or one of its variants
environments, it can increase collective

investment in the outcomes and avoid people feeling the need to take sides (more on how Oaxacan social movements have used these techniques in Chapters 6 and 8).

b. Involve staff, unpaid volunteers, and members in planning and decision making process, and don't relegate 'strategy' discussions to the board or senior managers *because pretending that only more senior staff can know what the organisation should do is insulting to the rest* (more on this in Chapters 3, 4, 5 and 8).

Your 'more like people' legend

c. When consensus can't be reached in choosing between two initiatives, try both, *because it might make a single answer clearer or it might demonstrate that there is no single right answer* (more in Chapter 8).

d. Explore 'Developmental Evaluation' and emergent outcomes *because predetermined outcomes limit our potential and distort our findings, hiding valuable learning and stronger accountability* (more on Developmental Evaluation in Chapter 9).

e. Avoid turning human stories into metrics of success *because it diminishes them and hides many of the most important truths of the work we do* (more on metrics in Chapter 9).

f. Don't strategise! Pay attention and adapt! *Because the world is too complex to predict and strategies make us less responsive to unexpected changes* (more on letting go of strategy in Chapters 1, 2 and particularly 8).

7. People Management

a. Encourage failures as well as successes *because if we pretend people won't fail, they'll just cover it up when they do, and we'll doom ourselves to repeating flawed approaches, without learning* (more on how Engineers Without Borders learned to 'admit failure' in Chapter 5).

b. 'De-specialise' your team, removing individual responsibilities and letting the group decide how to get things done together *because specialisation breaks-down shared responsibility for collective projects and gives people less opportunity to learn skills from each other in the process* (more on 'de-specialising' and new models of organising in Chapters 2, 6 and 8).

c. Encourage staff to use personal social media channels for work, if they want to, *because it doesn't feel like work, it helps the cause reach new crowds, and it encourages them to be more comfortable being themselves* (read about the Big Lottery Fund's experiments with personal social media use in Chapter 7, plus more in Chapters 2 and 4).

d. Regularly ask staff what they want from the job, and support them to get it, *because when they are happier, the organisation does better* (more on the importance of feeling good about work in Chapter 6).

8. Outside World

a. Make organisational learning and resources 'open source' for others to benefit from *because there are many others working towards good causes who could benefit from good information about your campaign emails, what helps your events succeed, or how you manage your payroll* (more on 'Open Source Organisations' in Chapter 5).

b. Actively support the work of other relevant organisations through your own channels *because they're working towards the same goals and you're not going to win on your own* (more in Chapters 3 and 8).

c. Share opportunities around a network, rather than centralising them *because when you hoard funding, opportunities, and media spots, you make others resentful* (more on the roles of organisations within movements in Chapters 3 and 6).

d. Let supporters suggest and act on their own ways to support the cause, with organisational backing, *because the people involved in your cause have far more ideas for how to advance it than the relatively tiny number you employ* (more about people finding their own paths to supporting your cause in Chapter 6).

e. Question how you organise your events, by experimenting with new venues, new catering, new formats and new contributors, *because the built-in assumptions in all of these realms perpetuate events that keep particular demographics comfortable, while alienating others* (more on subtle prejudices in Chapter 4).

9. Working Parameters

a. Support non-fixed working hours *because people have complicated lives to live beyond their jobs.*

b. Organise a 'Hack Day' for staff to work on whatever project or idea most inspires them for 24hrs and share the results, *because it sets the potential of creative staff free to create new ideas* (more on Hack Days and other non-directed working approaches in Chapter 5).

c. Give staff a free day/week to follow their dreams *because if you've hired good people, they're sitting on great ideas that could be a part of your organisation's work if you give them a chance* (more about how Google and other companies have used 20% time in Chapters 2, 5 and 6).

d. Let staff work however many hours they choose *because beyond manual labour, the quality and quantity of work we do are not determined by how long we sit at our desks* (more on how Netflix have used this policy in Chapter 6).

e. Let staff take as much paid leave as they want *because they are adults that know what work needs doing, and will work harder if their job helps them to be happy in the rest of their lives* (more on Netflix' policy in Chapter 6).

f. Support staff to informally train each other in a range of internal organisational functions (finance, fundraising, IT, HR, etc) *because they can more easily fill in for each other when needed, find new challenges for themselves, and better understand the organisation as a whole* (more on Semco and fluid jobs in Chapter 6).

g. Introduce a Results-Only Working Environments (ROWE) where all staff have full autonomy over everything except whether or not their work gets done *because it lets them figure out the best ways of doing their job, which may well be different from their colleagues' best ways of doing their jobs* (started by Best Buy and now used by many other US and international companies, more in Chapter 6).

Your 'more like people' legend

10. Salaries

a. Establish a 'social justice waging' system where staff are paid according to personal circumstances, such as dependents, debts, etc. *because equality makes for happier workplaces and having kids shouldn't mean you can't afford to work somewhere anymore* (more about how Platform use social justice waging in Chapter 6).

b. Train staff to understand organisational finances, and allow them to set their own wages *because it builds employee ownership and collective responsibility* (more on how Semco let staff set their own salaries in Chapter 6).

c. Pay enough that people aren't worrying about money, but not too much as to make it the main reason for the job *because high pay appeals to those concerned most about money, and low pay obviously makes it harder for people to feel invested in their work* (more about wages and motivation in Chapter 6).

d. Keep the salary range in an organisation relatively low *because inequality breeds resentment and poor working dynamics* (read The Spirit Level for more on the societal effects of inequality and think about how they might apply to an organisation).

11. Structures

a. Let the entire organisation become 'Senior Management' *because there are no shortage of examples, from social movements, to worker-run factories, where large groups don't need separate people to set their direction or organise their work* (more in Chapters 3 and 6).

b. Support ad hoc teams of 'Buddies, Bricks and Affinity Groups' *because small, interconnected, self-organising groups can be faster, more agile and more effective at many tasks than fixed, static teams* (read about how these models have been used Chapter 3).

c. Support co-management among staff, *because it can foster mutual accountability and reduce hierarchical power imbalances when those supporting each other are in an equal relationship* (more in Chapters 1, 2 and 6).

d. Scrap departments, make teams more flexible, and don't pin individuals to their job descriptions if they have broader interests *because each of these false divisions keep people from finding other people with whom they can accomplish amazing things* (more on alternative models in Chapter 6).

12. Hiring

a. Scrap job descriptions and look at project-based skills and knowledge requirements rather than individual requirements *because if you let a project-based group find their own roles, less will fall through the cracks and people will discover new strengths in the process* (more in Chapter 6).

Your 'more like people' legend

b. Emphasise candidate perspective in hiring to build a diverse staff *because different perspectives are often the key ingredient to a range of successes* (more on privilege in Chapter 4).

c. Hire only when there isn't someone else keen to shift their work within the organisation to address skills or time gaps *because encouraging more fluid movement between roles, teams and departments helps break down organisational silos* (more in Chapter 6 about when to hire new people).

Your more like people-finder

First Name	Last Name	Twitter Handle
Adam	Mansbach	@adammansbach
Alan	Rusbridger	@arusbridger
Avi	Lewis	@avilewis
Carne	Ross	@carneross
Chris	Coltrane	@Chris_Coltrane
Chris	Anderson	@chr1sa
Clay	Shirky	@cshirky
Dan	Pink	@danielpink
David	Pinto	@happyseaurchin
David	Graeber	@davidgraeber
Deborah	Frieze	@dfrieze
Dmytri	Kleiner	@dmytri
Emily	James	@emily_james
Harriet	Lerner	@harrietlerner
Jamie	Notter	@jamienotter
Jeff	Chang	@zentronix
Jen	Wilton	@GuerillaGrrl
Ken	Robinson	@SirKenRobinson
Lloyd	Davis	@LloydDavis
Maddie	Grant	@maddiegrant
Maurice	McLeod	@mowords
Naomi	Klein	@NaomiAKlein
Pamela	McLean	@Pamela_McLean
Paul	Barasi	@PaulBarasi
Peter	Wanless	@peterwanless
Phillip	Smith	@PhillipADSmith
Sam	Seidel	@husslington
Steve	Lawson	@solobasssteve

First Name	Last Name	Twitter Handle
Steve	Clift	@democracy
Steven	Johnson	@stevenbjohnson
Tim	Harford	@TimHarford
Veena	Vasista	@seeandconnect
Yeyo	Beltran	@yeyoenoax

Your 'more like people' finder

Group Name	Twitter Handle
Adbusters Magazine	@adbusters
Admitting Failure	@AdmitFailure
Big Lottery Fund	@BigLotteryFund
Creating the Future	@CreatingTFuture
Dadamac	@DadamacN
e-Democracy	@edemo
Engineers Without Borders	@ewb
Just Do It!	@JustDoItFilm
Mozilla	@mozilla
Occupy Sandy	@OccupySandy
Occupy Wall Street	@OccupyWallSt
Overseas Development Institute	@ODI_development
People & Planet	@peopleandplanet
Platform	@PlatformLondon
Runnymede Trust	@runnymedetrust
The HUB	@HUBworld
The RSA	@TheRSAorg
Ukuncut	@Ukuncut

Bibliography

Albert, Michael. *Parecon: Life after capitalism,* Verso, 2003. http://books.zcommunications.org/books/pareconv/Chapter6.htm#_VPID_45

Bakan, Joel. *The Corporation,* Viking Canada, 2004.

Bakunin, Mikhail. *Man, Society, and Freedom,* 1871.

Bassett, Laura. 'Susan G. Komen Foundation Elbows Out Charities Over Use Of The Word "Cure",' *Huffington Post,* 25 May 2011. http://www.huffingtonpost.com/2010/12/07/komen-foundation-charities-cure_n_793176.html

Berman, Sarah. 'Occupy Wall Street's new job: disaster relief,' *TheTyee.ca,* 10 November 2012. http://thetyee.ca/News/2012/11/10/Occupy-Sandy/

Bosley, Catherine. 'Town ditches traffic lights to cut accidents,' *Reuters,* 11 September 2007. http://www.reuters.com/article/2007/09/11/us-germany-traffic-odd-idUSGOR14512420070911

Brunton, Michael. 'Signal Failure,' *Time Magazine,* 30 January 2008. http://www.time.com/time/magazine/article/0,9171,1708116,00.html

Carroll, Rory. 'Here's the chocolate factory, but where has Willy Wonka gone?,' *Guardian,* 11 May 2007. http://www.guardian.co.uk/world/2007/may/11/argentina.rorycarroll

Chang, Jeff ed. *Total Chaos,* BasicCivitas Books, 2006.

Denham, Diana, ed. *Teaching Rebellion: Stories from the Grassroots Mobilization in Oaxaca,* PM Press, 2007.

Drucker, Peter. *Management: Tasks, Responsibilities, Practices.* Harper & Row, 1974.

Dubois, Frederic. 'The #OSJUBA event stresses early moves by net activists in South Sudan,' *South Sudan Info,* 13 August 2012. http://southsudaninfo.net/2012/08/the-osjuba-event-stresses-early-moves-by-net-activists-in-south-sudan/

Evans, Jon. 'In five years, most Africans will have smartphones,' *TechCrunch,* 9 June, 2012. http://techcrunch.com/2012/06/09/feature-phones-are-not-the-future/

Graeber, David. *The Democracy Project*, Allen Lane, 2013.

Harford, Tim. *Adapt: Why success always starts with failure,* Little Brown, 2011.

Hughes, Thomas. 'American Genesis,' University of Chicago Press, 2004.

INCITE! Women of Colour Against Violence, ed. *The Revolution Will Not Be Funded,* South End Press: Read. Write. Revolt. 2007.

International Association of Chiefs of Police, 'Discussion Paper on IACPs, Policy on Domestic Violence by Police Officers,' July 2003. http://www.vaw.umn.edu/documents/policedv/policedvpdf.pdf

Jaffe, Sarah. 'Occupy's afterlife — a dispatch from New York's dark zones,' *Jacobin Magazine,* 3 November 2012. http://jacobinmag.com/2012/11/power-to-the-people/

James, Emily. *Just Do It!* [documentary film], Left Field Films, 2011.

Jarvis, Brooke. 'Why everyone suffers in unequal societies,' *YES! Magazine,* 4 March 2010. http://www.yesmagazine.org/happiness/want-the-good-life-your-neighbors-need-it-too

Jenner, Mark. 'Tax avoidance costs UK economy £69.9 billion a year,' *The New Statesman,* 25 November 2011. http://www.newstatesman.com/blogs/the-staggers/2011/11/tax-avoidance-justice-network

Johnson, Steven. 'Where good ideas come from,' [video], *Riverhead Books*, 17 September 2010. http://www.youtube.com/watch?v=NugRZGDbPFU

Jones, Harry. 'Taking responsibility for complexity,' *ODI Briefing Paper* 68, August 2011.

Klein, Naomi and Avi Lewis. *The Take* [documentary film], Hello Cool World, 2004.

Kleiner, Dmytri. *The Telekommunist Manifesto,* Institute of Network Cultures, 2010.

Krippendorff, Klaus. 'Afterword,' *Cybernetics & Human Knowing,* Vol. 9, No. 2, 2002.

Kruglinski, Susan. '20 Things You Didn't Know About... Relativity,' *Discover Magazine*, 25 February 2008. http://discovermagazine.com/2008/mar/20-things-you-didnt-know-about-relativity

Lavaca collective. *Sin Patrón,* Haymarket Books, 2007.

Lerner, Harriet. *The Dance of Anger,* Harper Element, 1990.

Mintzberg, Henry, ed. *Management? It's not what you think!'* Prentice Hall, 2010.

Montgomery, David. *The Fall of the House of Labour,* Cambridge U P, 1989.

Notter, Jamie and Maddie Grant. *Humanize: Why people-centric organizations succeed in a social world,* Que Publishing, 2011.

Pew Research Center, 'Twitter Update 2011,' *The Pew Research Center's Internet & American Life Project,* 1 June 2011. http://www.pewinternet.org/Reports/2011/Twitter-Update-2011/Main-Report/Main-Report.aspx

Pink, Daniel. *Drive: The surprising truth about what motivates us,* Riverhead Books, 2009.

Pink, Daniel. 'Drive: The surprising truth about what motivates us,' *The Royal Society for the Arts,* 1 April 2010. http://www.youtube.com/watch?v=u6XAPnuFjJc

Pinto, David. *small book BIG THINK,* self-published, 2010.

Ross, Carne. *The Leaderless Revolution: How Ordinary People Will Take Power and Change Politics in the 21st Century,* Blue River Press, 2011.

Rusbridger, Alan. 'The Trafigura fiasco tears up the textbook,' *Guardian,* 14 October 2009. http://www.guardian.co.uk/commentisfree/libertycentral/2009/oct/14/trafigura-fiasco-tears-up-textbook

Schmidt, Jeff. *Disciplined Minds: A Critical Look at Salaried Professionals and the Soul-battering System That Shapes Their Lives,* Rowman & Littlefield, 2000.

Seidel, Sam. *Hip Hop Genius,* Rowman & Littlefield Education, 2011.

Semler, Ricardo. 'Managing without managers,' *Harvard Business Review,* September – October 1989.

Semler, Ricardo. *Maverick!: The Success Story Behind the World's Most Unusual Workplace,* Century, 1993.

Shirky, Clay. *Cognitive Surplus,* Penguin, 2010.

Sinclair, Paul. 'Grameen Micro-Credit & How to End Poverty from the Roots Up,' *OneWorldOnePeople.org,* 24 October 2011. http://www.oneworldonepeople.org/articles/World%20Poverty/Grameen.htm

Smith, Andrea. 'Without Bureaucracy, Beyond Inclusion: Re-centering Feminism,' *Left Turn,* 1 June 2006. http://www.leftturn.org/without-bureaucracy-beyond-inclusion-re-centering-feminism

Smith, Phillip and Dmytri Kleiner. 'What not-for-profit organizations need to know about free software,' *phillipadsmith.com,* 2 December 2004. http://www.phillipadsmith.com/2004/12/what-not-for-profit-organizations-need-to-know-about-free-software.html

Surowiecki, James. *The Wisdom of Crowds,* Abacus, 2004.

Taylor, Frederick Winslow. *Principles of Scientific Management,* 1911.

van Gelder, Sarah and YES! Magazine, ed. *This Changes Everything: Occupy Wall Street and the 99% Movement,* Berrett-Koehler, 2011.

Various. *Reflections on Now Activism,* self-published, 2006.

Vasista, Veena. 'Dear Gandhi, you've got me in a muddle...', *See & Connect,* 8 February 2012, http://seeandconnect.com/2012/02/08/be-the-change-really/

Vasista, Veena. 'Snowy Peaks: Ethnic diversity at the top,' *The Runnymede Trust,* 2010. http://www.runnymedetrust.org/uploads/publications/pdfs/SnowyPeaks-2010.pdf

Walker, Brian and David Salt. *Resilience Thinking,* Island Press, 2006.

Westley, Frances and Brenda Zimmerman and Michael Quinn Patton. *Getting to Maybe: How the world is changed,* Vintage Canada, 2006.

Wetendorf, Diane. 'When the Batterer Is a Law Enforcement Officer: A Guide for Advocates,' Battered Women's Justice Project, February 2004. http://www.vaw.umn.edu/documents/battererlawenf/battererlawenf.pdf

Wheatley, Margaret. *Leadership and the New Science,* Berrett-Koehler, 1992.

Wheatley, Margaret and Myron Kellner-Rogers, *A Simpler Way,* Berrett-Koehler, 1996.

Wheatley, Margaret and Deborah Frieze, *Walk Out Walk On,* Berrett-Koehler, 2011.

Wheatley, Margaret. *So far from home,* Berrett-Koehler, 2012.

Wikipedia contributors, "Free software," *Wikipedia, The Free Encyclopedia,* http://en.wikipedia.org/w/index.php?title=Free_software&oldid=564645195

Wikipedia contributors. "The Tyranny of Structurelessness," *Wikipedia, The Free Encyclopedia*, http://en.wikipedia.org/wiki/The_Tyranny_of_Structurelessness

Wise, Tim. 'Membership has its privileges: Seeing and challenging the benefits of whiteness,' *TimWise.org,* 22 June 2000. http://www.timwise.org/2000/06/membership-has-its-privileges-seeing-and-challenging-the-benefits-of-whiteness/

Bibliography

Expressions of Thanks

Firstly, my wife, Jen, deserves a massive shout out for supporting me through this whole process.

Then Paul, for having the early confidence in me and this project, and ultimately being the person to thank (or blame) for you reading this right now.

Thanks to my family – for encouraging me to do the seemingly crazy things I've always been inspired to do (even when they aren't the same crazy things that they themselves would have chosen for me).

To all the great people who inspired or offered feedback on the book: Veena, Aerin, Yeyo, Lorna, Suzanne, Nishma, Maurice, Tim, Adam, Derek, Matthew, David Pinto, Bembo, David Robbins, Dougald, Bonnie, Noel, Roger, Ed, Patrick, Jamie, Maddie, Jim Coe, Damon, Phillip, Megan, Doug, Clare, Pete, Pamela, Jim Cranshaw, Lloyd, Steve, Ian, Billy and Deborah.

Then there's all the wonderful people who contributed to the crowd-funding campaign: Aerin Dunford, Alex Farrow, Alexandros, Alicia Evans, Anake Goodall, Andrew Dickson, Andrew Murphie, Angille Heintzman, Angus McPhee, Anja S. Beinroth, Anonymous, Austen El-Osta, Bembo Davies, Ben Fraser, Ben Knight, Ben Schernick – Namibia, Beverly Green, Bob Goodfellow, Bonnie Foley-Wong - Founder & Chief Investment Innovator at Pique Ventures, Caedmon Ricker-Wilson – Humanist, camille bush, Carolyn Jane Davies, Casper ter Kuile, Catherine Marrion, Catherine Sawyer, Charlotte Pell, Chris Miller, Clare Cochrane, @clarewhite, Damien Austin-Walker - @b33god, Damien Zielinski, Damon van der Linde, Dan Slee of comms2pointo, Daryl Green, Dave Boyle – Brighton, Dave Oswald Mitchell, david pinto – founder of ecosquared, David Robbins, David Tross, David Wilcox, Dawn Reeves, Deborah Frieze, Derek Oakley, Diana Ralph, Doug Shaw – Consultant/ blogger/ speaker/ occasional troublemaker, Ed Anderton, Edward Saxton, Frauke Godat, George Wilkinson, Holger Nauheimer – host of the Berlin Change Days, hops, ID

Hicks, Iffat Shahnaz, James, Jamie Notter, Jan Teevan, jim coe, Joe Saxton, John Sargent, Jonathan James Todd (aka Billy), jonathan moore, jonny zander, Juliette Daigre, justin partridge, K Ludwig, Kai Millyard, Kathi Barrington, Kathleen Flaherty, Kathryn Binnersley, Kayle Donner, Kylee Bowater, Landon Yoder, Lauren Goff, Leo Salloum, Linda B, Lorna Prescott, Louise Barrington, Maddie Grant, Maria Haines – Llangollen, Mark Barratt, Mark Benfold, Mark Braggins, Mark Parker, Matthew Hayles, Maurice McLeod from Marmoset Media, Mike from StartSomeGood, Mohammad Ali Aumeer, Morgan Davie, Natalie Walker, Natasha Adams, Nehmi Klaassen, Neil Bachelor, nick beddow, Nick Drew, Nishma Doshi, Pam Dudman, Pam Elvy, Pamela McLean, Patty Barrington, Paul Barasi, Paul Smart, Paula Connaughton – lecturer at University of Bolton, Pauline Roche & Ted Ryan, RnR Organisation, People & Planet staff, Pete Speller, peter Collins, Peter Eversoll, Peter Wanless - Chief Executive of the UK Big Lottery Fund, Philippa de Boissiere, Phillip Smith, Pierre Marshall, Rachel Purkett, Randonn Swan, Rich Watts, Richard D. Bartlett, Director of Autonomy at Loomio, Robert O'Callaghan, Robin Davidson – Australia, Roger Clark, Rolf Kleef – internet trailblazer, Rosemary Frazer, Saffi Price, Sallie Lyons, Sandy McDonald – The ClanMaker, Seth Reynolds, Sharon Faulds, Shelagh Barrington, Shirley Ayres, Silvia Daole, Sofia Bustamante, 'someone who knows that hope is what we are left with,' Sophie Ballinger @sospot, Stephanie Cole @eseesea, Steve Bridger, Steven Bush, SURCO AC, Susanna Hunter-Darch, Susie R, Tim Gee, Toby Blume, Toby Lowe, Tom Baker, Tom Beale, Tom Dawkins, Tom Pollard, Tom Wragg - @T_Wragg, Tony Hall, Tony Tracy, Tony Wilton, Ursel, Veena Vasista, Wendy Lobatto, and Wiebke Herding, ON:SUBJECT. (Plus the 8 others who said they didn't want to be credited!)

To Majed Rostamian, for so generously and skilfully building morelikepeople.com.

To Serena Lee and Steve Lafler for making the whole thing look so awesome!

Of course to Dave Mitchell, for gently, but firmly working with me to edit the book into something you'll hopefully enjoy reading!

And to everyone else that is helping to make their organisations 'more like people!'

About the author

Liam Barrington-Bush is a 'cross-pollinator.' A grassroots activist disguised as an organisational change consultant; a youth organiser trying his hand as a social media trainer; a community development facilitator in investigative journalists' clothing.

His Twitter handle – @hackofalltrades – alludes to a life of dabbling between worlds, learning from each, but never getting so settled in any one field as to lose perspective on its place in a broader interdependent mosaic of understanding.

He co-founded a youth exchange between young hip-hop artists in Toronto and Havana in 2006 (Turning the Tables), led the UK National Council for Voluntary Organisations' (NCVO) work on online campaigning for two years, and co-founded Concrete Solutions (now 'more like people') under the tagline 'helping organisations to be more like people' in 2010. He made international headlines in 2011 for unexpectedly presenting a 'Greenwash Propagandist of the Year' award to a Canadian government minister visiting the UK to promote the Alberta tar sands and received a journalism fellowship (with his wife, Jen) to investigate Canadian mining operations in Oaxaca, Mexico in 2013, while writing, crowd-funding and self-publishing this book.

He is a regular guest lecturer in the Community Leadership programme at Birkbeck College in London. He has blogged, written articles and taken photographs for a range of publications, including the Guardian, Rabble. ca, and New Internationalist.

He has worked in Canada, Mexico, Cuba, Ukraine, Qatar and the UK.

liam@morelikepeople.org

@hackofalltrades

The story is just beginning...

Unlike most books, getting to the last page is no indication that this particular adventure is over. Now it's your turn.

Go to morelikepeople.com to see what other readers are saying about the book, the ideas in it, and their own experiments in 'helping their organisations to be more like people.'

To contribute thoughts and stories of your own, post a blog or a video (and tag it 'morelikepeople'), Tweet about it using the hashtag '#morelikepeople,' or just send me an email, if you'd like me to post something on your behalf (liam@morelikepeople.org).

The real potential in this book is in the growing body of knowledge and experience that it can help to spark and bring together.

But it's up to you to get it there!

Happy organising!

Liam (@hackofalltrades)

MORE
LiKE
PEOPLE Published by more like people press, September 2013.

Written by Liam Barrington-Bush.